The Changing
American Economy

D1369693

The Changing American Economy

Papers from the Fortieth Anniversary Symposium
of the
Joint Economic Committee of the
United States Congress

Edited by
David R. Obey and
Paul Sarbanes

Basil Blackwell

Library of Congress Cataloging in Publication Data

Fortieth Anniversary Symposium of the Joint Economic
    Committee of the United States Congress (1986:
    Washington, D.C.)
    The changing American economy.
    Includes index.
    1. United States – Economic policy – 1981–
—Congresses.   2. United States – Economic conditions
– 1981–   – Congresses.   I. United States.   Congress.
Joint Economic Committee.   II. Title.
HC106.8.F67   1986   338.973   86-17577
    ISBN 0-631-15394-2
    ISBN 0-631-15395-0 (pbk.)

British Library Cataloguing in Publication Data

United States. *Congress. Joint Economic Committee.*
    Fortieth Anniversary Symposium (1986: Washington, D.C.)
    The changing American economy: papers from the
    Fortieth Anniversary Symposium of the Joint
    Economic Committee of the United States Congress.
    1. United States – Economic conditions – 1945–
    2. United States – Economic conditions –
    1918–1945
    I. Title   II. Obey, David R.   III. Sarbanes, Paul
    330.973'092   HC106.5
    ISBN 0-631-15394-2
    ISBN 0-631-15395-0 Pbk

Typeset in 10 on 11½ pt Times
by Joshua Associates Limited, Oxford
Printed in the United States of America

Contents

Contributors

David R. Obey, United States Representative from Wisconsin, is Chairman of the Joint Economic Committee.

Paul Sarbanes, United States Senator from Maryland, was affiliated with the Council of Economic Advisors in the Kennedy Administration.

Walter Heller was Chairman of the Council of Economic Advisers under President John F. Kennedy and is Regents' Professor of Economics at the University of Minnesota.

James Tobin won the Nobel Prize in Economic Science and is Sterling Professor of Economics at Yale University.

John Zysman is Professor and Co-Director of the Berkeley Roundtable on the International Economy, University of California, Berkeley.

Stephen Cohen is Professor and Co-Director of the Berkeley Roundtable on the International Economy, University of California, Berkeley.

Felix Rohatyn is Chairman of the Municipal Assistance Corporation for the City of New York.

Lionel Olmer, formerly Under-Secretary of Commerce for International Trade under President Reagan, is a Partner in the law firm of Paul, Weiss, Rifkin, Wharton, and Garrison.

Robert Eisner is William R. Kenan Professor of Economics at Northwestern University.

Bennett Harrison is Professor of Political Economy and Planning at the Massachusetts Institute of Technology.

Chris Tilly is a PhD candidate in Economics and Planning at the Massachusetts Institute of Technology.

Barry Bluestone is Professor of Economics at Boston College.

Robert Kuttner is Economics correspondent for *The New Republic*.

Bernard Anderson is Senior Economist, Wharton Center for Applied Research, University of Pennsylvania.

Michael Piore is Professor of Economics at the Massachusetts Institute of Technology.

Lester Thurow is Professor of Economics and Management at the Massachusetts Institute of Technology.

Ray Marshall, formerly Secretary of Labor under President Jimmy Carter, is Bernard Rappaport Professor of Political Economy at the LBJ School, University of Texas, Austin.

Sheldon Weinig is Chairman of the Materials Research Corporation.

Kevin Phillips is a newspaper and broadcast commentator and publisher of *The American Political Report*.

Introduction

On January 16–17, 1986, the Joint Economic Committee of the US Congress celebrated its fortieth anniversary – and the anniversary of the Employment Act of 1946 which created the Committee – with a two-day symposium in Washington, DC on the state of the US economy. The papers and discussions presented at the two-day event examined the lessons of the past 40 years of economic policy and proposed future directions we should take. While everyone did not agree about the past or the future, there was unanimous agreement that the Employment Act had been a milestone in American public policy. Newly victorious in war, yet still scarred by the previous decade's grinding depression, the nation used the Employment Act to commit itself and its government to "useful opportunities, including self-employment, for those able, willing and seeking to work." If the private economy could not create enough demand for goods and services to keep employment high, then government would spur the economy to achieve "maximum employment, production and purchasing power." By creating the Joint Economic Committee in Congress and the Council of Economic Advisers in the Executive Branch to oversee the economy, the Employment Act formally embraced public, activist economics. *Laissez-faire*, the traditional notion that government and economy were separate and distinct realms, was over. In its place, the Employment Act ratified the primary objectives of the New Deal – Keynesian demand management, continued development of a social insurance system (e.g., Social Security, Unemployment Insurance, later Medicare, etc.), and the expansion of equal access to education and job opportunities. These principles became the basis of a bipartisan consensus on social and economic policy and, in general, the consensus met with great success.

This earlier consensus can be seen and felt when one compares the Joint Economic Committee's twentieth anniversary celebration with the fortieth anniversary celebration. Twenty years ago, the papers and speeches presented at the anniversary celebrations were filled with self-congratulations. Economists were riding high with the economy. If the

1950s had been a period of slow, steady growth, the 1960s were shaping up to be spectacular. The Kennedy Administration had formally embraced the New Economics of Keynesian demand management by increasing public spending, cutting taxes and following an expansionary monetary policy. The economy responded with five straight years of strong GNP growth and low inflation, with more growth still to follow through the rest of the decade. Productivity grew at a rapid pace of 4.2 percent, bringing with it the long-term consequence of better, higher-paying jobs for more Americans. Family income increased rapidly, and unemployment and poverty fell at a similar pace. To put this success in perspective, it is astonishing to recall that when unemployment rose to 4.8 percent in 1970, the issue dominated the Congressional elections of that year. It was no wonder that the economists, political leaders and laymen who met in Washington in 1966 to celebrate the twentieth anniversary of the Employment Act believed that continuous economic growth, full employment without inflation, and an equitable distribution of income were all within their grasp. Much still needed to be done, especially to reach out to those previously excluded, but these goals seemed easily manageable as long as the political will remained strong. The dismal science seemed far more joyous than ever before.

Unfortunately, the economic performance of the 1970s and 1980s shattered the buoyant optimism of the 1960s. And with the economy, the economic consensus also lost its sheen. Just as the Great Depression undermined traditional economic thinking and gave birth to Keynesianism, the slow growth and high inflation of the 1970s undermined confidence in Keynes. This shouldn't have been unexpected since advances in economics as in most social sciences are stimulated by events in the world as often as by the internal dynamics of the discipline. Economists and policymakers began to wonder if Keynes' system contained the seeds of its own destruction – a consistent bias toward the escalating prices as budget deficits and an expanding money supply stimulated the economy. In time, critiques of Keynesian economics multiplied, and new alternatives began to get a serious public hearing. As other economic indicators went the way of inflation, a trickle of dissent became a torrent. A brief look at the charts and graphs displayed in the appendix to this book tells a similar story. After 1973, almost every measure of economic health began to decline. Inflation roared at an annual rate of almost 8 percent throughout the 1970s and went as high as 14 percent by the end of the decade. At the same time, unemployment jumped as the economy did not grow fast enough to absorb all of the new workers needing work. Average unemployment for the decade was over 6 percent, reaching as high as 10.7 percent in 1983 and averaging 8.3 percent from 1981 through 1985. Productivity growth – the increase in output per man-hour of work – was slow throughout this entire period and continues to be weak, far below the

4.2 percent rate of growth which produced the rapid job and income gains of the late 1960s. Family income adjusted for inflation declined after 1973 and fell even more in the early 1980s. As incredible as it may seem to Americans accustomed to uninterrupted progress, Census Bureau data indicate that the average family is worse off in economic terms in 1986 than it was in 1973. Moreover, when unemployment increased and family income dropped, we stopped making progress against poverty (as officially measured) in the middle 1970s, and instead saw poverty rise precipitously during the 1980s. Despite sizable increases in "in-kind" benefits such as food stamps and Medicaid, poverty increased by every official and unofficial measure. At best, government aid kept up with falling income for the non-elderly poor; at times it fell behind.

The attempts to formulate a post-Keynesian position have been many, but none has been wholly satisfying nor borne out by the events of recent years. One of the most popular and influential critiques of Keynes has been leveled by the monetarist school, led by Professor Milton Friedman. In a nutshell, monetarists argue that increases in the supply of money determine nominal GNP growth, yet the monetarists also argue that attempts either to stimulate or cool off the economy by expanding or contracting the supply of money are doomed to fail because it is nearly impossible to time the intervention correctly. More often than not, monetarists contend, the effect of changing the supply of money will be felt just as the economy is moving into a phase different from the one the policy was designed to affect. As a result, fine tuning the money supply usually will have an unintended consequence. For example, rather than stimulate a sluggish economy into real economic growth, monetarists suggest that expanding the money supply will too often stimulate it into inflation. Their prescription is to abandon fiscal and monetary policies designed to offset the current phase of the business cycle, and instead to increase the money supply in a steady predictable fashion. However plausible their analysis, events have not borne out the theory in its entirety. Dramatic reduction in the money supply in 1981 wrenched the economy into the worst recession since the Great Depression. Although this clearly helped reduce inflation, it wasn't until the supply of money increased at a pace far in excess of what the monetarists prescribed that the economy resumed its growth and a powerful recovery began. Moreover, extremely large increases in the money supply in recent years, including 1985, have not rekindled inflation as the monetarists predicted. In fact, many economists are speaking of the dangers of deflation, i.e., falling prices, for the first time in decades.

Another contender for the post-Keynesian mantle was the rational expectations theory as exemplified in the writings of Robert Lucas and Thomas Sargent. Motivated by the price increases of the 1970s, these theorists argued that demand stimulation was easily anticipated by all economic actors, and thus rendered useless, or more often, inflationary. Taking a neo-classical position which emphasized the wisdom of traditional market clearing prices and wages, rational expectations theorists suggested that the retreat from activist positions would lead to a relatively painless disinflation. Moreover, monetary stimulation of the economy would become increasingly futile as a way to generate economic growth. Again, events have not borne out this theory. Constricting the supply of money in early 1980 and again in 1981 and 1982 led to first a brief and then a long, deep recession. Conversely, increases in the supply of money in late 1982 helped lead the way to recovery. In short, altering the supply of money mattered, and painful trade-offs between inflation and employment persisted.

Probably the most talked about theoretical challenge to Keynesian analysis has been "supply-side" economics. Taking off from Keynes' emphasis on stimulating demand, supply-siders argued that the real problem was inadequate *supply*. In their view, liberal activists had emphasized the need to create public and private demand for goods and services, but had created a welfare state and tax system which discouraged their production. Their answer was to cut taxes dramatically to encourage additional savings, investments and work. With additional supplies of labor and capital, inflation would disappear and sustained growth continue. In response to the claim that dramatic tax cuts would create large budget deficits, the more confident supply-siders responded that tax cuts would unleash such a torrent of additional work, savings and investments that we could reduce the budget deficit through additional growth and avoid inflationary bottlenecks through expanded production. Savings, investments, and productivity would all grow and thus solve the problems of the 1970s. Again, theory did not predict events. Budget deficits ballooned after the tax cuts of 1981, and economic growth came to a halt as the Federal Reserve Board tightened the supply of money to avoid runaway inflation. The resultant high interest rates and strong dollar continued to hamper American production and hinder American sales abroad. On the other hand, increased demand stimulated by rising budget deficits coupled with the strong dollar led Americans to buy foreign goods at unprecedented rates. Thus, while supply-side techniques did not stimulate increased inflation as some had anticipated, they did lay the groundwork for a trade and current account deficit of unprecedented proportions. Moreover, as a look at the Appendix indicates, low savings rates, low productivity increases and weak investment continue to hamper the economy.

If none of the analyses and prescriptions have proven adequate to the demands of the moment, they have none the less made trenchant contributions to our way of viewing the world. While Robert Eisner powerfully argues the continued importance of maintaining fiscal demand in periods of slack in his essay in this volume, Walter Heller notes that Keynesians cannot ignore the importance of monetary policy – and its inflationary possibilities – when offering policy recommendations. Nor can questions of "supply" be ignored. Lester Thurow, among others in this volume, makes it clear that increasing national savings (public and private) and investment are essential to improving productivity and long-term growth. Numerous contributors throughout the volume point out the importance of productivity for future growth and prosperity and all of them take the question of supply seriously. Where they differ from the "supply-siders" in general is in the belief that inflation and slow growth are not simply problems primarily created by the tax code, and thus solvable simply by tax incentives. Michael Piore, Ray Marshall, Sheldon Weinig, Lester Thurow and others argue that we must invest in people as well as in machines if we are to increase productivity and restore growth without inflation. Moreover, productivity improvements require improvements in how we organize the workplace. In short, supply-side questions are just as important to long-term sustained growth as maintaining adequate demand. But questions of supply must not be construed in narrow ways.

Robert Kuttner, Bernard Anderson, Bennett Harrison, Chris Tilly and Barry Bluestone point out the dangers of an approach that places all of its emphasis on tax incentives for individuals and corporations. Inequality and limited opportunities have their costs, they argue, as the nation wastes human talent that could enrich us all. These authors make it clear that it is foolish to insist that economic efficiency must come at the expense of greater opportunity and quality. The greatest periods of American growth and development were those in which we enlarged opportunity and pursued equality as well as efficiency. A number of contributors to this volume call for a renewed period of policy creativity that will accomplish for this generation what the GI Bill of Rights, the National Defense Education Act, and many other programs did for the last – create new opportunities for individuals to better themselves and in the process the nation at large.

One of the most striking contributions of the symposium and this volume is the importance given to international factors in determining our economic well-being. In the past, economic theory more or less assumed a closed national economic system. Yet, as almost every contributor to this volume suggests in one way or another, this is no longer the case. Kevin Phillips and Lionel Olmer warn that we must pay attention to foreign trade, foreign exchange rates, and international strategies pursued by governments in our increasingly interdependent world. John Zysman, Stephen Cohen, Lester Thurow and others, warn that America must constantly think about building an economy that remains competitive in world markets. If we don't, they warn, we will lose our home markets as well.

In the chapters that follow, there are no easy answers to complicated questions. These essays represent the reflections of some of the finest economic thinkers and policymakers on the lessons of the past and the solutions for the future. If they lack the brimming confidence of 20 years ago, or even the certainty of critics of a few years ago, they represent the mature reflections of individuals who have spent many years measuring the claims of theory against the facts of the world. They have seen the successes and the failures of the last forty years, and in each instance they have learned. Whatever their party affiliation or political ideology, each of these authors presents an argument for continuing the public economics tradition of the Employment Act of 1946. While specific circumstances may change, and policies along with them, their vision of an activist economics thrives.

PART I

Forty Years of Economic Change

1

A Public Economics of Growth, Equity, and Opportunity

DAVID R. OBEY

The year 1986 marks the fortieth anniversary of the Employment Act of 1946. That Act not only established the Joint Economic Committee and the Council of Economic Advisers, but also formally acknowledged the responsibility of government for promoting the growth of employment and output in the American economy. It thereby ratified the key lesson of the New Deal – that our modern economy needed an effective "public economics" to build the foundation necessary for private initiative to lift the economy onto a sustained path of growth and prosperity.

The Employment Act grew out of a widespread fear that our economy would have difficulty managing the transition from war to peace without the active effort of government. The economy had grown at an incredible 12 percent per year under the stimulus of government's war-induced demand, and there was concern that demobilization would bring about a collapse of demand which would shove us once again back into a Great Depression.

To help meet the challenge of demobilization, the Employment Act mandated that the federal government use "all practicable means" to "promote maximum employment, production and purchasing power."

A set of charts, which forms the Appendix to this book, tracks the performance of the American economy over the last 40 years, in meeting the goals of "maximum employment, production, and purchasing power."

The pattern is striking. On a whole range of key indicators, the American economy performed very well during the first two decades after the war, but fell off noticeably during the decade of the seventies. And in spite of some recent talk about the economy entering a "new era" of growth, the data suggest that today's policies have not reversed the 1970s pattern of uneven growth and persisting problems in our economic structure.

The strong performance of the American economy in the two decades after the war was neither an accident nor a matter of purely private initiative. Instead, our enormous growth during this period was the product of good fortune in our economic circumstances combined with good sense in public policy.

We had the good fortune to emerge victorious and intact from a war which devastated the economies of the other major nations of the world. But we also had the good sense to craft policies like the Marshall Plan and the Bretton Woods monetary system which would foster growth in the rest of the world and create demand for American products.

We had the good fortune to welcome most of our servicemen back to the civilian economy, but had the good sense to provide them with the skills they needed to be productive members of the new economy. The GI Bill and the National Defense Education Act assisted tens of millions of Americans in obtaining an education, and in the process gave the economy the skilled labor it so urgently needed. I myself would not be in Congress today if I had not been lucky enough to receive a graduate fellowship to study Russian government under NDEA.

We had the good fortune to see a strong progressive labor movement emerge in the context of the war effort, and the good sense to reinforce positive labor–management relations after the war with laws and practices which protected the rights of labor and provided for wage increases sufficiently large to purchase the output of industry.

We had the good fortune to discover the power of government demand in promoting recovery, and then had the good sense to craft fiscal and monetary policies to maintain adequate private demand once the war was over.

We had the good fortune to be blessed with abundant and fertile farm-land, and the good sense to put that land into ever more productive use. As a result of such policies as soil conservation, agricultural extension, land reclamation and rural electrification, agricultural productivity in the post-war period grew at *six times the rate* of the previous 40 years.

In short, the policies of the 1950s and 1960s did a good job in meeting the challenges which that era presented. But the 1970s presented us with a set of new challenges which seemed beyond the reach of our old policies.

Inflation was the principal problem of the 1970s. Budget deficits resulting from Lyndon Johnson's failure to pay soon enough for the war in Vietnam left us poorly positioned to cope with two oil price shocks and a steep jump in food prices following the failure of the Soviet grain harvest. The assumption that wages should keep pace with inflation quickly transformed these isolated shocks into a generalized level of inflation throughout the economy.

Faced with significant inflation, the old policies of active demand management appeared helpless. Traditional macroeconomics, trapped by the dismal logic of the Phillips Curve, offered no cure for inflation except deliberate recessions and higher unemployment to cool off the economy.

Equipped with only this understanding of the problem, we wound up running macroeconomic policy in reverse, using fiscal and monetary tools not to promote growth but to induce recession. This was the infamous era of "stop-go economics," as the economy lurched from inflation to credit crunch and back to inflation again.

Soon, even "stop-go" policies failed to produce growth, and we repeated the late 1950s experience of producing both high unemployment and high inflation at the same time – the famous "stagflation."

The failure of conventional policies in meeting the challenges of the 1970s led to some extraordinary experimentation in public policy. A Republican President, Richard Nixon, expanded the welfare system twice as fast as his Democratic predecessors as the private economy failed to generate sufficient jobs and income for the poor. That same Republican abandoned the gold standard and imposed wage and price controls, hardly "conservative" solutions and indicative of the confusion of the times.

Democrats fared no better. Jimmy Carter came to office on a promise to use both fiscal and monetary policy to stimulate growth sufficient to lower the unemployment rate from the "intolerable" figure of 7.4 percent. He left office after totally reversing course, with the nation adopting an extraordinarily restrictive monetary policy, which helped create double-digit interest rates and still kept unemployment at unacceptably high levels.

The failure of both Democrats and Republicans to devise policies which effectively met the challenges of the 1970s set the stage for a radical policy departure in the 1980s. Rather than interpreting the 1970s as a period where policy failed to meet the challenge of reality, the Reagan Administration blamed the failures of the decade on the policy itself.

In this formulation, the best public economics was no public economics. President Reagan himself said: "Government is not the solution to our problem. Government is our problem."

These views, strongly reminiscent of the economic philosophy of the 1920s, were supported by some apparent new departures in economic theory. Although monetarism and "supply side" economics contradicted each other in crucial respects, they were fused into the theoretical foundations of the new economics. Monetarism argued that a steady and predictable rate of growth in the money supply would reduce inflation without causing a recession. Supply side economics argued that a tax cut would liberate a huge reservoir of work, savings and investment, producing enough growth to finance the tax cut and bring the budget into balance.

In retrospect, this radical departure has had some significant successes. Inflation was brought down dramatically, and the country experienced a sense that things which had gotten out of control were now back in hand.

But these successes were purchased at a huge price. Inflation was brought down but, despite the predictions of monetarism, only at the price of a recession longer and deeper than any since the 1930s. And the recovery from that recession was purchased with unprecedented increases in both budget and trade deficits, not the huge outpouring of growth and investment predicted by "supply side" economics.

In the face of this mixed record, there is no point in rehashing the 1980 debate about economic policy. It will change no minds. The important question before us now is: Where do we go from here? We must disregard old debates, comfortable partisanship and our own ideology, and face the fact that since the mid 1970s the economy has grown at a slower pace than before and neither political party seems to have mastered the art of designing economic policies that will produce "maximum employment, production and purchasing power" without inflation.

The need to move on, the need to find a new set of economic policies has been dramatically intensified by the passage of the Gramm–Rudman amendment. Its passage signalled the widespread recognition that under the policies put in place since 1981 the numbers really did not match, and that today's policies have not been living up to their promises. We can no longer paper over problems with mountains of debt, and hand the next generation the bills for today's indulgence.

But while Gramm–Rudman calls a halt to the folly of present policy, it does not by itself constitute any sort of solution to the economic challenges ahead. The bill closes off an old avenue for policy, but does not by itself open up a new one. That new avenue can only be opened if all of us, the President, the Congress, both political parties, and the economic leadership of this country face the fact that the country cannot confront new realities with old political promises. While Gramm–Rudman would not have been the route I would have chosen to drive home the need for a new set of policies, I have very much welcomed the chance it provided to re-open the real debate about economics and economic policy.

I believe that an economy must achieve three basic goals if it is to be judged successful by a democratic society with America's set of values. First, it must produce an adequate and sustained rate of economic growth. Second, it must distribute the benefits of growth in a way which most citizens believe is fair. Third, it must provide opportunities for all individuals to realize their full human potential.

The first goal must be economic growth. Growth is essential for making the economy work in both a technical and a human sense. Strong growth makes it easier for an economy to adjust to the technological and competitive changes of modern life by transforming economic life from a zero-sum game in which I can win only if you lose – to a positive-sum game in which all can win if we all contribute to the recipe which will help expand the pie.

Strong growth produces rising incomes, and with it the sense of optimism and self-confidence which helps hold a society together. Growth demonstrates the country is working. It nurtures a spirit of generosity and caring about those less fortunate, and helps build the social consensus which keeps our society and government working together.

Strong growth is the only viable solution to many of our most pressing problems. The Third World debt problem can only be resolved through strong growth in the world economy. The threat of protectionism and economic nationalism, which once drove the entire world economy deeper into the Great Depression, will not be averted without solid sustained growth in the industrialized world. And stronger growth at home and abroad is essential to an orderly reduction in the enormous federal deficit.

Since the early 1970s, our economy has not enjoyed the kind of rapid economic growth we need. In 1985, we managed to achieve only a 2.2 percent rate of growth in real GNP, which merely equalled the average GNP growth rate for the five years of the 1980s. Weak growth produces a host of economic and social negatives. With slow growth, institutions become rigidly defensive, adjustment slows down, hope diminishes, opportunities contract and people become fearful and anxious.

Slow growth imposes its greatest burdens on the young, who have not yet made a place for themselves in the economic structure. Recently, there has emerged a chorus of criticism of today's younger generation for being "materialistic" and "selfish." They may be more materialistic; I do not know. Theologians and sociologists will have to determine that. But it is human nature to think more about yourself and less about your neighbor if a decade of slow economic growth seems to be squeezing your opportunity to provide things for your family which you always thought were just around the corner.

Here are some examples.

In 1973, the average 30-year-old earned $23,500 in today's dollars. By 1983, the average had dropped to $17,520. A young man leaving home in the 1950s and 1960s could expect by age 30 to be making 33 percent more than his father did when that young man left home. Today's 30-year-olds on average are making 10 percent less than their fathers were making when those 30-year-olds left home. And they are not experiencing the kind of vigorous earnings growth during the early part of their work lives that previous generations enjoyed.

When two wages do not seem to bring a family the same standard of living one wage did 15 years ago, when young couples fight to be able to afford their first home, and when 55 percent of children living in single-parent families are being brought up in poverty, it is no wonder that members of this generation think more about themselves than their neighbors. Our challenge is to broaden both their income opportunities and their field of vision.

But growth alone is not enough, not in this society. Successful economies also must manage to distribute the rewards of growth in a manner which citizens believe is fair and just.

The term "fairness" has taken a good deal of abuse recently, with poll-sters telling us that most people take it as a codeword for "giveaways" to the idle and unproductive. But fairness is not synonymous with welfare, and we do ourselves a great disservice to dismiss the concepts of fairness and justice from our discussions of economic policy. To me, and to most Americans, a fair economy is one where rewards are distributed on the basis of hard work and where those willing to work can achieve a middle-class standard of living.

But today, it is getting harder and harder to earn a middle-class standard of living. Real earnings fell steadily throughout the 1970s, and have not rebounded in the present recovery. The number of prime age individuals who work but are still poor has soared, increasing more than 60 per cent since 1978.

At the other end of the income distribution, the rich, who derive much of their income from the ownership of capital, not from work, are expand-ing their share of national income. According to the Census Bureau, the gap between the richest American families and the poorest has widened in recent years, and now stands at its highest point since they began keeping statistics in 1946. No one can make me believe that the American economy cannot be efficient without this much inequality. Nations such as Germany and Japan grew faster than we did during the period 1960 to 1985, yet have far less inequality than we do. And our own period of most rapid growth came about when income disparities were less than they are today.

In fact, growing inequality undermines the social consensus which is an essential prerequisite to growth. The divine right of property is no more sustainable in a democracy than the divine right of kings. Policies which pursue growth without regard to a fair distribution of both costs and benefits are likely to generate a populist resistance from those left out. That resistance will inevitably deny the country what it badly needs to plan and prosper – continuity.

Finally, a successful economy must meet the test of opportunity. Economic institutions are created to serve the needs of people, not the other way around. Successful economies are those which provide adequate opportunity for all citizens to realize their full potential as human beings, a realization which comes largely through work. The ability to provide work for all who want it is thus the key test of a society's ability to deliver on the promise of opportunity. By this standard, the United States still has a long way to go. Although the American economy has generated an impressive number of new jobs, we seem incapable of reducing the problem of unemployment or delivering on the promise of full employment. During each recession, the unemployment rate climbs to new highs, but each recovery also leaves the unemployment rate higher than at the peak of the previous recovery. Our inability to deliver on the promise of full employment has greatly complicated our problems in dealing with the poor. We cannot make the poor the central focus of economic policy, but the poor are human beings to whom, in the words of Willy Loman's wife, "some attention must be paid."

When a national news magazine such as *Newsweek* makes the homeless the subject of its cover story, can we truly ignore the fact that for too many people the world of Charles Dickens does not just exist in *A Christmas Carol* which we see yearly on our television sets?

In the past, we have paid attention to those whom the economy left behind through "welfare." And for many, the sick, the disabled, there is no alternative except welfare. Not many de-institutionalized mental patients will be browsing among the want-ads for computer programming jobs or even for street sweeping opportunites. Yet we knew then and are even more certain now that, for most, welfare is a second-best solution. Increasing the ranks of the dependent is not good for the recipients or for society.

The programs that worked to build a middle-class America were *opportunity* programs, not *welfare* programs. It was only when we failed to deliver sufficient opportunity that we were forced to expand the ranks of the dependent. We need to renew our commitment to full employment and expanding opportunity, or risk making America an economy that works only for those with sharp elbows.

Realizing the three goals of growth, fairness and opportunity will not be an easy task. The world of the 1980s and 1990s will present us with a new and complex set of challenges which must be met in order to reach these objectives.

We face the difficult challenge of reducing the massive federal deficit without precipitating a recession or eliminating those government programs which are essential to economic growth. But the challenges are greater than simply getting our budget house in order. We must do that, but we cannot allow Gramm-Rudman and the necessity of budget control to push us into a policy of disinvesting in things that can help make this country grow.

We will need to meet the challenge of competition in an increasingly integrated world economy, or become a second-class economic power with a declining standard of living. We will need to meet the challenge of increasing the growth rate of the world economy, or face a crisis of insufficient demand, increasing protectionism and unpayable debt. We must meet the challenge of increasing our own rate of productivity growth, improving the quality of our workforce and raising the incomes of our workers. We must find new ways of moving people from welfare to the work world or we will cripple the humanity of welfare recipients and exhaust the patience of the taxpayer.

Meeting these challenges will require the active cooperation of all of our citizens and intelligent, effective partnership between the public and the private sector, between workers and management. Economics is not just mathematics and models, it is also sociology and politics. It involves recognizing the importance of human motivation and acknowledging the economic importance of political decisions around the world. Policies which emphasize only market forces and individual self-interest cannot create the sense of social justice or define our true *national* interest in ways which will enable us to devise effective responses to the myriad challenges ahead.

Our past five years of experiment have proven that a purely private economics does not provide all the answers. To get the economy moving again, it is time to return to the spirit of creative pragmatism in the public sector which animated the Employment Act of 1946. It is time to move on to new arrangements which face new realities.

Previous waves of public creativity have brought us such conspicuous successes as the Marshall Plan, the GI bill, the public highway system, Social Security, unemployment insurance, Bretton Woods and the new economics of demand management which reduced the pain of recession.

It is time for another wave. It is time to once again search out, in the words of the Employment Act, "all practicable means" of achieving growth with equity, and prosperity with justice.

2

The Public Policy Experience

WALTER HELLER

I've been asked to do the impossible: examine 40 years of progress – and occasional retrogress – under the Employment Act of 1946, as later amended; the Joint Economic Committee's role in this saga; the present state of our quest for greater growth, equity and opportunity; and what direction that quest should take in the future. I was tempted to ask: "Is *that* all?"

In a period when government activism, especially in economic affairs, is under attack – indeed, when President Reagan, charming, disarming, and sometimes alarming, tells the country that government's impact on the economy is somewhere between baneful and baleful and that the greatest contribution he can make is to get government's clammy hands out of our pockets and government monkeys off our backs – against that background, the Joint Economic Committee's fortieth anniversary is an especially appropriate time to take stock of the role government has played and should play in the economy.

Economic Performance

First, with respect to *comparative economic stability*: excluding the Great Depression of the 1930s – after all, *in*cluding it would make all comparisons a statistical cakewalk for economic activism – but *ex*cluding it, we find that the prewar economy spent roughly a year in recession for every year of expansion. Postwar, it has been one year in recession for every *four* years of expansion. Pre-1930 recessions were not only much longer but much deeper than postwar recessions (with a standard deviation relative to trend growth that was twice as great prewar as postwar). The shape of the typical prewar cycle was a deep symmetrical V, but, postwar, it was more of a shallow checkmark.

Second, as to *comparative economic growth*: here, updating some of the late Arthur Okun's numbers, I find that the era of economic activism wins again. Compared with an average real growth rate of 2.8 percent from

1909 to 1929 (and 2.3 percent from 1929 to 1948), the postwar pace was a hefty 3.8 percent for the first 25 years before slowing down after 1973 and lagging even more in the eighties.

Third, as to the *comparative use of our GNP potential*: the postwar activist economy operated far closer to its potential than the prewar economy. Measuring the "net gap" under the trend lines connecting prosperity years, one finds that the gap averaged 5 percent of GNP, prewar, even leaving out the Great Depression, but less than *1* percent postwar (from 1948 to 1979).

Now, where has that progress come from? You would not expect me to give the same answer as Richard Nixon gave an audience in Jackson, Mississippi, during the 1960 campaign when he noted that the Mayor told him that they had a doubling of population during his 12 years as mayor. Nixon went on to say: "Where has that progress come from? That progress has not come primarily from government, but it has come from the activities of hundreds of thousands of individual Mississippians, given an opportunity to develop their own lives."

Contrary to Mr. Nixon's answer, I would agree with Okun that the improved performance record, especially the greater economic stability, must be credited to public policy. As he put it, "It was made in Washington." The automatic stabilizing effect of a larger public sector – both on the tax and on the spending side – undoubtedly played an important role. Coupled with it was an aggressive fiscal-monetary policy that, while not always on time and on target, assured private decision-makers that recessions would be relatively short and shallow and that great depressions were a thing of the past.

Poverty

Paralleling the improved economic performance in the postwar era of economic activism was a dramatic decline in the incidence of poverty. From an estimated 33 percent of the population in 1947, poverty fell by one-third, to 22 percent, by 1960 – a decline that must be attributed primarily to economic growth plus some increases in public assistance and transfer programs. Then came the uninterrupted growth of the 1960s coupled with the War on Poverty and other Great Society programs, which cut the remaining poverty in half. The President's 1985 *Economic Report* (p. 264) – I cite that rather than his assertion that "in the early sixties we have *fewer people* living below the poverty line than we had in the later sixties after the Great War on Poverty got under way" – shows us that the percentage of the population in poverty dropped steadily from 22 percent in 1960 to 19 percent in 1965 to 12 percent in 1969, and then bottomed out at 11 percent in 1973. From then until 1980, growing transfer payments just managed to offset sluggish economic performance, and poverty stayed in the 11–12 percent range until it shot upward in the 1980s. More of that later.

Perhaps the most gratifying testimonial to the success of activist socio-economic policy is the striking advance in the economic status of the elderly. Since the media have recently discovered and hence covered this phenomenon at length, I need only to cite one or two salient facts: 25 years ago, 35 percent of older Americans (65 and above) were in poverty. By 1984, that number had dropped to 12.4 percent, two points lower than the poverty rate for Americans overall.

Down Memory Lane

Now, let's turn to some of the pages in our postwar economic history, partly to make a few points about good and bad policy and *about the reshaping of the 1946 Magna Carta as the decades passed*. In doing so, one should not, of course, forget Jackie Gleason's dictum that "the past remembers better than it lived" and the companion warning that "reason is to nostalgia as wind is to fog."

The early postwar years were really vintage years in our fiscal policy annals. We ran appropriate surpluses (that alone shows I'm dealing in ancient history) in 1947 and 1948. Then, in mid-1950, the Joint Economic Committee, in one of its finest hours, recognized the inflationary potential of the Korean War and led the charge to reverse gear, i.e. take the tax *cut* that was halfway through the congressional mill and help convert it into a tax *increase*. But I must add that not *everyone* followed, e.g. I remember vividly Muley Doughton, the 88-year-old Chairman of the Ways and Means Committee, sternly asserting "If I thought that even one dollar of that $10 billion was for those new-fangled ideas about fighting inflation instead of sending guns and tanks and planes to our boys in Korea, I'd vote against it." As I recall, my response would have done credit to Cap Weinberger. We got $7 billion of the $10 billion out of Congress. When Ike dismantled the Truman price-wage controls in 1953, demand had been so successfully curbed that wages and prices hardly budged. In fact, 1952–56 were years of calm on the inflation front. But the 1953–60 period, with three recessions in seven years, was hardly activist policy at its best, especially during the 1959–60 period of too-tight fiscal-monetary policy.

Then came the Golden Sixties, truly watershed years, with a revitalizing of the Employment Act of 1946. President Kennedy asked us to return to the letter and spirit of that Act. He ended equivocation about the intent of the Act by translating its rather mushy mandate into a concrete call for meeting the goals of full employment, price stability, faster growth and external balance – all within the constraints of preserving economic freedom of choice and promoting greater equality of opportunity. He went on to foster a rather weak-kneed anti-recession program in 1961 and a powerful growth-promoting tax cut program in 1962–64. In that process, I counted six firsts for presidential economics:

1. He was the first President to commit himself to numerical targets for full employment, namely 4 percent unemployment and 4.5 percent growth per year.
2. He was the first to adopt an incomes policy in the form of wage-price guideposts developed by his Council of Economic Advisers. The guideposts, flanked by sensible supply-side tax measures to stimulate business investment – training and retraining programs, and the like – helped maintain a remarkable period of price stability in 1961–65, namely, only 1.2 percent inflation per year.
3. He was the first President to shift the economic policy focus from moderating the swings of the business cycle to achieving the rising full-employment potential of the economy.
4. He was the first to move from the goal of an annually or cyclically balanced budget to a balanced budget at full employment, a goal that Gramm-Rudman is grinding into the dust.
5. As a capstone, he was the first to foster a tax cut not to cope with recession (there was none), but to propel the economy to its full employment potential.

All of that may have been old stuff to economists, but it was bold new stuff for a President. I recall that the big tax cut proposal was greeted with grave scepticism by the community at large, but the JEC helped carry the mail and the message. Most vividly, I remember the JEC hearing early in 1963 which was distinguished, first, by Gardner Ackley's pioneering exposition, with charts and all, of the tax multiplier concept to the Committee, and, second, by my gaffe on the Puritan Ethic. When Martha Griffiths asked me why it was that the American people seemed so reluctant to accept this bonanza of the Kennedy tax cut, I suggested that it might be the Puritan Ethic. The next day, Johnny Byrnes, the Ranking Minority Member of the Ways and Means Committee – and a worthy predecessor to Bob Dole as the ranking wit in Congress – wound up his attack on me with this zinger, "I'd rather be a Puritan than a Heller!"

Those were the halcyon days of economic policy. Aided and abetted by the Fed, the 1964 tax cut worked like a charm. In mid-1965, just before the July escalation in Vietnam, we saw the happy combination of an inflation rate of only 1.5 percent; unemployment coming down steadily to 4.4 percent; defense expenditures continuing their four-year decline from 9 percent of GNP in 1960 to 7 percent of GNP in 1965; and the cash budget running $3 billion in the black. Then came the dark years of Vietnam.

Unlike 1950–51, we did not reverse fiscal gears in spite of the timely warnings of the Joint Economic Committee and the economists, both inside and outside the government, who were advising President Johnson.

A case in point was my trip from Minnesota to the LBJ Ranch in late 1965 to plead for a tax increase. In the midst of an interlude of deer hunting on Lynda Bird's "back 2000" from the LBJ-driven white Cadillac convertible – with George Hamilton as shooter and me as spotter – LBJ turned to me – perhaps, I should say, turned on me – and asked: "What do you want me to do, call Congress back into special session and rescind the repeal of those temporary excise taxes?" A wise and wily man. (As some of you will recall, those temporary excise taxes had been on the books since 1933 and were universally regarded as a good riddance.) He did not propose any tax increase until early 1967, and no tax action was completed until 1968, long after the inflation horse was out of the barn.

But that was an excess-demand horse, the kind we understood, the kind that even I warned against in my rather exuberant Godkin Lectures in 1966, those lectures in which I had said: "Nothing *suc*ceeds like success, but the London *Economist* unkindly corrected that to "nothing *ex*ceeds like success." My references to the "treasured but treacherous territory around full employment" and to the fact that "prosperity without a wage-price spiral" was "a goal that has hitherto eluded not only this country but all of its industrial partners in the free world" were understandably ignored.

As I put it in testimony before the JEC in July 1970, "there are no magic formulas, no pat solutions, no easy ways to reconcile full employment and price stability. No modern, free economy has yet found the combination of policies that can deliver sustained high employment and high growth side-by-side with sustained price stability." That was all well and good, as far as it went, but, in light of the experience of the 1970s, it did not go nearly far enough.

The policy travails of the seventies are too well known to require lengthy review. But a couple of points are worth underscoring:

1. First is the Nixon fiasco of freezes and phases serving as a facade for pumping up the economy with tax cuts, spending increases, and a rapid run-up in the money supply, with sure-fire consequences of an over-heated economy.
2. Second, superimposed on that were the supply shocks in 1973–74 that served to consolidate stagflation – oil prices quadrupling, food prices jumping 40 percent in two years, and other world raw material prices doubling in about the same time. The shocks, of course, were not just to the price level, but to the economics profession, led by Keynesians. We learned the sad lesson that, as to wages and prices, what goes up, propelled by overstimulative monetary-fiscal policy and a series of

external shocks, does not necessarily come down when the fiscal-monetary stimulus and supply shocks subside. We've learned a lot about sticky wages and prices that stay in a high orbit even without visible means of fiscal-monetary support. At least, they stayed there until we administered a dose of sadomasochism – better known as the double-dip recession of the eighties, the deepest since the Great Depression.

One should not recite the economic sins of the seventies without acknowledging one bright fiscal episode, namely, the tax rebate and tax cut enacted in the second quarter of 1975. Granted, it was a bit late to blunt the recession, but it provided a welcome boost to an economy that had fallen into what, until topped by the recession of the early eighties, was the deepest postwar recession. The 1975 tax cut was a winner in both size and timing. Though prices behaved very well in 1976, when inflation averaged 4.8 percent (with the help of good crops and no increases in the real price of oil), the combination of an overly strong expansion (partly resulting from economists' overestimates of GNP potential) and the second oil price shock soon pumped inflation back into the double digits. The seventies were a time for economists to be mighty humble – though I suppose one should bear in mind Golda Meir's admonition: "Don't be so humble, you're not *that* great."

As one surveys the whole postwar period, activist economics and New Deal intrusions into the marketplace can surely take credit not only for building in strong defenses against depression, but for a quarter century of sharply reduced instability and high-octane operation of the economy. Within that framework, one can criticize anti-recession fiscal policy as often too little and too late, monetary policy as sometimes too easy and other times overstaying tightness. The far-too-late and considerably-too-little tax increase to finance the war in Vietnam, coupled with excessive monetary ease in 1967–68, has to go down in the annals as one of the flat failures of postwar fiscal-monetary policy. And the stagflation experience of the seventies still hangs like a pall over expansionary policy today. Still, it is worth reminding ourselves that, even in the face of high performance of the economy, inflation in the 1949–1972 period averaged only 2.3 percent and rose above 6 percent only once (during the Korean War). If inflation was the price of activism in public economics, it was a long time in coming.

The Haunted Prosperity of the 1980s

Now, we pass through the economic portals into the eighties, the age of anti-government. Some of this actually began with that social liberal but

fiscal conservative, Jimmy Carter. I don't refer to his deregulation of transportation, communication and finance where competition has a fair
chance to do well what regulation did badly. Nor do I refer to the harnessing, where possible – that is, without sacrificing public purpose and values
– of market incentives, the profit motive, private self-interest to the
accomplishment of public purpose. Using taxes or auction rights to make
depollution profitable and pollution costly is a case in point. But I do refer
to sloughing off functions and responsibilities on the grounds that delivery
of the services has been inefficient in the past, or on the grounds that there
is an inevitable too-costly clash between efficiency and equity.

But I digress from the subject at hand, our haunted prosperity of the
1980s, a perceptive term borrowed from Al Sommers of the Conference
Board. Exactly what is it that haunts our prosperity in this new era of
belittled government?

First, it is *slow growth*. After enjoying *4.2* percent annual real growth in
the sixties, and managing to average 3.1 percent even in the seventies, we
have slipped to less than 2 percent in the first six years of the eighties. Even
if we optimistically assume that there will be no recession in the next four
years and an average 3 percent growth rate, the decade would come out
with just a *2.4* percent real growth rate. And even if we adjust these
numbers for the slowdown in the growth of the labor force, the eighties as
a whole seem destined to go into the economic annals as a period of pallid
performance.

Second, we are haunted by *resurgent poverty*. The percentage of our
population in poverty jumped by one-fourth from 11.7 percent in 1979 to
15.3 percent in 1983. Recovery brought the poverty rate down to 14.4
percent in 1984, but, leaving aside the Reagan years, this is still the highest
rate since 1966. And speaking of the role of public policy, one should note
that without *cash* transfers by the government, the poverty rate would be
25 percent and that with *noncash* transfers, like food stamps, the rate
comes down to 9 percent. But even that 9 percent is a surge of over two-
fifths in poverty since the late seventies. In addition to the Great Recession, the tax and budget cuts of the early eighties undercut the incomes of
the poor and boosted the incomes of the wealthy. The House tax overhaul,
embodying more generous earned income credits, standard deductions,
and personal exemptions, would be a welcome first step in reversing this
doleful story.

Third, we are haunted by *wasted potential*. With the unemployment rate
still stuck at about 7 percent, and with utilization of our manufacturing
capacity stuck at 80 percent throughout the third year of expansion, we
are wasting a big chunk of our productive capacity, presumably as a means
of safeguarding the great and welcome gains that have been made on the
inflation front.

Fourth, *productivity* advances have fallen far short of expectations. A respectable performance in manufacturing has been more than offset by disappointing productivity gains elsewhere in the economy.

Casually correlated with this change for the worse in growth, poverty and wasted potential are some economic policy shifts that haunt us:

1. One has to start with that *monstrous tax cut of 1981*. Look at the grisly progression, or rather retrogression: (1) a Korean War buildup, more or less fully financed by three tax increases in 1950–51; (2) the Vietnam War buildup, with a too-late, too-little tax increase; and (3) a Reagan defense buildup, the biggest in peacetime history, coupled with the biggest tax cut in all history, a combination guaranteed to produce the biggest deficit in history.

2. From 1950 through 1979, the *Federal deficit* averaged less than 1 percent of GNP. Now, that $220 billion deficit is running at well over 5 percent of GNP, and most of it is structural rather than cyclical. The huge deficits and high interest rates have spawned an overvalued dollar and enormous *trade deficits*. From roughly $25 billion in the late 1970s, readily financed by a flow of earnings from overseas investments, the trade deficit has zoomed to $150 billion, with no offset from service earnings, as we are now a net debtor nation.

3. The dismal record on *savings and investment* is another ominous concomitant of the huge budget deficit. Far from being in an investment boom, we have been on a consumer binge financed by liquidating our assets abroad, by gorging on a huge flow of imports, and by depressing national saving and investment to the lowest level since the 1930s. Since this runs counter to popular impression, let me cite chapter and verse. First, net *private* saving – individual plus business saving minus replacement investment – ran close to its long-run level of 8 to 9 percent of GNP in 1984. Second, half of it had to be used to finance the Federal deficit with the result that the *national* saving rate fell from 8 percent to just over 4 percent. Third, only by sucking huge amounts of foreign saving was net investment rate held at about 7 percent of GNP. But savings and investment by Americans have dropped to the lowest levels in 50 years.

Apart from such damning economic developments, the eighties have also seen the rise and fall of what Herb Stein aptly calls "punk-supply-sidism," to distinguish it from sensible classical supply-side policies for investment, productivity, and growth that we all subscribe to. Alan Blinder put the matter neatly when he said, "Monetarists offered statistical evidence with no theory. New Classicists offered an elegant new theory with no evidence. Combining the best of both tactics, supply-siders offered neither theory nor evidence." And that makes another point. With super-supply-sidism falling flat on its face, with monetarism failing to deliver, and with rational expectations, elegant as the theory is, proving to be a nonstarter in the policy sweepstakes, Keynesians have regrouped, built Milton Friedman's natural rate of unemployment into their models, developed a credible theory of wage-price rigidities, and seem to be regaining the intellectual and policy-oriented high ground in economics. By being eclectic, pragmatic and realistic, the Keynesians have made a remarkable comeback. (If you get the vague feeling that I am grinding an axe now and then, you're quite right.)

Where Do We Go from Here?

Where should activist economics go from here? There are plenty of new ideas floating around – and even a few *good* new ideas – but none will make much difference unless we restore the essential conditions for faster and more sustained economic growth and stop the consumption being fostered by our irresponsible fiscal policies. It is worth reminding ourselves that it will take a skilled balancing act to put the economy back on the track of long-term growth while maintaining our expansionary momentum in the near term.

Clearly, the vital first step is to shrink the gigantic deficit that is leeching the lifeblood out of growth by absorbing over half of our private savings. One has to hope that a Gramm–Rudmanized budget process will lead to a "deficit disarmament conference" and an agreement to couple tax increases with bearable budget cuts.

Second, even as we move fiscal policy toward restriction, we must maintain and even step up the level of aggregate demand in the economy. That's where the high-wire balancing act comes in, namely, offsetting the reduction in aggregate demand from a more restrictive fiscal policy by running a more stimulative monetary policy. That, in turn, means keeping one eye on the substitution of investment for consumer spending as the budget deficit shrinks and interest rates fall and the other eye on the shift of demand from imported goods to domestically produced goods and services as the trade deficit shrinks, and not getting cross-eyed in the process. As a matter of fact, in an open-economy world, we have to keep a third eye on our trading partners. As we shrink our imports and expand our exports, the impact on foreign economies will be damaging unless we find some effective way at last to develop some constructive international cooperation in economic policy. There is nothing in the market economy that, left to itself, will make the necessary adjustments. Lester Thurow, for one, has presented a challenging agenda of moves we can and should make on this front, several of them involving judicious *increases* in public programs.

Third, we will need to adjust our structural policies, applying the classical supply-side precepts designed to beef up our productive capacity and productivity – everything from boosting investment in physical infrastructure, in human brain power, and in research and innovation, to stimulating private saving and investment.

Lurking in the background of this whole process will be the perennial trade-off question: is an attempt to improve our growth and expansion performance going to reignite inflation?

What does past experience tell us about the need to curb our appetites for expansion and faster growth in order to forestall inflation? Is it possible that we are misapplying past experience, that we are like the cat that sat on a hot stove and now won't sit on a cold one? The trade-off between unemployment and inflation may well have moved in our favor. With the hard core of inflation, namely, wage norms, coming down sharply, with plenty of excess capacity in the economy, and with these tendencies buttressed by falling oil prices and soft world commodity prices, isn't it time to test the waters with a more expansion-oriented and growth-oriented policy as outlined above?

Yet, there's no guarantee that growth alone will reduce inequality—and worse, that with the incidence of poverty shifting so strongly to single-parent families and their children, there's no guarantee that growth will lift *all* the boats.

Isn't it about time that the richest country on earth, as we still are, in terms not only of wealth *per capita* but of the annual flow of goods and services *per capita* (as shown by the Kravis–Summers studies at the University of Pennsylvania); with the lowest taxes (at about 29 percent of GNP) of any advanced country in the world, with even Japan now having passed us; and with the least socialized industrial economy on earth (as established by late-seventies IMF data and a recent update by the London *Economist*); isn't it about time that we stopped asking the poor and the near-poor to take the main brunt of the buildup of our defenses?

As a citizen of this richest, lowest-tax and least socialized of countries, I read with disbelief the accounts of the hundred cuts we are inflicting on ourselves under the $11.7 billion Gramm–Rudman sequestration this year. And that is only one-sixth of what's coming next year. Cuts in funding of national parks, of new drug approvals, of health and education services, of IRS enforcement, of the Social Security Administration – that is just a sampling of items on this year's hit list. Wait till *next* year's! We, the leaders of the Western world, cannot afford those things? The mind boggles.

And isn't it about time that we came out and said that it is a shameful thing to be gorging ourselves on imports and feasting on resources that ought really to be devoted to investment and growth, all in the name of hands-off economics and in the wake of staggering deficits and a White House that sees taxes, not as the price we pay for civilization, but as the root of almost all economic evil? And isn't it time to stop shortchanging the future, as we are, by stunting growth and running up huge foreign debts in what Rudy Penner calls a case of "fiscal child abuse?"

The fear and loathing of deficits in Congress is palpable. The JEC and the Congressional Budget Office have spearheaded the drive to bring some sanity into fiscal policy. Indeed, the record shows – as Norman Ornstein's study for the American Enterprise Institute so clearly demonstrates – that the Congress, "through the broad sweep of American history, has struggled to restrain the growth of Federal spending and to limit deficits and the public debt, through direct action and through periodic adjustments of its own structures to minimize the deleterious effects of political pressures." Thanks to courageous congressional initiatives led by Senators Dole and Domenici in 1982 and by those two and others in 1983–84, with the President playing tag-along, the deficit is at least $100 billion a year less than it otherwise would have been.

So, while there is much to be said for a brave new world of innovation in public economics, our *first* order of business is to clear the fiscal decks for action, promote growth with some fairly orthodox measures, and use a modest portion of our vast wealth and taxable capacity to share more of our affluence with the poor and disadvantaged. That may be a bit old-fashioned, but show me something new-fashioned that would be better.

Pursuing this thought, let me close with some words of hope with which Joseph Kraft ended his last column:

> Except in its blindest moments, the United States is not a country that sins against the light . . . Normally, on the contrary, the United States plays host to a humane society. Few things, certainly not the tyranny of abstract numbers, drive us to barbarous, even unfeeling behavior. So my hunch is, when all the figures come up on the table, when Gramm-Rudman is in its heaven, Americans will figure out a way to beat the odds. We will balance welfare and defense and investment and social improvement in a rough way that does not blight vast numbers of lives. Both in dealing with the Russians, and in dealing with ourselves, we will make good the promise of a turnaround year.

Amen!

3

The Economic Experience

JAMES TOBIN

As we observe the fortieth birthday of the Employment Act, the auguries of its future are mixed. On the negative side, the objectives to which the Act committed federal economic policy – maximum employment, production and purchasing power – command little support in word or deed among legislative and executive makers of policy. The Council of Economic Advisers, the major institution established by the Act to implement that commitment, has lost status and influence. Its attention has shifted to lesser goals. The Joint Economic Committee, more faithful to the original mandate but ever handicapped by its lack of legislative function, has difficulty getting its voice heard. The ideology dominating economic policy since 1980 rejects the premises of the Act, denying that federal interventions can improve the performance of the economy.

On the positive side, the economic climate over the foreseeable future is more clement than it has ever been since the twentieth birthday party. Nothing now on the horizon threatens the historically extraordinary series of external shocks that dominated the scene and preoccupied policy-makers throughout the world from 1966 to 1981 – notably the Vietnam War and the two oil crises of the 1970s. Now the OPEC cartel is collapsing and energy prices are falling. What is missing is commitment and confidence to take advantage of the benign climate of this decade.

Consider the complacency, resignation and indifference with which the stagnation of the economy these last eighteen months has been accepted. The recovery that began in late 1982 stalled in June 1984 at 7 percent unemployment, give or take a couple of tenths, and at about 80 percent capacity utilization. My esteemed colleague Herb Stein has interpreted the experience to signify that those numbers are equilibrium values, "natural rates." I was dismayed to find him subscribing to Panglossian macroeconomics. In my own view, this low-level stability reflects not an optimal equilibrium but the inadvertence or excessive caution of the monetary authorities. Certainly the architects of the Act, and those who took it seriously over its first quarter century, would not have been content. They would not brag about real GNP growth barely fast enough to keep high unemployment rates from rising further, nor congratulate themselves on avoiding outright recession. Observing that wage and price inflation rates are subsiding and seeing no bottlenecks or shortages on the economic landscape, they would wish to push the economy with deliberate speed towards higher utilization of its capacity to produce.

Unemployment and Inflation

The Employment Act did not specify any numerical target for unemployment. That was wise, because feasible targets have varied from time to time and will vary in future. Particular Administrations and Congresses may adopt and announce numbers – like the 4 percent of the Kennedy years – but only as interim goals to be reconsidered with experience. It was a great mistake for the congress to enshrine in the Humphrey-Hawkins Act numerical goals for unemployment and inflation that were in combination patently unachievable in the 1970s, in contrast to the 1960s. The result was that policymakers could ignore not only the numbers but the spirit that motivated them.

The Employment Act is directed first of all to fiscal and monetary policies affecting aggregate demand for goods and services. Inflation is the systemic constraint on the use of demand stimulus to lower unemployment and to increase utilization of productivity capacity. All six recessions the United States has suffered in the last 30 years can be attributed to deliberate policies to restrict aggregate demand in order to bring inflation rates down. The counter-inflationary objectives were generally achieved, but with serious interruptions to economic growth and long intervals of high unemployment and excess capacity. Distaste for rising inflation rates, and indeed for persistent inflation above 5 percent, is a strong revealed political preference of the American public. There is good reason, therefore, to keep enough slack in labor and product markets to avoid substantial risk of triggering a spiral of accelerating prices.

The natural rate of unemployment already mentioned is conceptually the lowest "inflation-safe" rate obtainable by expansion of aggregate demand, the lowest rate that fiscal and monetary policies can be expected to achieve. Unemployment may be, probably is, still excessive at that rate, but further reduction requires structural reform along with fiscal and monetary demand management.

It is important to be clear about what the inflation limits to demand management do and do not mean operationally. First, no one can be sure what the inflation hazards are at any unemployment rate in given circumstances, only that they are greater at 7 percent than at 8 percent and at 6 percent than at 7 percent. Second, no one can guarantee that there is zero inflation risk; it would be silly and wasteful to run the economy with so many resources idle that inflation risk was negligible. Third, the hazard to be avoided is a continuing, pervasive acceleration of prices. One-shot boosts of particular prices and even of general price indexes are bound to occur, especially in cyclical recoveries; they are not a problem even though they make statistical measures of annualized inflation rates temporarily high.

Today we do not know what the inflation-safe unemployment rate is, even if we could agree on how little inflation risk that concept should imply. I don't know; Herb Stein doesn't know; Paul Volcker doesn't know. The fact that inflation rates rose at successively higher unemployment rates – from 3–4 percent in the late 1960s to 5 percent in 1973 and 6 percent in 1979 – is doubtless an influential reason for caution today. However, I think this history is useless evidence for policy in this decade. It tells us nothing about normal labor and product markets today; if it describes any natural rate, it is the "natural rate" of energy consumption and oil imports in the trying decades of the 1970s.

Now there is good reason to believe the natural rate of unemployment is well below the current rate of 7 percent. Both wage inflation and commodity price inflation are still declining. Workers and their unions are still desperately afraid of losing jobs. Employers are scared of losing markets, and in many cases of going broke. Both are frightened of foreign competition. Changes in industrial structure and comparative advantage have hit particularly hard those industries and unions whose price and wage behavior used to set extravagant patterns for a large part of the economy. So long as these benign conditions prevail, I think we should persist in gradually reducing the slack in the economy.

The situation today reminds me of the early 1960s. Two recessions in 1957–58 and 1960 had taken unemployment from around 4 percent to 6 or 7 percent and reduced inflation from a peak between 4 and 5 percent in the mid-fifties to less than 2 percent. Nevertheless, influential opinion in the Federal Reserve and elsewhere opposed measures to expand aggregate demand, on the grounds that they would be inflationary and that the increases in unemployment were structural rather than cyclical. These diagnoses and fears turned out to be groundless in the 1961–65 expansion, which lowered unemployment to 4 percent without adding perceptibly to inflation. Although 4 percent unemployment is not a realistic objective for aggregate demand policy now, we can surely lower the rate to 6 percent or less.

The gains from completing the recovery and boosting the utilization of existing productive resources are insufficiently understood and appreciated. Unemployment is privation for those affected, often pushing them below the poverty line. Unemployment compensation does not make them whole, materially or psychologically. Most unemployed are not even eligible. But from a society-wide point of view, unemployment is a waste of productive resources, whether or not the individuals unemployed suffer hardships.

The unemployment rate is a convenient cyclical barometer of macro-economic performance; production, capacity utilization and incomes are all strongly negatively correlated with under-utilization of labor. So is the overall incidence of poverty, far beyond the personal privations of those unemployed. Each point unemployment is lowered gains from 2 to 3 per-cent of GNP, about $100 billion. Of that, some $40–50 billion would be saved by businesses, households and governments – the federal deficit would go down by $25 billion – adding to domestic investment or diminishing overseas borrowing. No tax incentives or other supply-side nostrums could do as much for saving and investment. For this reason, the high employment commitment embodied in the Act of 1946 is important, indeed essential, for long-run growth.

Demand Management and Structural Policies

Why is unemployment so high at "full employment?" That is, why is the inflation-safe unemployment rate so high? What explains its distressing and apparently inexorable upward drift these past 20 years? Perhaps the "natural" rate is just a moving average of actual rates; perhaps the recessions engineered to cope with the inflationary shocks of the 1970s have left us an unpleasant legacy. Perhaps, as suggested above, the natural rate today is a lot lower than generally believed. Anyway, it is too high.

The time to fix the roof is when it is not raining. Structural unemploy-ment, beyond the reach of macroeconomic demand policies, afflicts disproportionately certain vulnerable demographic groups, teenagers, young adults, minorities. Labor markets are very imperfectly competitive. The interests of unemployed outsiders are insufficiently represented in wage-setting decisions and negotiations, where the claims of insiders and senior job-holders take excessive precedence. Prior to 1981 Administra-tions and Congresses were at least concerned with these problems. They sought to ameliorate them by both labor market and wage-price policies, not very successfully, to be sure. Those approaches are not fashionable today. But the problems are still there, and the issues will recur.

I suggest that this would be a good topic for major study by the Joint Economic Committee. The agenda could include a number of ideas of how to lower the inflation-safe unemployment rate: improvements in public education; relaxation of minimum wage laws and other regulations that limit the downward flexibility of wages and prices; encouragement of labor contracts that relate wages to firms' revenues, profits or labor productivity; penalizing by unemployment insurance surtaxes employers who raise wages while they are curtailing employment or while unemployment is high in their localities; annual economy-wide guideposts for wages and prices, with compliance induced by tax-based rewards and penalties.

Demand Side, Supply Side

Clear thinking about macroeconomic policies requires distinction between aggregate demand and aggregate supply and between the effects of policies on demand and supply. Potential real GNP is the output the economy can produce with unemployment and capacity utilization at their inflation-safe rates. Its growth trend depends on the growth of productive resources, labor and capital, and on productivity-rising technological progress. Its level also depends, as noted above, on the amount of slack in the economy deemed necessary to contain inflation. Structural reforms, including "supply-side" measures, may increase potential GNP and/or its growth rate. But experience suggests that such effects are small and slow, difficult to discern and predict. The sources of productivity growth are elusive; its decline in the 1970s remains a mystery to the leading students of the subject. The supply-side measures of the 1980s have yet to bear fruit in potential GNP.

Actual real GNP fluctuates irregularly around the potential trend, generally in response to demand-side shocks or to policy-induced changes in aggregate demand. The two kinds of demand management policies available to the federal government are fiscal and monetary. Choices among the several fiscal and monetary instruments may also affect potential GNP, in the future rather than contemporaneously. We must distinguish short-run demand stabilization from long-run growth in potential output, and sort out the effects of policies on these two goals.

Fiscal Policy as Demand Management

The sponsors of the Employment Act expected fiscal policy to be the main instrument of short-run demand management, and it was in fact actively used. In almost every recession prior to the most recent pair of 1979–82, fiscal stimulus, temporary or permanent, was deliberately applied to promote recovery. It took the form of extra purchases of goods and services (e.g. public works) or transfer payments (e.g. enlarged social security or unemployment benefits) or tax cuts. In 1964 income taxes were cut during a recovery, in order to keep it alive. On several occasions fiscal instruments were used to restrain aggregate demand during booms; taxes were increased sharply during the Korean war and belatedly during the Vietnam war.

Deliberate changes in budget programs and revenue legislation, sometimes adopted in the interests of macroeconomic stabilization, are to be distinguished from the built-in automatic contributions of the federal budget to stability. Without programmatic or legislative actions, tax collections fall during recessions and rise during recoveries and booms; likewise certain expenditures, especially transfers to the unemployed, the poor, and other victims of hard times, move counter-cyclically. As a result, private purchasing power falls less than business activity in slumps and rises less in prosperities. Built-in stabilizers do not prevent or reverse cyclical swings, but they do reduce their amplitude.

The well-known counter-cyclical movements of federal budget deficits or surpluses are just the mirror image of the partial stabilization of private spending power. Large budget deficits have usually been passive symptoms of weakness in aggregate demand throughout the economy, rather than indicators of increased active fiscal stimulus. The "high employment budget deficit," now returned to popularity as the "structural deficit," corrects for these cyclical effects, measuring what the budget outcome would be under existing programs, entitlements and tax codes if the economy were operating at a constant rate of utilization of potential output. Changes in this deficit (often a surplus in the past) are a fairly accurate measure of the changes in aggregate demand due to fiscal policy, whether for stabilization purposes or for other reasons.

The stronger are the built-in stabilizers, the less need is there to resort to discretionary changes in the structural budget in the interests of demand management. Presidents Kennedy and Johnson, seeking to reinforce the automatic stabilizers, proposed some semi-automatic triggers for altering certain taxes and expenditures for counter-cyclical stabilization, but Congress did not act upon their proposals.

The use of fiscal tools for demand management does not necessarily bias the federal budget either to chronically higher deficits or to chronically higher expenditures and taxes. It is true that the budget has been much bigger relative to the economy since World War II than before. This was due to the much larger permanent burdens of national and international security on the United States, and to the growth of social security, Medicare and Medicaid, and other transfer programs. It is also true that the larger size of the budget, given that expenditures are stable or counter-cyclical and tax revenues are pro-cyclical, both strengthened the built-in stabilizers and facilitated discretionary demand management. Until 1981 structural deficits were small, generally less than 1 percent of potential GNP, and often negative. The public debt grew more slowly than the economy, falling from more than 100 percent of GNP at the end of World War II to 25 percent in the 1970s. The size and growth of the budget, expenditures and revenues both, raise political issues regarding the nation's priorities as between various public programs and taxpayers' private interests. Those are quite separate from the uses of fiscal policies as instruments of macroeconomic management, functions that can be performed whether the federal budget is much larger or much smaller than it is today.

Monetary Policy as Demand Management

Monetary policy, decided and executed by the Federal Reserve System, also operates on aggregate demand – though indirectly, by altering the availability and cost of credit to households, businesses and state and local governments, by affecting the values of their existing assets and debts, nowadays by influencing the foreign exchange value of the dollar and the competitiveness of American products in world markets, and by influencing the expectations of economic actors about all these variables. In principle, within broad limits, anything that fiscal policy could do to aggregate demand, monetary policy could also do, or undo. The two are substitutes for one another in demand management, although their side effects, including their implications for long-run growth of potential output, may be quite different. As policy instruments, they are also substitutes, in the sense that their settings are technically – and in the United States today also administratively and politically – independent. The Fed is not compelled to print money to finance government deficits; it is free to do the reverse, to monetize less public debt and tighten its policies when fiscal stimulus is strong.

The fact that the two kinds of policies are substitutes has an important implication that is insufficiently appreciated. In doses of equivalent effect on aggregate demand, fiscal and monetary policies have pretty close to identical effects on output relative to prices. The "natural" rate limit to demand expansion remains about the same whether it is approached by monetary stimulus of fiscal stimulus. There is no way to twist the outcome more in favor of output and employment and against price and wage inflation by altering the mixture of monetary and fiscal dosages. In particular, in given circumstances of the economy there is nothing intrinsically more or less inflationary in monetary expansion than in equivalent fiscal stimulus. I will acknowledge one qualification to these propositions below, in discussing international implications of the fiscal–monetary mix, but the central point will stand.

Over the past 40 years, particularly over the last 15, monetary policy has overtaken fiscal policy as the principal regulator or macroeconomic performance. In the 1940s many Keynesian economists were, because of their reading of experience during the Great Depression, as skeptical of the potency of monetary measures as they were enthusiastic about the newfound potentials of fiscal management of aggregate demand. (They were misreading Keynes, in my opinion.) Until 1951, the Federal Reserve remained a prisoner of its wartime commitment to support federal securities' prices at par; essentially there could be no independent monetary policy with interest rates thus frozen. Even after its liberation by the Accord of 1951, the Fed's strategy of "leaning against" the cyclical winds was more a monetary built-in stabilizer than an active control of the economy. In the 1960s, and especially in the 1970s under the influence of monetarist critics, the Fed assumed a more active and independent role. The Fed is, after all, well positioned to be the major arbiter of macroeconomic developments. The Federal Open Market Committee has ten or more moves a year to the Congressional budgetmakers' one.

The Decline and Fall of Compensatory Fiscal Policy

In the past 40 years discretionary active fiscal policy has fallen in the esteem of both policy makers and economists. Lags in decision making and implementation meant that expenditure changes, and even tax and transfer changes, were likely to take effect too late to do their intended good, and might even do harm. New theories, stressing the importance of expectations in the behavior of consumers and businessmen, questioned the effectiveness of temporary fiscal measures. For example, the temporary income tax surcharges President Johnson belatedly persuaded Congress to pass in 1968 were judged to have disappointingly small effects on taxpayers' spending. The increasing complexity of the annual budget-making process in Congress in the 1970s produced delays that diluted the value of the macroeconomic considerations involved in the decisions. This was unfortunate and ironic, coming at the same time as procedural reforms designed to enhance the rationality of budget-making by requiring Congress to decide consciously on the budget as a whole and by providing members of Congress via its new Budget Office with better independent economic and budgetary intelligence than they ever had before.

At the same time, the grip of monetary policy on the economy was strengthening. As the Federal Reserve drifted towards monetarism and geared its policy to announced targets for growth of monetary aggregates, its policy was leaning much harder against all winds and was less accommodative to fiscal stimuli. The structure of the financial system became more monetarist too. The velocity of money became less responsive to interest rates, for several reasons. When nominal interest rates are high, businesses and households have strong incentives to economize their holdings of cash, irrespective of marginal changes in interest rates. Together with banks, they also have strong incentives to arrange *de facto* interest payments on their deposits, including transactions accounts. Now previous legal limits on interest payments to depositors are well on the way out.

However, the greatest blow to the use of fiscal policy in demand management came with the Reagan Administration's budgets, beginning in 1981. Drastic tax cuts plus rapid build-up of defense spending, incompletely offset by cuts in civilian expenditures, generated deficits, actual and structural, far larger relative to the economy than in any previous peacetime experience. Federal debt rose to more than 40 per cent of GNP in four years.

The Reagan budgetary programs, as they were phased in over several years, were heavy stimuli to aggregate demand during the recovery that began in late 1982. This was counter-cyclical fiscal policy with a vengeance. Of course, it was serendipitous; the Administration officially scorned Keynesian ideas of demand management. The Reagan budgets had two quite different motivations. One was supply-side confidence that cuts in tax rates would tap vast reservoirs of work effort, saving and enterprise, and thus greatly speed the growth of the economy and even balance the budget. Even if successful, this strategy had more to do with long-run potential GNP than with short-run demand-side recovery. The second was a political strategy designed to achieve the Administration's prime ideological goal, the shrinking of civilian government: cut taxes, then use the public outcry against the resulting deficits to bludgeon Congress into cutting non-defense spending.

The Gramm–Rudman "solution" to the nation's deficit problems does not restore fiscal policy to effective partnership in demand management. To the contrary, it is likely to be the *coup de grâce* – if it really takes effect, and at least as long as it lasts. Of course, it was already true that the sheer magnitude of the structural deficits ruled out counter-cyclical fiscal policy for all practical purposes; certainly any extra fiscal stimulus to combat recession is now unthinkable. Gramm–Rudman not only formalizes that incapacity but makes matters worse. In case weakness of the economy adds to prospective deficits, the legislation mandates additional expenditure cuts to meet the prescribed schedule for reduction of the deficit (actual, not structural). Such cuts would tend to make the economy weaker still. Thus the built-in fiscal stabilizers that served us well for 40 years are to be replaced by mandatory destabilizers. There are, to be sure, some escape hatches in the law, but they are inadequate to prevent the perverse responses just described.

Over the foreseeable future, therefore, Federal Reserve monetary policy will be macroeconomic policy. Without built-in and discretionary fiscal stabilizers, the monetary authorities will have to act more boldly to preserve stability in the face of the inevitable surprises. Fortunately, since its policy shift in 1982, the Fed has become quite pragmatic.

In the 1970s, and especially in the three years after October 1979, the

Fed imposed upon itself targets for the growth of intermediate monetary aggregates, M-1, M-2, and so on. Having staked its credibility to the financial markets on the realization of these targets, the Fed was reluctant to deviate from them even when adherence to them had unintended and unwelcome macroeconomic consequences. This dilemma became acute and dangerous in 1982, when an unanticipated and persistent decline in the velocity of money meant that sticking to the targets implied a further severe decline in nominal and real GNP. Eventually Paul Volcker and his colleagues chose the economy over M-1, to universal relief and with no loss of credibility. That policy shift turned the economy from recession to recovery, and since then Fed policy has been oriented more to macro-economic performance, as measured by variables that really matter – GNP, prices, exchange rates, interest rates – than to money-stock growth targets. The Fed has recognized that velocity is volatile, the more so because of recent institutional, technological and regulatory changes, and is prepared to adjust money growth to compensate for persistent velocity changes even if it requires transgressing and revising its M targets.

The Fed has, it is true, allowed the economy to stagnate over the last year and a half, but that seems to reflect its macroeconomic judgment rather than its concern for money-stock targets *per se*. The corollary is that the Congress should make its own judgments about the desirable paths of real GNP and unemployment, and convey them to the Federal Reserve. After all, these are the most important economic decisions the federal government makes. Responsible elected officials should not evade them. Twice a year the Federal Reserve reports to Congressional committees its monetary targets for the coming quarters and its "projections" for GNP, prices, and unemployment. Since the Fed has been shifting emphasis to macroeconomic performance and downgrading money-stock growth, these projections can be interpreted as its basic targets. The committees should take them seriously in the hearings, both *ex ante* and *ex post*. (The economy fell short of the Fed's February and July projections for GNP in the second half of 1985.)

The immediate challenge is the transition to a tighter fiscal stance and to a better policy mix. It should not be allowed to bring on recession or prolong stagnation. If fiscal policy is about to be tightened severely, by Gramm–Rudman or by normal legislative process, the Fed should lower interest rates significantly, even if this requires unusually high money growth during the transition. If so, and only if so, will we reap the benefits of an improved mix of fiscal and monetary policy.

The Monetary–Fiscal Mix Today and Tomorrow

Reaganomic fiscal policy led to an extreme monetary–fiscal mix, beyond feasible sustainable limits. Even while slack remained in the economy these past three years, the Federal Reserve felt it necessary from time to time to contain the speed of recovery propelled by massive fiscal stimulus. Thus real interest rates, even after-tax rates on US Treasury obligations, which had been elevated sky-high during the Fed's recessionary anti-inflation crusade after 1979–82, remained above the economy's long-run growth rate after the Fed shifted gears to recovery. This constellation is a recipe for unending and accelerating growth in ratios of federal deficits and debt to GNP. The high net internal costs of the debt alone guarantee such instability, which is of course accentuated by a "primary" deficit (that is, on transactions unrelated to existing debt) of about 2.5 percent of GNP. Although the 40 percent debt/GNP ratio already reached is not itself disastrous, runaway growth of that ratio is not a viable long-run future.

As I stressed above, the same total dose of demand stimulus can be given in various mixtures of monetary and fiscal medicine. The short-run consequences for output, employment and prices will be very much the same. Important side effects will be different. The principal differences are in the uses of national output, in particular the relative shares of private and public consumption on the one hand, and real investment on the other – to put it more basically, the relative shares of present- and future-oriented economic activities. Generally speaking, a loose-fiscal tight-money policy mix, of which the 1980s present an extreme example, encourages present consumption relative to investment for the future.

I should at this point interject some caveats regarding the identification of future-oriented, growth-oriented, policy with tight budgets. Some deficit-increasing expenditures are future-oriented, for example public investments in infrastructure, research, education and environmental protection. It would be silly to cut these out in blind ideological belief that only private capital formation matters to the future productivity of the economy. Those outlays should be considered on their merits, weighed against shopping centers and casinos in the private sector as well as against robots and computers. Bob Eisner is right about this, and the JEC could take the lead in insisting on capital accounting for the public sector in the United States, about the only civilized country where it is not done. Moreover, some deficit-increasing tax reductions increase private investment instead of, or along with, private consumption. Careful attention to the content of government budgets is essential to appraise the effects of particular fiscal-monetary mixes. These caveats do not, however, save the United States' policy mix of recent years from the charge that it has been pro-consumption and anti-growth.

Comparing the year 1984 with 1978, the last preceding year of normal prosperity, I find that fully 97 percent of the growth of real final sales (GNP less inventory investment) was destined for private consumption or government purchases of goods and services. The Reagan macroeconomic strategy failed completely in its objective of tilting the disposition of national output toward private investment in the interests of speeding up productivity growth. While increased domestic fixed investment did amount to about 23 percent of the increment of real GNP, this was almost completely offset by the decline in Americans' foreign investment, i.e., our net exports. Domestic capital formation mortgaged to foreigners will not benefit our children and our children's children.

While the tax legislation of 1981 (modified in 1982) gave incentives for private saving and investment, its immediate and direct effect was to add massively to the government's dissaving. The second effect swamped the first. Anyway, there is no evidence that the tax cuts enhanced households' propensity to save. Although new tax incentives may have helped revive business investment in 1983 and 1984 – this too is debatable – high real interest rates worked the other way, especially on residential construction, which did not enjoy similar concessions.

The same recovery could have been engineered with much less fiscal stimulus, with deficits in the normal range of postwar experience, and with real interest rates several hundred basis points lower. There would have been more domestic investment and much more foreign investment; we would not have the large trade deficits that have crippled American manufacturing and agriculture.

These international implications of United States macroeconomic policies have been the most surprising and disturbing feature of recent experience. Although they corresponded qualitatively to economists' textbooks, we too were unprepared for their magnitudes. There is a powerful new mechanism by which high interest rates reduce demand for goods and services. It is a product of the regime of floating exchange rates, which replaced the Bretton Woods system of fixed parities in 1971–73, combined with the high international mobility of interest-sensitive funds, free of exchange controls, passing through worldwide markets of marvelous technical efficiency. In the 1980s high US interest rates attracted funds into dollars, appreciated the exchange value of the dollar, and made American goods uncompetitive at home and abroad. The excess of imports over exports (3 percent of GNP) has become a major drag on aggregate demand and the source of counter-productive political pressures for protectionism.

At the same time, the dollar prices of goods with unchanged foreign currency prices fell; since these have some weight in American price indexes, the appreciation of the dollar assisted our disinflation – accounting for perhaps 10 percent of the decline in the Consumer Price Index from 1980 to 1984. This effect is an exception to the rule I stated above, that for a given impact on aggregate demand the mix of outcomes between prices and quantities is independent of the mix of demand management policies. A loose-fiscal tight-money mix does yield somewhat lower prices for the same output. However, this gain accrues only to the one country pursuing the policy. Our trading partners suffered extra temporary inflation because of the appreciation of the dollar, which inflicted on them higher local prices for goods (including oil wherever produced) invoiced in dollars. For the same reason, we will not be able to keep those disinflationary gains of recent years related to the appreciation of our currency. As the dollar depreciates and restores some of our lost competitiveness in world markets, we will have to pay back the disinflation we borrowed from our friends overseas. Consequently, the exception to the rule is not, in my opinion, a weighty justification for the bizarre policy mix the United States drifted into during this decade.

Summary and Conclusion

(1) The objectives of the Employment Act should be restored to high priority in federal economic policy. It is high time to break the dismal upward trend of unemployment. The climate is favorable; the stagflationary shocks of the 1970s are behind us. Stagnation at 7 percent unemployment is over-cautious when no signs of inflationary pressure, either from wage costs or from demand, are visible. So long as these benign conditions obtain, federal demand management policies should aim to reduce gradually the unemployment and excess capacity rates. Under present circumstances, this task falls to Federal Reserve monetary policy.

(2) Since 1982 the Fed has been gearing its policies less to money-stock targets and more to macroeconomic performance. Its semi-annual projections of GNP can be taken as indicators of its desired path for the economy. Congress should welcome and reinforce this trend, make its own targets for the economy known to the Fed, and hold the Fed responsible for macroeconomic performance, as measured by variables that really matter: GNP growth, prices, unemployment.

(3) The inflation-safe unemployment rate, though surely significantly lower than the current rate, can only be estimated with further experience in today's environment, and even then with uncertainty. It is probably too high for the nation's economic health. Structural policies and reforms will be needed to make it possible for demand management policies to aim at lower rates of unemployment. These have to do with government regulations, labor and product markets, wage- and price-setting institutions. The JEC has an opportunity to contribute to the design of such structural changes. The time to fix the roof is when it is not raining.

(4) The tight anti-inflationary monetary stance of 1979–82 and the Reaganomic fiscal programs from 1981 on have given the United States an unprecedented, extreme and bizarre mix of demand management policies. The tight-money/easy-budget combination is not viable in the long run. It results in real interest rates on public debt higher than the

sustainable growth rate of the economy. This is a recipe for unending rise in the debt-to-GNP ratio, especially because the primary budget is also in deficit. The policy mix runs counter to long-run growth because it encourages present-oriented uses of GNP relative to future-oriented ones. The mix has resulted in a large current account deficit in US international transactions, i.e. in massive net borrowing from the rest of the world. Although the appreciation of the dollar bought us some extra disinflation, it was borrowed from our trading partners and will have to be repaid eventually. The temporary disinflationary gains do not justify our policy mix, nor should their reversal deter us from moving to a more normal and better mix or from completing our presently stalled recovery. A tighter-fiscal and easier-money mix will lower interest rates, depreciate the dollar, and improve the competitiveness of American industry and agriculture. It will also be better for long-run growth. All these consequences are to be welcomed.

(5) Fiscal policy, once the mainstay of demand stabilization, is now the junior partner of monetary policy. The extreme size of current and prospective budget deficits, actual and structural, rule out budgetary changes as counter-cyclical tools. The Gramm–Rudman remedy is almost worse than the disease, since it mandates perverse pro-cyclical movements in fiscal stimulus. The Federal Reserve will need to be active and bold in order to keep the economy free of recession during the transition to tighter fiscal policy, *a fortiori* to complete the recovery and sustain growth.

(6) Once the transition is made, there is good reason for optimism that the rest of the century can be one of stability and growth, the more so if pragmatic realism is substituted for ideology in the management of the economy. As an aged veteran soldier of the cause of the Employment Act, I am unavoidably dismayed by the wholesale dismissal on all sides of pre-1980 ideas and policies. I look forward to the day when some of the forgotten "golden oldies" will be rediscovered and hailed as "new."

4

The International Experience

JOHN ZYSMAN and STEPHEN COHEN

This paper contends that production is changing in such profound ways and at such rapid rates as to seriously threaten our nation's place – and the places of most other nations – in the international economic hierarchy. We are, in brief, in the midst of a major industrial transition.

Transition is a word that triggers a reaction – usually bored annoyance. After all nothing is more permanent than transition, especially in economics. A healthy economy is always in a state of transition. Indeed, as that oldest of professorial remarks has it, it was Father Adam who turned to Eve on the way out of Eden and announced: "I guess we are entering a period of transition." Technology is always changing: think of the railway, the motorcar, the electrical grid, Saran wrap. And competitors are constantly struggling for a new product, new process and new kinds of efficiency. That's what makes the game so constructive; it keeps us on our toes and busy citing Schumpeter. This paper argues that the transition is real and colossally consequential.

I

Two principal forces – (1) changes in international competition and (2) changes in production technology – are driving the changes in the world's economies. The first motor force is the relatively rapid and massive exposure of major segments of American manufacturing and services to international competition that is different in extent and in kind from anything we have previously experienced. Over the past generation America preached to itself and to others a doctrine of interdependence. But it was the other nations that were interdependent on each other, and in the US

Major portions of this paper appear in Stephen Cohen and John Zysman, *Manufacturing Matters* (Basic Books, New York, 1986). Research for the larger work from which this paper was drawn was supported by special grants from the Carnegie Forum on the Education and the Economy and the Office of Technology Assessment, US Congress to the Berkeley Roundtable on the International Economy (BRIE).

we were independent. As late as 1970 imports into the US totaled only $40 billion; by 1980 they had climbed to $245 billion and by 1984 to almost $350 billion. Until only yesterday imports in manufacturing averaged around 4–5 percent of sales and were easily balanced by exports; now they are about 25 percent of sales and some 70 percent of US industries are subject to foreign competition. The abrupt change in scale was matched by a change in kind. Old competitors, located mostly in Western Europe, caught up from an unnatural lag in the kind of production that created the wealth and power of the United States – complex manufacturing in such industries as autos, chemicals and aircraft. They accumulated or dug up capital. And they have never been behind in the fundamentals – education and the ability to create technology. But more important, new competitors have come on line, most prominently across the Pacific. To speed their development, many of the most successful of these new competitors have shaped economic structures, institutions and policies that are marginally, but crucially, different from ours, in small and crucial ways. We call these economies Developmental States. Japan is the most successful, and the biggest, but it is not the only one. Japanese competition in all lines of production – ranging from the highest technology products such as VLSI semiconductors and optoelectronics through complex manufacturing such as automobiles and consumer electronics to such advanced services as banking and process engineering – has, more than any other factor, been responsible for the current debate on American competitiveness.

The Developmental State

Since we cannot here review a long series of country and sector stories, let us at least briefly consider some fundamentals of the Japanese case. The Japanese government exerted influence on the economy during its boom years of the 1950s and 1960s in two important ways. First, it was a gatekeeper controlling the links between the domestic and international economy. It was in T. J. Pempel's terms an "official doorman determining what and under what conditions capital, technology and manufacturing products enter and leave Japan."[1] The discretion to decide what to let in and, at the extreme, out of Japan permitted the doorman to break up the packages of technology, capital and control that the multinational corporations represent. In almost all cases, neither money nor technology could in itself allow outsiders to buy or bull their way into a permanent position in the Japanese market. This closed market then gave Japanese firms a stable base of demand which permitted rapid expansion of production and innovation in manufacturing.

Second, government agencies – most notoriously MITI – sought to orient the development of the domestic economy. Although government bureaucrats did not dictate to an administered market, they have consciously contributed to the development of particular sectors. MITI is not so much a strict director as a player with its own purposes and its own means of interfering in the market to reach them. Government industrial strategy assumes that the market pressures of competition can serve as an instrument of policy. It is not simply that the government makes use of competitive forces that arise naturally in the market, but rather that it often induces the very competition it directs. This intense, but controlled, domestic competition substituted for the pressures of the international market to force development. The competition is real, but the government and private sector work together to avoid "disruptive" or "evasive" competition. We do not need to select between cartoon images of Japan, Inc. or a land of unfettered competition. It is the particular interaction of state and market in Japan that is interesting.

Seen from the perspective of the firm, government policy helped provide cash for investment, tax breaks to sustain liquidity, research and development support and aid to promote exports. These public policies – the web of policies rather than any individual element of it – changed the options of companies. Without the protected markets the initial investment could not in many cases have been justified by private companies. Without external debt finance, the funds to expand production rapidly would not have been available to the firms. Within a protected market, the easy availability of capital and imported technology was bound to attract entrants to favored sectors.

However MITI viewed the stampede for entry which it had encouraged and the resulting battle for market share, which limited profits, as excessive competition that had to be controlled. The intensive domestic competition was controlled by a variety of mechanisms that included expansion plans agreed to jointly by government and industry, debt financing of rapid expansion that made the bankruptcy of major firms a threat to the entire economy and hence unthinkable, and the oft-cited recession cartels. The dual facts of purposive government influence on economic outcomes and real market competition are reconciled by seeing the system as one of controlled or limited competition.

The very success of Japanese industrial development – combined with intensifying pressure from Japan's trading partners – has begun to loosen the network of relations that characterized the developmental state, and on which the strategy of creating advantage in world markets rested. Many formal restrictions on entry to the Japanese market have been lifted. Serious trade problems still remain, however. As long as Japan had to borrow generic technologies on which to build its growth and had underdeveloped potential markets that could be seized by domestic or foreign producers, formal closure of markets was essential to a system of orchestrated development. Now less formal obstacles to entry may matter as crucially to competition in advanced technology as formal restrictions did a generation earlier.

Japan's imports of manufactured goods remain dramatically below those of the other advanced countries, and have not increased as a proportion of the national economy since the early 1970s. Japan's unique trade characteristic is the tendency, relative to its trade partners, not to import manufactures in sectors in which it exports. The system of administrative guidance that affects government programs of finance and procurement, the Byzantine distribution system, and the habits of private coordination amidst competition all evolved slowly. Indeed, the Japanese state still exercises a leadership role and exerts substantial influence in high-technology industries on the one hand, and declining or mature industries faced with oversupply on the other.

There is a crucial interplay between these two sets of interventionist policies that is likely to continue to spark problems in international markets and enduring tensions between Japan and its trade partners. Promotional policies in which the risks of domestic oversupply are at least in part insured against or underwritten, depending on how one chooses to characterize the particulars of Japanese policies, encourage bursts of investment for domestic demand that translate directly into export drives. Now that Japanese producers tie domestic investment decisions directly to world market strategies, the relationship between strategies in the Japanese market and their impact in the American market is immediate. There is a pattern of aggressive promotion of advancing sectors and of determined insulation and cushioning of mature sectors. This amounts to confining open international competition in the domestic market to sectors in which major Japanese firms are dominant worldwide or at least able to withstand foreign entry into the home market, and to sectors from which Japanese firms are absent. It implies sustaining closure in those sectors that are under pressure from abroad.

The Japanese system may slowly open and become fully integrated with its advanced-country trade partners. But other would-be Japans stand in line. The challenge of the developmental state will not pass from the contemporary scene.

II

The second major force is a technological revolution in production, spreading across major segments of manufacturing and services. It is built on the advent for mass application of microelectronics-based telecommunications and automatic control technologies. Its emblematics are the semiconductor, the computer, the robot; potent combinations of these technologies are CAD, CAM and CIM. Their buzzword translations into business startegy, economic policy debates and social anxiety include computerization, flexible production, deskilling, reskilling, dislocation – a second industrial revolution.

These two forces – technological change and the new scale and nature of international competition – interrelate and compound; competition drives the development of the technologies, the rates of their diffusion and, just as important, the ways they are used. In turn, the use of these technologies is a major component of the new strategies throughout the economy for responding to foreign competition. Their combined effect is to propel America smack into the middle of an industrial transition we didn't ask for and we may not be prepared to cope with terribly well.

The Eroding Competitiveness of American Industry

In this era of fundamental industrial transition, American producers are not doing very well. Precisely because the changes are basic and likely to prove enduring, the outcomes of industrial competition today will matter powerfully tomorrow. The trade conflicts that have pushed their way onto the front page are not ordinary trade frictions about cars or blouses or semiconductors. They involve serious, long-term conflicts about shifting national positions in the world economy. The wealth and power of nations are the stakes. Once American firms dominated world markets; now they must adjust to them. A mere twenty years ago Europeans wrote books about the American Challenge and the Secrets of the Giant American Firms while they fretted about technology gaps and undoubted American advantages in product, production process, marketing strategy and management techniques. Now we read about the East Asian Edge, Japan as Number One, and flexible production in Italy while we worry about innovations in production and management coming from abroad. Unfortunately, the evidence is substantial that the American position has eroded dramatically.

Measured each of seven different ways – by unprecedented trade deficits in manufactured goods, declining shares of world markets for exports, lagging rates of productivity increases, eroding profit margins, declining real wages, the increasing price elasticities of imports and the eroding position in world high technology markets – American industry confronts a severe problem of competitiveness that it has never known before. Each measure has its limitations and can, perhaps, be explained away, but taken together they defy easy dismissal and portray a serious long-term problem.[2]

It is misleading to conclude, as many do, that America's comparative advantage in high technology goods translates into a secure position in international trade in high technology, let alone in manufactures in general. Comparative advantage means, in the end, the thing you do less worse than you do others – not the thing at which you are better than your foreign competitors. It is misleading to conclude that since there is no rapid "deindustrialization" the path along which American manufacturing is evolving is healthy or secure. American adjustment to the new world economy is quite troubled. It is not only statistical indicators that tell the story. There is something going on underneath. Japanese producers, for example, have established real competitive advantages in a range of complex manufactured products. These advantages rest on a wider diffusion of advanced technology, as in steel, in greater investment in automated production technologies, as in segments of the electronics industry, and an approach to mass production which uses fewer labor hours per unit than American companies in a broad range of consumer durables from machine tools through automobiles.

Though symmetry is the organizing principle of economic theory, as many students learned practicing origami in Economics 101, it is not the organizing principle of international competition. Temporary disequilibria brought about by superficial causes – as the overvaluation of the dollar is generally treated – can have profound and enduring consequences. Foreign companies that establish sales distribution networks, and even brand recognition in the US market will tend to hold them as the dollar declines. The super-profits garnered by foreign industries as a result of the dollar's high have in many cases been used for reinvestment in more efficient production that will generate a competitive edge in the years to come. It is perhaps worth noting that when the dollar rose by almost 50 percent between 1980 and 1984, the prices of imported goods declined by only 2 percent. That means – despite what we are regularly told – it is not so much the US consumer who has benefited from the high dollar as much as foreign producers, middlemen and retailers, according to the *New York Times*, Dec. 9, 1985. Similarly, US corporations that moved production to offshore factories during a period of a high dollar will not necessarily move their facilities home when the dollar falls. Indeed, as we argue below, the move abroad to find cheap labor may preclude a strategy of sustained production innovation at home. The moves made during the era of the super-dollar may thus have more than long-term locational consequences but may adversely affect the strategic choices of firms as well. Such traditional notions as symmetrical effects and rubberband responses, where the system goes back to the predisturbance equilibrium, are inappropriate organizing principles. Strategic choices made in response to one set of factors – often relatively small factors – can have consequences that are not likely to be reversible and be far greater in scale than what caused them.

III

The key to American adjustment to a transforming world economy and an evolving technology may prove to be the capacity to remain, or better still become once again, competitive in manufacturing processes. This can be seen clearly by considering the international market pressures to which firms and industries must respond and the technologies to which they must adapt. First the low-cost labor of the newly industrializing countries has permitted firms in those nations to penetrate the markets of the advanced countries. In labor-intensive goods that are sold on the basis of low cost, advanced country producers cannot compete without protection or basic strategic shifts. They must either reorganize production, making labor-intensive production into a game of automation, or alter their mix of products, and with it marketing and corporate strategies. Second, in consumer durables industries such as autos and televisions, competitive advantage rests on the mastery of complex manufacturing processes, as well as on distinct product and marketing strategies. Those processes are being revolutionized by microelectronics. Finally, in advanced technology sectors, the ability to implement new engineering and scientific knowledge in products and production is critical. The basic science and many of the generic engineering concepts used in these industries are in the public domain. The ability to commercialize these ideas successfully and produce the products competitively is the basis of advantage.

American producers over the last years have moved their production offshore, not simply to be closer to their foreign markets, but to find inexpensive labor and components to reduce the cost of products they sell in the United States. Offshore production has been spawned both by the pressure of imports and by competition among American firms. It has been sustained by policy both in the United States and in the countries where export platforms have been located. In the last years some American firms have found another reason to move production abroad. They have sought to escape some of the consequences of the high value of the US dollar.

The move abroad is cumulative, that is it builds on itself in two ways. First, an offshore production network that is a real alternative to a domestic net has been built up. When the first producers went abroad they had to supply many of the component parts and production services from an American base. Their suppliers often moved offshore with them, to be closer to the point of final production and to capture some of the same advantages of aid and low-cost labor. Foreign component makers also began to supply American offshore producers. For example, the American semiconductor industry has found that when their clients move offshore, they begin to buy components from offshore sources as well. In some cases American firms have subcontracted their production abroad, transferring the product and production knowhow. This has often speeded the emergence of their own competitors. In fact, once component sources are offshore there is often a temptation to move product assembly offshore: as product assembly moves, additional moves offshore of component suppliers are again encouraged. Once the bulk of production is offshore, there comes a moment when it is seriously tempting to move product engineering abroad. This is not fanciful. We have heard such discussions in American firms. Let us be clear, though, the move offshore gives a one-time labor cost advantage. Production innovation and investment in capital offshore are required to sustain that advantage.

Second, after years of moving abroad to find cheap labor to produce existing products at lower costs, American firms build up an expertise in the management of offshore production. They do not build up an expertise in managing the implementation of the most advanced production technologies or in designing or redesigning product to facilitate automated production in the United States. Over time, the perception that foreign competition could be met by offshore production took form and force! Even a few years ago, when it was already evident that the Japanese had massively invested in production, some in the semiconductor industry were still calling for more offshore locations as a viable response. Some major corporations have built formal models to set a framework for these choices, but the models (in our view) are built on quite incorrect assumptions about exchange rates and leaning curves that serve simply to justify their biases.

We do not intend to exaggerate. There are many goods or pieces of production processes which, because they cannot be effectively automated, absorb enormous amounts of labor and have limited transportation costs, are clear candidates for offshore production or assembly. As programmable automation emerges the mix of activities which can be carried out in the United States will expand. We suggest simply that earlier moves offshore were often taken without clear attention to the possibilities of traditional automation and that the earlier moves offshore may blind firms to the possibilities and needs of automating at home.

America cannot maintain its wealth or high wages economy by only playing a role as laboratory for the world, producing the ideas and prototypes and handling distribution and advertising and sales in our own market, while others make the products. If we can't make the products, our technology edge will erode. After several rounds of product innovation, the innovative initiative will pass to the firms that make the products. They end up understanding the market and the product in a way that permits them to become the technology leader. Experience in steel, consumer electronics and autos alone ought to convince us of this.

The proposition is simple. *Lose control of the manufacturing or produc-*

*tion process of your product and you risk losing control of both the techno-
logy and the final markets*. A firm or a nation's industry cannot survive at a
substantial production disadvantage to its major competitors.

Common to these three categories of competition is the importance of
manufacturing processes to retaining industrial competitiveness. The
revolution in manufacturing is as important as the more often noted
acceleration in the pace of product innovation. When pressed by low-cost
producers, American companies can sometimes transform a labor-
intensive production process into one that is technology-intensive. This, of
course, involves substantial displacement of labor, a reorganization of the
labor that remains, and changes in corporate habits. Sharp dislocations of
workers and communities have generally produced political trouble that
disrupts the adjustment process. Competitive position over time, in a
broad range of products such as consumer durables, rests squarely on the
ability to master the most advanced manufacturing techniques. Even in the
so-called haven of high technology, the long-run competitiveness of firms
and the national economy will rest on translating product advantage into
enduring market position through manufacturing expertise. Manufacturing expertise is, in this period of fundamental change in production
processes, critical. The central capacity required to remain competitive
will prove to be dynamic flexibility, the capacity to adjust rapidly to new
market and production conditions. That flexibility will turn on corporate
strategies and structures, the capacities of the people throughout the
production system, and the national technological infrastructure to
develop and diffuse new production technologies and approaches.

The distinction between *static* and *dynamic* flexibility is to us critical,
not the differences in techniques used to be flexible. *Static flexibility*
means the ability of a firm to adjust its operations at any moment to shifting conditions in the market, to the rise and fall of demand or the changes
in the mix of product the market is asking for. It implies adjustment within
a fixed product and production structure. Flexibility has come to mean a
whole variety of ways of adjusting company operations to the shifting
conditions of the market. The term is used to refer to the ability of a firm
efficiently to vary its strategic direction, level of production, composition
of goods, length of the work day or week, level of wages, organization of
work or any of a variety of other elements of operations.

The techniques to achieve flexibility can thus be technological or
organizational. Firms may employ new programmable machine tools to
increase the efficiency of batch production or reach an agreement with
unions to reduce the number of job categories. The reduction of the
number of job categories in the new United Motors (the GM-Toyota
venture in Fremont, California) permits easier changes on the shopfloor.
American Airlines announces it is reducing the number of full-time
employees in many airports, shifting to part-time personnel, in order to

increase its operational flexibility. A worker buy-out of a steel plant in Weirton, Va. permits a wage reduction, the workers accepting "wage flexibility" because they have a stake in the company profits. In static terms – that is at any given moment – increased flexibility means greater capacity to adjust to short-term market changes. Static flexibility, consequently decreases risk that the firm won't be able to adapt to changes in the number and types of goods demanded in the market, it increases the ability to adopt quickly to changed conditions.

Dynamic flexibility, by contrast, means the ability to increase pro-ductivity steadily through improvements in production processes and innovation in product. Burton Klein presents the notion well.[3] He argues that Japanese firms, and auto firms originally,

> have evolved a practice that can be described as dynamic flexibility ... contrasted with static flexibility, dynamic flexibility is not concerned with producing more than one product (e.g. cars and light trucks) on a single production line – although the Japanese do this too. Rather it is concerned with designing production lines in a way that they can quickly evolve in response to changes in either the product or production technology. In other words, the central pre-occupation is to get ideas into action quickly ... (In practice in Japan) the main purpose of dynamic flexibility is to make rapid changes in production technology for the purpose of lowering costs and thereby improving productivity.

We agree with Klein that "continuing productivity gains presuppose advances in relevant technologies and a keen desire to make good use of this progress." All studies of post-war economic growth in the advanced countries highlight that technological advance, not the simple increase in the number of machines or the amount of capital or labor employed, is at the core of sustained increases in productivity and economic develop-ment. Indeed where R and D expenditures have dropped, productivity increases have fallen in latter years. Increased productivity permits lowered costs or, depending on the response of competitors, higher wages and profits.

Dynamic flexibility is the corporate capacity to develop and introduce these technological advances. A commitment to such flexibility in Japan is reflected in the structure of the market for computer-controlled manu-facturing equipment. In Japan many firms develop internally their own production equipment. "Almost every Japanese auto company has a large machine tool operation in which 200 to 400 people do nothing but create new tools, which are quickly introduced into the production process." When successful, these machines are often then sold on the market. In Japan as a consequence the machine tool market is highly fragmented, shared amongst many producers who are developing equipment for their own internal purposes and then selling it on the open market. In the United States, where less production equipment development occurs internally, the market for programmable machine tools is highly concentrated, that is, shared amongst a few big producers. The result, which we return to, is that American firms tend to introduce production innovations periodically, moving from one plateau of best practice to another. The Japanese, studies suggest, move through continuous and iterative production innovation, steadily improving the production process. In fact, the Japanese system with greater flexibility has achieved greater productivity gains over the last years than the more rigid American ones.

Technological advance inherently involves risk; new ideas may not work in practice or may not work as well as hoped. Consequently, dynamic flexibility involves a management of levels of risk sufficient to match what competitors are doing. Levels of risk, Klein argues, vary from industry to industry. A norm emerges within a given sector. Partly this is a product of the possibilities inherent in the technologies of the moment. If the potential returns are very high and the risk relatively low, one or another firm in a sector may take the risk of product development. Partly the risk norm, the propensity to engage in risk, depends on the intensity of competition in the industry. In the United States, in our view, firms in many oligopolistic sectors had established a low norm of technological risk that was part of a competitive truce or at least a corporate Geneva Convention about the terms of civilized combat that reduced the need to take risks. American firms in a variety of sectors suddenly confronted competitors from foreign sectors where the norms of risk – partly a reflection of the pace of development – were higher. American firms were caught off-balance, and the results are evident.

Static and dynamic flexibility are inextricably linked. Static flexibility to short-term shifts in market conditions can be achieved in a variety of ways; how it is achieved will affect the long-term capacity of the firm to introduce the evolving technology on which its product and production position depend. A decision to move production offshore may be taken because it will allow lower wages and or because it will make it easier to shut plants during downturns. The move offshore, it seems to us, makes it harder to steadily improve the production process itself. A decision to reduce skill levels in domestic plants to reduce skilled-worker resistance to technological development may eliminate the very skilled workers required to implement new production technologies effectively. In a similar vein, firms may have to choose between short-term economies of scale which involve large fixed costs in the form of investment in equipment and the long-term necessity of responding to evolving technologies, which may involve smaller and less efficient plants. Japanese and American firms have made different choices. "Japanese plants for producing cars are only about one-third as large as comparable American plants," ostensibly to permit greater dynamic flexibility.

A period of economic transition is a time when "dynamic flexibility" is of predominant importance. Our contention is that the crucial change now is the transformation of manufacturing, not the replacement of industry by service. The transformation of manufacturing does not simply mean that a few "sunrise" manufacturing sectors, such as personal computers, are assuming the importance once held by certain traditional manufacturing sectors, such as automobiles. Rather, as we shall see in a moment, computers have begun to alter the production process throughout industry. The transformation is occurring because the new high-technology sectors are agents of change, sources of innovation, within the traditional sectors. Much of "high technology" really consists of producer goods – goods used to make other products. As individuals we do not buy a bag of silicon chips, we buy the products that incorporate semiconductors, or we buy products that incorporate semiconductors that have been made by machines that also incorporate these omnipresent chips. We do not buy high-speed computers or mainframe computers, we buy products that are developed or processed on those machines. It is for aircraft design and now automobile design that supercomputers are purchased. The insurance industry long ago became a dominant buyer of mainframe computers and even minicomputers. *The proper object of our concern should be how the new technologies spread throughout the economy as part of a national response to changing competition. We must have a national economy that can absorb and apply the new technologies.*

IV

America has a choice. Our economic and indeed our technological future will be a product of political decisions. It is not simply a choice of whether we do well or badly, but of the kind of society the economy we create can support.

The need for choice is urgent, for America is not adjusting well to the changing world economy. The evidence is overwhelming that our competitive position in international markets has eroded. We are displaying rigidity where flexibility is required. Even the credibility of the counter-arguments that the problem is centrally one of exchange rates or can be managed by increasing service exports is crumbling. Furthermore, many of the debates are simply poorly formulated. It is not a matter of de-industrialization, of whether American industry disappears or not. It is a matter of the composition of the manufacturing base. For example, we have been happy exporting capital goods to Developing Nations and importing the finished product made with those machines on the grounds, correct we believe, that America should position itself in the segments of industry that can sustain high wages. Should we be equally content that America now imports the high value-added textile and apparel machinery built in Europe and Japan with high wage labor to produce low value-added textiles and apparel produced with low wage labor? And how should we feel about imports now taking more than 50 percent of our market for advanced machine tools – far more than that if we omit protected sales to defense contractors.

The task is to assure a dynamic adjustment to shifting market and technological conditions that will sustain our high-wage economy. We must sustain the ability to generate and apply product and process innovation. It is not just a matter of innovation, but of the ability to exploit innovation in the market. Technology diffuses quickly and when sold as licenses captures few rents. The lessons of the last years make that very clear. Using technological innovation to create and hold market positions for entire industries requires a deep and broad effort. Technology spreads quickly, leaving few advantages in the simple creation of scientific or technological knowledge or in the investment in simple machines. Thus, all depends on how that knowledge is used throughout the economy. That in the end rests in the investment in people, human capital, not narrowly in engineers or scientists – though certainly that – but broadly in the community as a whole.

Our policy problem is not a matter of capturing gains from others, but of assuring our own abilities to participate fully in the possibilities of the new economy that is emerging. Policy can expand our capacity to make the multiplicity of adjustments that will be required. It can help to upgrade a nation's position in international competition in a substantial and enduring way. Like much in economic reality, but little in economic theory, the relationship is not symmetrical. Policy, all by itself, can hold back an economy that has most other things going for it: Argentina is a recurring reminder. But policy, however enlightened and astute, can (by itself) only contribute to the upgrading process. It can't do it alone. But the contribution can be very important.

The thing policy is least able to do is to have *no* impact on a nation's competitive position. And that, of course, is what conventional economics sternly prescribes for it. That policy cannot simply go away, or be "held-harmless" in its impacts on the economy, is true not only for America, but for any complex, modern society. Like it or not, government affects the economy – both as a direct economic actor (taxing, spending and, often, doing) and as a set of all-pervasive and ever-changing rules. That truth is compounded by the fact that economic reality today consists of several large and complex economies that are all heavily policy-impacted. One nation's policies affect another nation's position. Were it achievable, policy neutrality in all nations might well be the best rule for the system as a whole (though not necessarily for any one nation in that system). In the absence of such universality, it loses any claim for being the best rule for any particular nation.

These thoughts take us right into another core notion that has shaped our policy debate, the forbidding doctrine of Comparative Advantage, remembered by the millions who once took Economics 101, in rather the same way as Latin declensions are remembered by their parents. Revealed comparative advantage, to give it its full name, is the economic doctrine that addresses foreign trade. It tells a nation what its economy will specialize in: the British (because they wrote the text) in manufacturing textiles; the Iberians (because they believed it and lost), in port wine. A nation should, and will find itself specializing in those activities where it is the most efficient (or at least inefficient) compared to all the others. Having a comparative advantage in something, say machinery, or better yet, complex manufacturing, does not mean that you are world-class good at it, or even better than the other guy. It means that you are just less worse at it than at other things. Your wage level tells you how good you are.

American policy debate on trade is formulated by the prevalent view of comparative advantage in American economics. Our policy choices are framed by the notion that comparative advantage is revealed, not created. A nation finds its comparative advantage by looking backwards in the trade statistics. It does not choose it by looking forward in its policy councils. Policy should not try to create comparative advantage. We are constantly told that nations who subsidize exports are only deluding themselves and, at the same time, subsidizing our consumers. Pull away the subsidy, and things will rubberband back to "normal." Enduring comparative advantage cannot be created by policy.

It is of course true that in a strict, definitional sense, comparative advantage cannot be created. But saying that is a little like saying, as the economists do, that foreign trade will always balance out. Prices simply need time and freedom to adjust. That is true, but nugatory. If, for example, we were to let the price of the dollar adjust to the point where one dollar equaled one yen, we could sell the entire economics building at the University of Chicago, brick by brick, to the Japanese to use as disco space. The trick is not to balance trade; it is to balance trade at a high-wage level. Similarly, we always have a comparative advantage in something. That is the way the thing is defined. The interesting question is, in what? Can we keep it in activities that pay a high wage? Government policy, we argue, can to a significant degree move that list upwards (or downwards).

V

In brief, the outcome of America's passage through the industrial transition need not be exclusively the affair of impersonal and imperturbable technological and economic forces. There is room for choice and action. That is the good news. The bad news is contained in that same sentence: there is room – and need – for choice. Just because we have a choice about our future does not mean that we will take advantage of that opportunity, use it well and even enjoy the freedom and responsibility choice provides. We have a political system that we cherish that is artfully constructed to avoid clear choices. And we have an economic ideology based on a notion of choice, that minimizes the opportunity and desirability of making important, strategic ones.

There is a spectrum of possible economic futures open to us. At one end lies an internationally competitive US economy in which highly productive, educated workers use new technologies flexibly to produce a broad range of high value-added goods and services. They thereby earn the high wages necessary to sustain both the standard of living to which many Americans have grown accustomed and most aspire, and the open society that has been so closely linked with a strong and open economy. At the other end of the spectrum lies the real danger of a competitively weakened economy in which a small minority of high-skilled jobs coexist with a majority of low-skilled, low-wage jobs and massive unemployment. Living standards – perhaps along with social equality and political democracy – would deteriorate rapidly as, in order to compete, manufacturing and services move more and more value-added offshore and automation strips the labor content from the remaining US goods and services.

The transition sets the agenda of change, but there is nothing inevitable about the outcome.

Notes

1. T. J. Pempel, 'Japanese foreign economic policy: the domestic bases for international behavior,' in *Between Power and Plenty*, ed. Peter S. Katzenstein (University of Wisconsin Press, Madison, 1978), p. 139.
2. Stephen Cohen, David Treece, Laura D'Andrea Tyson and John Zysman, *Report of the Presidents' Concession on Industrial Competitiveness*, vol. 3 (Washington, DC, 1984).
3. The discussion following relies heavily on Burton Klein, 'Dynamic competition and productivity advances,' in *'The Positive Sum': Strategies Harnessing Technology for Economic Growth* (National Academy of Sciences, Washington, DC, 1986).

PART II

The Challenges We Face

Introduction

In the last few years, business and economic news has been dominated by talk of deficits and debt. The subject of federal budget deficits has vexed economists for many decades. Most recently, a new deficit has come to dominate our thoughts – the trade deficit. The United States has a growing imbalance between what we produce and sell to others, and what they produce and sell to us.

In addition to deficits, we are also troubled by debt. Again, we are not just concerned about the federal debt, i.e. the accumulation of past deficits, but mounting private debt as well. Household and corporate debt now stands at a record level of 165 percent of gross national product. As a result of the trade and current account deficits we are now a debtor country, i.e. we owe foreigners more than they owe us, for the first time since the beginning of World War I.

Although most of us are familiar with the increase in the size of the federal deficit, a few facts are worth repeating for purposes of illustration. In 1960, the federal budget had a surplus of $0.3 billion and a surplus again in 1969 of $3.2 billion. However, the remaining years of the 1960s were years of modest budget deficits, as well as very strong economic growth, leaving us with $5.7 billion average annual budget deficit for the decade. In the 1970s the average annual deficit grew to $36.4 billion as the economy slowed and inflation mounted. The most dramatic increases have come in the 1980s when deficits of unprecedented size averaged $134.5 billion from 1980 to 1985 and $201.8 billion from 1983 to 1985. From an economist's perspective, perhaps the most important statistic is one that measures deficits as a percentage of GNP. In the 1960s deficits on average were 0.8 percent of GNP, in the 1970s 2.1 percent of GNP and in the 1980s to date 4.4 percent of GNP. From 1983 to 1985 deficits have averaged 5.6 percent of GNP, seven times the figure for the 1960s.

Economists differ greatly over the effects of deficits. They also differ over how to measure them. Do you account for inflation? Compare them against assets? Include state and local accounts? etc. What are the effects?

Do public deficits crowd out private investors? Or stimulate the economy into growth? Force up interest rates? Generate trade deficits?

Robert Eisner addresses many questions about federal deficits in his controversial article in chapter 7. Eisner takes the neo-Keynesian position that deficits can play a useful role in stimulating a weak economy, but also reminds us that they may be troublesome in a different economic environment. Eisner emphasizes, however, that we must be able to measure deficits correctly before we can predict their effects. Since we do not measure correctly it has been difficult to create appropriate theory and pursue appropriate policy.

In chapter 5, Felix Rohatyn brings the perspective of both policymaker and investment banker to bear. As Chairman of New York City's Municipal Assistance Corporation, which oversaw the financing of a bankrupt city, and as chairman of the investment firm of Lazard Frères, Rohatyn warns that corporate debt has exploded beyond rational grounds. Often using unstable financial instruments, firms and individuals have pursued their own short-term gain in ways which threaten the stability of the entire financial system. Rohatyn warns that complete deregulation of financial markets threatens us with chaos and calls for continued public scrutiny – compatible with the proper functioning of free markets – over the financial sector.

Lionel Olmer, former Undersecretary of Commerce for International Trade in the Reagan Administration, points out in chapter 6 to the dangers posed by the US trade deficit. Olmer warns that industrial firms must learn to produce more efficiently, but he emphasizes the tremendous burdens they must bear because of inadequate public policies. Olmer argues that economic policy must focus on the United States as an actor in an international economy, and to date this has been ignored.

The challenges posed by deficits and debts of various types are serious, each of these authors concludes. They can only be solved by a public policy which understands when government action helps, and when it hinders, a healthy market economy. Yet all agree that the resolution of these problems will determine the success of our nation's economy for the remainder of the century and beyond.

5

Financial Instability

FELIX ROHATYN

A few days ago the Federal Reserve Board adopted a rule to limit the more extreme types of junk bond takeovers by applying the margin rules (i.e. a requirement to put up 50 percent of the required capital) to a bid by a shell corporation. This rule is largely symbolic since it will affect relatively few takeovers, is easily circumvented and is aimed at the most extreme cases of leverage. The reaction was stupendous. Every agency and department of the Federal government attacked the Fed and Paul Volcker as if they had come out with a plan to nationalize the economy. Editorials screamed in the *Wall Street Journal* and many others, summarized by the following excerpt from a full page editorial in the *New York Post*: "Properly interpreted, then, the effects of this improper new rule will be to curtail the rights of stockholders, to reduce the value of their investment by reducing the number of potential buyers, to encourage foreign ownership of US corporations, to damage the financial services industry, to remove an important incentive for corporations to use their assets efficiently, and to make the economy generally more sluggish." The only rational interpretation for this dramatic overkill was that our most responsible financial leader, Paul Volcker, was being forced out as Chairman of the Fed in order to promote and protect the most extreme kind of unfettered speculation seen in the country since 1929. Fortunately for us, Paul Volcker stood firm; how long he can last under these circumstances is an open question. The New Deal is dead; so are the Fair Deal and the Great Society. However, the Casino Society is here and it is here with a vengeance.

I have seen the evolution of mergers and takeovers from the conglomerate merger era of the 1960s, through the growing acceptability of large, "hostile" takeover bids during the 1970s, to the current wave of huge transactions, with offensive and defensive tactics that often go beyond the norms of rational economic behavior. I am not here to argue against the ability of corporations to make acquisitions or to reject being acquired. Takeovers do not have to be friendly; they have to be fair and they have to

be soundly financed. Current takeover tactics, both in the legal and financial area, run counter to those principles.

Arguments for new or additional regulation or legislation should be
based on national interest issues. The issues involved here are twofold: (1)
The integrity of our securities markets; (2) The safety of our financial institutions.

They are both jeopardized by what is happening today as a result of
excesses in connection with takeovers.

These excesses, let me hasten to add, are not limited to the takeover
field. They are part of a general pattern of speculation in securities,
commodities, currencies, etc. They are part of a trend of excessive risk-
taking on the part of financial institutions seeking "performance" at the
expense of safety. They are the result of a climate of rapid deregulation
with inadequate preparation as to the results in certain areas.

A series of events is eroding the climate of confidence required of our
financial institutions. Among these were the financial collapse of several
government securities trading firms which led to crisis in the Ohio and
Maryland Savings Bank Systems, the financial collapse of the Penn Square
Bank which led to the quasi-nationalization of the Continental Illinois
Bank and the demise of the Seafirst Bank, and the repeated credit scares of
Third World borrowers. Every one of these events shakes the confidence
needed by our financial system. They are, however, only the tip of the
iceberg. Our banking system is still exposed to large risks. Many are under
the illusion that the Third World debt problem has been resolved as a
result of a series of rollovers; recent events in Argentina, Brazil and
Mexico with a combined external debt of $250 billion may create a rude
awakening. Elsewhere, if the price of oil were to drop by 20 per cent, not
unthinkable under present circumstances, the problems of banks with
large energy loans would be compounded by the problems of large oil
companies so elegantly restructured as a result of takeover raids and
greenmail. To the trillion dollars of Third World bank loans, we have to
add the dramatically increased use of debt, both conventional debt and
junk bonds, in all types of takeovers and leveraged buyouts and the risk
involved if we were to enter a serious recession. One does not have to be
Cassandra to be concerned about the safety of our financial institutions
and their vulnerability to sudden jolts.

By the end of 1985, American corporations will owe a total of $1.56
trillion, the highest in our history. After adjusting for inflation, debt has
grown at 8.69 percent per annum in 1984 and 1985 compared with 2.7
percent from 1975 to 1983. Corporate debt exceeds total net worth by 12
percent. Total borrowings now represent 81 percent of the external
sources of funds of corporations compared to 56 percent in 1975. As a
result, corporate debt has replaced equity financings, with stocks as a
percentage of external funds declining from 35 percent during 1975 to 14

percent currently. American corporations are far more vulnerable coming out of the 1980–82 recession than they were after the 1974–75 recession. Since 1982, cost of servicing debt has been absorbing 50 percent of the entire cash flow of corporations while during the 1976–79 recovery the cost averaged only 27 percent of cash flow. The combination of deflation, deregulation and a strong dollar makes this a very dangerous equation.

In the securities markets, especially in the takeover field, we also find troublesome excesses. Over the long run, the capital markets self-correct, but sometimes abuses become so widespread that the markets must be helped by legislation or regulation. Today that is the case in respect to takeovers. The abuses fall into several general categories: (1) unequal treatment of shareholders as part of offensive or defensive corporate actions; (2) unsound financial structures as a result of excessive leverage; (3) destabilizing impact of large-scale arbitrage and other short-term trading activities as an integral part of mergers and takeovers, and the market volatility thus created. I would like to examine each of these briefly.

(1) The basic concept of our securities laws, which have been the basis for the world-wide appeal of our securities markets, has been full disclosure, non-manipulation, and equal treatment of all shareholders. The most basic elements of stock ownership, i.e. equal voting rights and equal equity ownership for all common shareholders, are now under attack. Both the techniques of current takeovers as well as concurrent court decisions undercut these concepts. For instance, the NYSE is under pressure to permit the listing of common shares with unequal voting rights; and the recent Unocal decision in Delaware permits, in certain cases, unequal payment among common shareholders.

In tender offers, two-tier takeover bids heavily favor professional traders to the detriment of non-professionals. Bids that are made "subject to financing," in many cases directly or indirectly financed by junk bonds, permit the bidder to manipulate the markets without committing himself to purchase. The resulting activity by arbitrageurs and short-term traders creates speculative accumulations which, in the parlance of the trade, "put the company into play." Whether the result is "greenmail" or a "white knight" rescue, the result is a large profit for the raider, at minimal risk. The third-party, or "white knight" takeover, if it occurs, takes place purely to satisfy speculative positions taken as part of the raid.

Because of these tactics, defensive maneuvers have been devised that are equally damaging to shareholders. The payment of "greenmail" is the most obvious and, in many ways, the most old-fashioned of these maneuvers. Selective repurchase of stock, "lock-ups," "crown jewel options," "shark repellent" and "poison pills" of one kind or another, all have been designed to enable managements and boards of directors to impose themselves between the shareholders and takeover bids. These tactics have been used, sometimes indiscriminately, against bona fide bidders as well as against the more pernicious types. In some of the more extreme cases, i.e., in the defense of Carter-Hawley-Hale in the face of a 100 percent offer from The Limited and in the defense of Unocal against a partial offer from Mesa Petroleum, the courts permitted the target companies to selectively repurchase their own shares from some, but not all, shareholders. The result, in many cases, is to find companies burdened with excessive debt and their remaining shareholders badly damaged. Phillips Petroleum, Unocal, Carter-Hawley-Hale are all examples of this type of operation.

(2) As a result of this activity, financial structures are seriously eroded. I have mentioned above several examples of companies which, in order to remain independent, have depleted their equity and taken on excessive debt. Several of the largest takeovers were brought about as a result of raids, financed by junk bonds, on the target companies which were then acquired by third parties. A large part of the oil industry has been badly damaged as a result. Chevron-Gulf, Occidental-Cities Service, Mobil-Superior occurred as a result of raids or the threat of raids. The deterioration in their combined balance sheets has been dramatic. The premiums received by the acquired shareholders have been paid by the debt of the acquiring companies and, ultimately, by their shareholders. Far from being a healthy restructuring, the oil companies involved are cutting exploration sharply, a practice our country will pay for dearly when the next energy crisis occurs. In the meantime, as a result of their high levels of debt, they could be in serious difficulty, in the near term, if the price of oil continues to decline. If one were to write a scenario about how to get the United States into trouble as far as energy is concerned, it would be hard to improve on what is happening.

It is in the area of large takeovers that the junk-bond phenomenon is particularly hazardous. High-yield, unrated debt, in reasonable amounts, is a perfectly acceptable financing vehicle for many companies ineligible for investment-grade credit ratings. It is a different story, however, when this type of debt, in the billions of dollars, is used to substitute for equity in the takeovers of very large companies.

The risk in this type of operation is twofold. First, in the actual security of the paper. If the takeover is successful, the servicing of very high levels of debt, at rates of interest in excess of most target return-on-investment, requires significant asset dispositions which may not always be possible or desirable. It is an approach that also completely fails to take into account the fact that a large corporation is an entity with responsibilities to employees, customers and communities, which cannot always be torn apart like an erector set. The alternative to a breakup requires significantly improved operating performance which is very often much easier said than done. Indeed, in looking at many of these raids, one is left to wonder if the intent is really to acquire control or simply manipulate a third-party takeover in order to make a profit with little or no risk.

The second element of risk in this type of paper is liquidity. Much of this paper is privately placed, among a small group of private investors initially, and subsequently to financial institutions such as savings banks, insurance companies and pension funds. Over the last several years, $75 to $100 billion in junk bonds have probably been placed. In many instances, no large-scale, liquid public market exists in these securities and purchases and sales are handled through private transactions. Many of the investing institutions are in financial sectors under considerable pressure at this time.

To protect themselves against this type of takeover, companies have begun large-scale restructurings of their own whereby they assume significant amounts of additional debt in order to shrink their equity and increase the price of their stocks. ARCO and Litton Industries are the most recent examples of this trend, the latter shrinking its capital base by more than one-third. Whether in the long run this is sound financial policy and good for the country is open to question. It is highly probable, however, that these restructurings are driven more by the fear of these types of takeover than by straightforward economic forces.

Junk bonds, of course, are not the only source of excessive leverage in recent takeover activity. Large-scale leveraged buyouts and "going private" transactions have been financed by bank and institutional loans in the tens of billions of dollars as well as by junk bonds. The result is more and more substitution of debt for equity and less and less stable financial structures. In 1984, a year of strong economic growth, the equity of American corporations shrank by nearly $100 billion. It was turned into debt.

(3) Added to this combination of unequal treatment of shareholders and unsound financial structures is the market speculation which has become an integral part of the process. Very large pools of money are managed by arbitrageurs looking for rapid returns; some of these pools, incidentally, are financed by junk bonds. Very large pools of money are in the hands of raiders, similarly financed. This creates a symbolic set of relationships which has as its basic purpose the destabilization of a large corporation and its subsequent sale or breakup. It creates, at the very least, the appearance, and often the reality, of professional traders with inside information, in collaboration with raiders, deliberately driving companies to merge or liquidate. The process is driven by the ability of raiders to make tender offers "subject to financing," thereby avoiding costly commitment fees, and getting a free ride if they are bought out with "greenmail" or the target company is taken over by a white knight. St. Regis Paper, Gulf Oil, Cities Service were forced to merge as a result of this process.

In summary, what does all this add up to?

1. At a time when we are trying to encourage long-term investment, this activity encourages speculation and short-term trading
2. At a time when we are trying to strengthen our important industries to make them more competitive, this activity weakens many of our companies by stripping away their equity and replacing it with high-cost debt
3. At a time when our financial institutions (banks, savings banks, insurance companies) are under considerable pressure, this activity preempts more and more general credit and causes the weakest sectors to acquire large amounts of risky and possibly illiquid paper to show performance. Much of this paper has never been tested in a period of economic downturn.
4. At a time when we need to continue attracting capital from all over the world, our securities markets appear to be more and more under the control of professionals and insiders. The rights and privileges of shareholders appear to be continually eroded.
5. Institutional investors such as pension funds, S&Ls and insurance companies are behaving more and more like short-term traders than like long-term investors.

I believe that these issues are sufficiently serious to warrant the relevant regulatory authorities and the Congress to consider more stringent regulation coupled with new legislation.

These actions should be part of a total package of legislation and/or regulation. They should all be interconnected. It would be unreasonable to remove defensive devices such as "poison pills" from a company's use unless abusive takeover tactics were limited in a similar vein.

In the area of excessive uses of credit, whether junk bonds or otherwise, I believe that regulation as opposed to legislation can handle most of the problems. The SEC and its tender offer rules, the margin rules and the capital requirements set by Federal and State regulators or banks, insurance companies and savings institutions, can deal with most excesses if the regulators decide to act or are directed to do so. This is also true of insider trading and market manipulation by professionals where the SEC has ample authority.

It may be worth exploring some form of taxation on tax-exempt institutions such as pension funds if they engage in short-term trading activities and if their holding periods are below one year.

I have made my living, for more than 30 years, negotiating hundreds of mergers and acquisitions for a variety of corporate clients. Most of these were the result of negotiated agreements; some were bitterly contested, hostile takeovers. I hope to continue this activity for many more years. I believe it to be an integral part of the service an investment banker should provide his clients and that it is an important and constructive factor in maintaining a competitive market place. There is no question in my mind that thoughtfully negotiated mergers have a better chance of achieving their objectives than multi-billion dollar takeovers, or major restructuring, decided upon over a weekend, as a result of a raid. None the less, there should be room for many types of transactions in our market system, but very clear lines should be drawn between what is acceptable economic and corporate behavior on the one hand, and what is runaway speculation on the other. This is not the case today.

There are always arguments against any changes. Regulation and legislation are, inevitably, imperfect and may, unwittingly, restrict perfectly valid activities. However, the integrity of our securities markets and the soundness of our financial institutions are vital national assets. They are being eroded today and regulatory and legislative actions are required to protect them. If this does not occur, the regulatory backlash, a few years from now, will go far beyond anything discussed here.

6

The Competitive Challenge

LIONEL OLMER

The staggering trade deficit which the United States continues to accumulate (it should reach more than $140 billion for 1985) has rippled through the US economy like a fierce summer storm. But, unlike a hurricane, the consequences of the trade picture will batter the American industrial landscape for many years to come.

There has been a $117 billion swing in the trade account of manufactured goods between 1980 and 1985: from a $13 billion surplus to a $104 billion deficit. The volume of exports of manufacturers was roughly 15 percent less in 1984 than it was in 1984; and, although the value of manufactured exports last year was 8 percent higher than in 1981, fully 40 percent of this increase was the result of defense-related procurement. Total imports of manufactures grew by 53 percent, and, despite the recent decline in the value of the dollar, there are no indications whatsoever that the deluge of foreign imports will subside appreciably at any point in the near future.

The short- and long-term effects of this situation are many and varied; from the perspective of most manufacturers, particularly small and medium-sized businesses, they are almost always painful. While larger corporations have also been hard-hit, often they have had the resources with which to adjust. There are indications, however, that the sustaining nature of the trade deficit is forcing even the "giants" to adopt new means of doing business in order to remain profitable. Unfortunately, the new approaches add up to a seriously diminished national capacity to manufacture.

"Globalization" is an old term given new meaning in the context of corporations developing strategies to accommodate tougher foreign competition and an overvalued dollar:

1. Major elements of manufacturing have been moving offshore at an accelerating rate.
2. Investment by US companies in their foreign affiliates has expanded fourfold over investment in domestic activities in the past year.

3. Domestic manufacturers are increasing their reliance on foreign components.[1]
4. Employment in manufacturing in the US has remained stagnant at roughly 1979 levels, and hundreds of thousands of workers have been displaced from factories which no longer produce automobiles, textiles, steel, or footwear.
5. In relative terms, job losses in the US have also been substantial across a wide range of value-added products such as cameras, televisions, consumer electronics, telephones, copying equipment, and, more recently, in many high technology areas as well.
6. When new equipment is purchased to improve productivity in the factory, it has often been of foreign, not of US, origin.
7. It is not unusual to find companies with a long history of exporting giving up foreign markets or serving those markets from offshore facilities.
8. Finally, as alternatives to US-led exports, some companies have turned to licensing their technology in lieu of selling their products, or to joint ventures and mergers with foreign partners as the only practical means of remaining profitable.

Are these phenomena due mainly to the strong dollar or to unfair trade? Are they a function primarily of slow economic growth abroad and thus relatively less demand for US goods; or to a loss of markets in Latin America because of its debt problems; or have American companies lost the will and the ability to compete?

Virtually everyone in and out of government seems to agree that all of these factors have contributed to the trade deficit and are thus forcing a fundamental restructuring of America's economic base. There remains serious disagreement, however, on the relative weight of each factor and, more importantly, on whether this reshaping process is inherently harmful. Some argue that it is beneficial – a sort of "creative destruction," which in the end will forge a more vibrant America out of the transient discomfort of industrial adjustment.

The optimistic prognosis holds that the world is becoming more economically interdependent; that American society is increasingly dominated by the development, distribution and consumption of information and that most of the jobs it will ever need can be generated by the vast and unlimited services sector rather than from the smokestack industries whose time has passed.

Still others have argued that a large US trade deficit was a boon not only to the international economy (i.e., that America must serve as the engine of world growth), but also that the deficit held inflation in check during the economic expansion in 1983–84. That is, when the American economy was growing at 8 percent annually, it was a good thing that the trade deficit lopped off what would have been 2 percent additional growth. But with the economy growing at a sluggish 3 percent annual rate, the loss of 2 percent growth becomes not a boon but a burden.

But there are many reasons why sustained trade and current account deficits (the latter being a broader measure of the international exchange of goods and services) are inordinately unhealthy and why they merit strong measures by government to reverse their upward movement:

1. The current account deficit for 1985 of about $125 billion is nearly twice as much as a percentage of US gross national product as it has been in the country's entire 210-year history (3 percent now, heading to 4 percent – some would say 5 percent within a few years – while the previous high was 2 percent in the 1870s during an unprecedented industrial and railway expansion boom). Financing such enormous deficits means international financial markets will be flooded with US dollar assets, threatening higher interest rates to keep foreign investment coming into America, and risking, ultimately, a loss of confidence in the US economy.
2. To bring down the deficit it will be essential that the US experience a sizeable surplus in manufactures trade, simply because a surplus from any other source isn't likely: the US will of necessity remain dependent on importing various raw materials and petroleum (which has equaled roughly half of the trade deficit); it cannot expect a significant increase in the surplus of agriculture exports (the existing surplus is by no means assured); and growing interest payments on America's foreign debt are eroding its position as a net exporter of services.

Thus, the responsibility for lowering the deficit will fall necessarily on manufacturers.

At the very time when it is urgent that the US experience a surplus in manufacturing exports, it may be that much of its industrial base, having left America's shores or having abandoned export strategies, is no longer able to compete in international markets. Moreover, during periods of slack demand, much less during a recession, US companies will be hard pressed to retain their existing markets, much less recapture what they have lost to foreign suppliers, many of whom have invested heavily in developing strong and lasting relationships with their US customers.

The United States, the leader of the world community, must maintain a strong industrial base which is capable of responding on short notice to a call for mobilization of its defense structure. This is not to say that it must – at whatever cost – maintain the ability to produce "everything" needed in whatever the mobilization scenario; that is impossible, clearly. Yet, US government officials must remain sensitive to what is happening to the industrial structure as a result of trade and economic policies which have been pursued sometimes without consideration of their national security implications. The list of "essential" industries could get temptingly large, even out of control, if restrained only by the strength of the political constituency involved. It would thereby represent an open invitation to full-scale protectionism for the sake only of sustaining a domestic presence which otherwise would not be viable. Such a result would be highly undesirable ... but the risk to Western security of a "hands-off" policy is far greater.

Evidence of the executive branch's agreement that the problem is a serious one is reflected in the Administration's intense effort to engage the leading industrial nations in a multi-part, cooperative program designed to:

1. bring down the value of the dollar (and, thereby, increase the international competitiveness of American products);
2. cause other leading industrial democracies to stimulate their economies (and, thereby, increase their demand for goods, including from the United States);
3. encourage commercial banks to extend new loans to the debt-ridden nations in the developing world;
4. aggressively pursue the further opening of foreign markets for US goods and strictly apply trade laws to prevent unfair competition from injuring US companies.

But, the higher the deficit becomes, the greater will be the burden on the manufacturing sector to post a surplus and this means that even greater pressures will be placed on each of the four parts of this program.

The consensus on Capitol Hill also seems to be that the situation is reaching something close to desperate proportions. Unfortunately, this perception is too often accompanied by a belief that the deficit is, in largest measure, the result of the wily trading tactics of our allies, mostly the Japanese, who use a combination of government and financial assistance, protected home markets, and lower wage and capital costs, to dispatch their American competitors to second class status. And so, months of frustrating debate have led to several versions of a trade bill designed to legislate "an even playing field" in order to deal "effectively" with the Japanese.

Would that it were so simple!

It is misleading at best to imply any substantial connection between all of the real and imagined unfair trading practices of the major trading nations, and the size of the US trade deficit. If all the markets in the world were open on an equitable and balanced basis, and no nations were permitted to sell products at prices below fair value or with the benefit of government subsidies, it would merely dent – by less than 10 percent over several years – the $140–150 billion trade deficit; it certainly would not immobilize its negative movement.

In attempting to analyze causes, one startling statistic reveals the significance of the value of the dollar to the trade balance: in 1979 US labor costs were 25 percent lower than those in the Federal Republic of Germany; in 1984 they were 25 percent higher. And, while labor costs in the US were never lower than those in Japan, the latter climbed to two-thirds of US labor rates in 1978 and remained roughly at that level until recently when, because of the strong dollar, they fell again to one half those in the United States. Individual companies are extremely hard-pressed to overcome such competitive disadvantages, even in businesses which are more capital- than labor-intensive.

But the strength of the dollar, although very significant, perhaps even the most important cause, is still only one among several important factors.

It is vital that policymakers not focus on this or any other single cause; rather, it is essential that they remain keenly attentive to the mix of contributory factors so as to design a mix of solutions. For example, since no more than 5–8 percent of the US trade deficit should be attributed to unfair trade practices, it makes little sense to "retaliate" indiscriminately against Japan or East Asian NICs and risk the loss of valuable markets for US farm, aerospace, power generation, office equipment and other high technology products.

Unfortunately, it also appears that the lowered value of the dollar at the level experienced over the last four months will not of itself do very much in the near future to the size of the US trade deficit. For when the trade account is disaggregated, a number of revelations appear which, taken together, diminish greatly the prospect that a moderately lower dollar (meaning 20 percent less than its 1985 high) can have more than a moderate effect on the trade deficit:

1. 25 percent of US imports of manufactures originate in Japan, but the dollar appreciated less than 20 percent against the yen between 1980 and 1985.
2. 20 percent of total US imports of manufactures enter from Canada, yet the US dollar appreciated only about 6 percent against the Canadian dollar between 1980 and 1985.
3. 16 percent of US imports of manufactures are shipped from the East Asian NICs, and their currencies are essentially "pegged" to the US dollar so that changes in the latter are generally matched by adjustments to the former.
4. Although the dollar appreciated by a staggering 73 percent average with respect to the French franc, West German deutschmark and British pound, imports from these countries increased only about half as much.
5. Import prices since 1980 have not been lowered as might be expected

with a strong dollar, but, rather, they have actually risen slightly, indicating wider profit margins on foreign products and therefore an ability of exporters to cut prices along with a declining dollar.

So, if it isn't an elimination of unfair trade practices, nor a sustained reduction in the value of the dollar, how about loss of markets in the developing world, especially Latin America?

Indeed, roughly 40 percent of the deterioration in the US manufactures' deficit between 1980 and 1984 was due to export surpluses of developing countries and the loss of markets in Latin America.

Yet Brazil, Mexico and other Latin American economies simply must post export surpluses in order to pay interest owed on accumulated debts. And these favorable trade balances cannot be maintained only by government-imposed cutbacks on imports, as was the case during 1983–84. Imports, especially of essentials to the manufacturing process, are necessary to stimulate economic growth. Any further restraint on growth would give rise to a threat of social instability in certain countries in the developing world – and it would obviously mean a continuing loss of market opportunities for US exporters.

There is not a simple "yes" or "no" answer to the question as to whether US companies have "lost" the ability to compete internationally, even in the absence of the exchange rate phenomena of recent years which have reduced so dramatically their price competitiveness. Evidence abounds of industries which have failed to modernize, which turn out products lacking in quality and reliability, or which have allowed runaway costs far in excess of efficiency improvements. Yet, it is instructive to note the sharp upturn in US productivity growth of the last five years and observe that for the first time in the post-World War II era, it has equalled that of Western Europe.

Largely due to efficiency improvements and new investment in manufacturing equipment, output per worker in the United States increased twice as fast from 1979 to 1984 as it did between 1973 and 1979.

Still US productivity growth lags far behind that of Japan and in the largest single source of America's trade deficit with that country, the automobile sector, it is unlikely to catch up in the near term. Analysis suggests that despite the $80 billion investment by Detroit in retooling and in research and development over the last several years, Japanese manufacturers have maintained at least a $2,000 per car cost advantage over comparable US motor vehicles. In 1986, Japanese (and Korean) motor vehicle manufacturers will increase their market share in the US by a substantial percentage. Direct investment within the US by foreign producers will also be accelerated but not nearly fast enough to offset perhaps as much as an additional $8–10 billion of trade deficit in this sector's account.

Nevertheless, there are many industrial goods produced in the US that are fully competitive internationally, or that would be, *except* for the strong dollar. One could say with some optimism that a substantial segment of American industry is poised for a comeback; as the value of the dollar declines, as economic growth rebounds elsewhere, as the pressures to open markets succeed, as commercial bank lending to Latin America resumes, these companies will be prepared and capable of exporting.

The answer to the US trade deficit is that there is no single, adequate policy response to the accumulated imbalance and its effects on US manufacturing. It will be necessary to "fix" a number of things which haven't worked or which are acknowledged without argument to be unsatisfactory.

Stamping out unfair trading practices; opening markets; beginning a new multinational round of trade talks next year to improve existing rules and to establish new rules for trade in services, stimulating economic growth so as to create increased demand for US goods, bringing down the value of the US dollar so as to make these goods more competitive; pressing Japan to do more to reduce its surplus; encouraging commercial banks to renew lending to Latin America and, finally, reducing the US federal budget deficit, are all manifestations of legitimate concern. They cannot be criticized . . . except by those who wonder whether these measures – even collectively – will be enough. If they are not sufficient, or if only of limited success, those in the US who have been committed to the pursuit of free trade may be convinced – or forced – by stark circumstances to turn elsewhere for solutions.

The Administration is taking the right tack in its comprehensive approach; will our trading partners do their share?

Most importantly, if the Administration's answers are inadequate, or if the Western democracies do not cooperate, American industry will find itself in a hole so deep that subsequent government intervention to salvage its badly damaged remnants may take the form of highly protectionist (and politically irresistible) trade legislation. And this would be neither in America's interests nor the world's.

This year, 1986, might well prove to be a watershed . . . for the international trading system as well as for America's domestic industrial structure.

Note

1. An agreement reached last year between Japan and the US to end tariffs on semiconductors and computer parts, although heralded as a major achievement on behalf of free trade, was in fact stimulated within the US private sector by companies more desirous of eliminating duties on what they *import* from Japan and elsewhere in Asia rather than on what they export. The savings in duties on imported parts is expected to exceed the duties on exports from the US by at least ten to one.

7

The Federal Budget Crisis

ROBERT EISNER

There has always been a certain amount of hysteria surrounding the federal debt and deficits. Politicians and pundits compete in their proclamations of future disaster and the attribution of its causes.

The real story is that federal budget deficits *can* have great consequences for the economy. These may be good, as well as bad, but we cannot begin to know the consequences of deficits until we measure them correctly. When we do, we find that they can still be too large, but they can also be too small.

The underlying significance of government budget deficits is that they add to public debt, and hence to private holdings of that debt. Paradoxically, the federal debt, however fequently viewed as a burden to the government or the future taxpayers, is wealth to those who own it. Whatever their concerns for the government's fiscal responsibility, the holders of all those deficit-financing Treasury notes, bills and bonds feel richer for having them. And the richer they feel, the more they try to spend now and plan to spend in the future.

Since federal deficits add to federal debt, which thus adds to private wealth, they can be expected to increase aggregate demand, or spending. If the economy is booming along at full employment of its resources, further increases in demand raise prices and encourage inflation. But if there is slack in the economy, deficit-induced demand stimulates output and employment. The method of financing deficits, whether by interest-bearing debt or the creation of money, which is properly viewed as non-interest-bearing debt, will also affect the levels of demand and spending and their allocation to consumption and domestic and foreign investment. It is these issues of the impact of deficits on the economy and not misguided moral imperatives which are properly central to our concerns.

But for deficits to matter, they must be *real* deficits. A real deficit is one

This paper has drawn very considerably on my book, *How Real is the Federal Deficit?* (The Free Press, New York, 1986). Earlier sources include my joint articles with Paul J. Pieper in *The American Economic Review* (March 1984) and *The Public Interest* (Winter 1985), and my own paper in *The American Economic Review* (May 1984).

which increases the real debt of the government to the public and hence increases the public's perception of its own real wealth. It is thus vitally important to correct for inflation. Inflation in effect generates an "inflation tax," eating away the value of the public's holdings of those Treasury notes, bills and bonds, or the cash which they back.

One failure to adjust measures of the deficit for inflation has yielded a number of anomalies which have confused analysis and bedevilled policy-making. For with all our deficits, the general trend of real federal debt – the debt adjusted for inflation – has been downward. On a *per capita* basis it has indeed gone down very sharply over most of the last 40 years, until 1980. And the government's net worth, the difference between its assets – financial and real – and its liabilities, moved from red to black. The Employment Act of 1946, which established the Joint Economic Committee along with the Council of Economic Advisers, wisely committed the government to policies aimed at maximizing employment and purchasing power. Fiscal policy, particularly decisions as to total spending and taxes and consequent surpluses or deficits, have been properly recognized as essential in implementing this commitment.

For a good deal of our post-World War II history, fiscal policy has been helpful. It has laid a framework for relatively high-employment and substantial prosperity and economic growth. There have also, however, been substantial failures, particularly in the 1970s and early 1980s. The coexistence of apparently large and increasing budget deficits, inflation, *and* growing unemployment seemed to some to indicate a breakdown in the framework for fiscal policy which had guided the United States and much of the world since the catastrophe of the Great Depression of the 1930s. In fact, what was at fault was not our view of basic economic relationships. It was rather mismeasurement of critical variables. Very simply, we had confused real and nominal values.

From the standpoint of macroeconomic policy, a *real* federal deficit is one which adds to the real value of federal debt held by the public. This is not the same as the nominal deficit because changing interest rates in themselves change the market value of existing debt, and inflation, which affects interest rates, also serves to reduce the real value of that market value of debt. Further, to the extent that the Treasury runs a deficit and borrows in order to finance lending to farmers, homeowners, businesses or students, the gross debt will rise more than the net debt of government. Thus, in table 7.1, we note that, despite repeated budget deficits, the real value of federal debt declined sharply from 1945 to 1980. Indeed, the net debt *per capita* in 1972 dollars fell by almost three-quarters, from $4,017 at the end of 1945 to $1,032 at the end of 1980. It then more than doubled, from $1,032 to $2,183 by the end of 1984. At that time, however, the net debt *per capita* was still little more than half of what it had been at the end of 1945.

Table 7.1 The real value of federal debt, 1945–1984

(1) Year	(2) Gross public debt	(3) Net debt	(4) Budget surplus or deficit (−)	(5) Net reval. of net debt	(6) Change in net debt	(7) Net debt per capita	(8) Change in net debt per capita
			Billions of 1972 dollars			1972 dollars	
1945	681.6	562.0	−111.0			4,017	
1950	459.1	351.0	17.2	−32.0	−44.0	2,305	−343
1955	455.4	323.0	7.3	−16.0	−21.3	1,947	−165
1960	421.1	300.5	4.4	11.0	8.5	1,663	21
1965	426.0	289.0	0.7	−11.9	−10.4	1,487	−73
1970	415.3	268.4	−13.6	1.9	15.4	1,309	61
1975	445.9	277.0	−55.2	−16.0	57.3	1,283	255
1980	495.9	234.9	−34.3	−36.7	−1.0	1,032	−17
1984	730.7	516.7	−78.6	−9.5	86.7	2,183	350

Full accounts of sources and methods of this and subsequent tables are to be found in Eisner, *How Real Is the Federal Deficit?*

Table 7.2 Federal budget surplus or deficit and change in real net debt, billions of dollars, 1946–1984

(1)	(2) Surplus or deficit (−) on national income accounts	(3) Interest rate effects	(4) Price effects	(5) Adjusted surplus or deficit (−)	(6) Off-budget items	(7) Revaluation on gold	(8) Decrease (+) or increase (−) in real net debt in current $
1946	3.5	0.4	52.5	56.4	−2.1	−3.7	50.7
1950	9.2	2.9	15.0	27.1	−0.2	−3.3	23.6
1955	4.4	3.8	6.0	14.3	−0.7	−0.6	13.0
1960	3.0	−9.8	2.3	−4.5	−1.1	−0.2	−5.8
1965	0.5	3.1	5.9	9.5	1.9	−3.7	7.8
1966	−1.8	−1.7	8.1	4.6	−1.4	−0.5	2.7
1967	−13.2	4.4	8.0	−0.8	−0.2	−0.4	−1.4

Year						
1968	−6.0	1.1	11.5	6.5	−3.5	1.9	4.8
1969	8.4	7.5	13.4	29.4	−1.9	−2.9	24.6
1970	−12.4	−14.0	12.2	−14.2	−0.0	0.1	−14.1
1971	−22.0	−3.9	12.5	−13.4	−1.5	1.3	−13.6
1972	−16.8	4.3	12.4	−0.1	−1.3	5.4	4.0
1973	−5.5	3.4	21.3	19.1	−1.5	11.3	29.0
1974	−11.5	−2.0	31.2	17.7	0.0	18.4	36.1
1975	−69.3	−2.5	23.2	−48.6	−5.4	−18.0	−71.9
1976	−53.1	−12.6	21.1	−44.6	−5.1	−3.4	−53.0
1977	−45.9	16.1	29.2	−0.6	−8.6	5.8	−3.3
1978	−29.5	19.1	43.2	32.9	−8.7	12.3	36.5
1979	−16.1	4.6	43.6	32.1	−4.7	69.4	96.8
1980	−61.2	13.7	55.1	7.6	−12.1	6.3	1.8
1981	−64.3	−3.7	49.7	−18.3	−13.1	−47.8	−79.2
1982	−148.2	−62.4	33.4	−117.2	−6.8	−18.2	−202.3
1983	−178.6	42.3	35.1	−101.2	−13.3	−7.9	−122.4
1984	−175.7	−20.6	42.1	−154.1	−16.5	−23.1	−193.7

The major discrepancies between budget deficits and increases in net debt suggest that our conventional measures of the budget deficit are devoid of much of their presumed economic relevance. They are particularly misleading in periods of substantial and varying inflation and high and fluctuating nominal interest rates. For these contribute to large net revaluations of existing debt which are a major factor, generally *the* major factor, in the discrepancy between conventional measures of nominal budget deficits and increases in net debt. The exact relation between changes in the real value of the net debt, measured in current dollars, and the budget surplus or deficit may be seen in table 7.2. First, a surplus itself reduces the debt and a deficit increases it. Higher interest rates, however, also lower the market value of debt, and increases in prices reduce its real value. In addition, off-budget outlays increase the debt while increases in the market value of Treasury holdings of gold reduce the real net debt.

The decrease (increase) in real net debt in current dollars is actually the sum of the surplus (deficit) in our national income accounts, interest rate effects (par-to-market adjustment), price effects (nominal-to-real adjustment), off-budget items, and the net revaluations on Treasury gold. To secure a measure of the impact of the surplus or deficit on the financial wealth of the individuals and business of the private sector or, more properly all sectors other than the federal government, we should add to the surplus in national income accounts only the interest rate effects and the price effects. And since this measure changes in the financial wealth of the economy outside of Washington, it is this "adjusted surplus" or "adjusted deficit" which, as we shall show, will weigh heavily on the ebb and flow of the nation's economy.

Since in the last four decades there has always been some inflation, which reduced the real value of the debt, the adjustments have generally moved the budget toward surplus. Thus, surpluses in the official national income accounts in the early post-war years were larger by our adjusted measure. Where there were deficits they were usually lower in the adjusted measure, or they became surpluses.

Some particularly interesting reversals are recorded. In 1973 and 1974 there were moderate deficits by the official national income account measure. With inflation accelerating in response to oil price shocks, our adjusted budget was in substantial surplus.

But the most remarkable differences between official and adjusted budget measures show up in the 1977–80 Carter years. The 1977 deficit of $46 billion is turned into a virtually balanced budget. The 1978 deficit of $29 billion is converted to an adjusted surplus of $33 billion. And the deficit of $61 billion which caused so much consternation in 1980 appears now as an adjusted surplus of $7.6 billion.

What then was really going on? Mesmerized by those official deficit figures, most observers insisted that our fiscal policy was irresponsibly expansionary. That justified Federal Reserve Chairman Paul Volcker's tight money policy as "the only game in town" to stop inflation.

But the rising interest rates associated with escalating inflation, reinforced by the restrictive monetary posture, had been driving down the market value of the public's holdings of federal debt. And that inflation itself was further reducing its real value. The purchasing power of the public was thus shrinking, not growing.

An inflation-adjusted budget would have told us that we were actually running a surplus. We were suffering from a tight fiscal policy *and* tight money. But everyone looked at the official deficit. The tricks played by inflation were ignored, or never seen.

Public concern and confusion regarding federal deficits and their contribution to federal debt are fueled by curious federal accounting practices. If major corporations kept their accounts in the same manner as the federal government, the demand for real red ink would grow substantially. Many a profitable business would seem to be operating at a loss and, in government parlance, would be showing a "deficit." This would show that, like the federal government, American businesses have been going more and more into debt.

Can we compare the federal debt with that of private business? Take a look at table 7.3. The gross debt or liabilities of General Motors grew from $2.6 billion to $27.9 billion from 1970 to 1984. The debt of IBM grew from $2.6 billion in 1970 to $16.3 billion in 1984. Similar records of increasing debt can be found for almost every successful large business in the United States.

Table 7.3 Assets, liabilities and net worth, General Motors and IBM, 1970, 1980, and 1984

(1) Item	(2) 1970	(3) 1980	(4) 1984	(5) 1970–1984
	Billions of dollars			Percent change
General Motors				
Assets	14.2	32.2	52.1	+268
Liabilities	4.3	13.0	27.9	+546
Net worth	9.9	19.2	24.2	+146
IBM				
Assets	8.5	24.5	42.8	+401
Liabilities	2.6	9.6	16.3	+530
Net worth	5.9	15.0	26.5	+345

Data for 1984 are from annual reports. "Net worth" figures are what GM denotes as "net assets," and IBM as "stockholders' equity." IBM figures for 1980 have now been reclassified to conform with 1984 presentation. They show 1980 assets at $26.8 billion and stockholders' equity at $16.6 billion.

Table 7.4　Federal and other debt as percent of GNP, 1952–1984

(1) Year	(2) Federal	(3) State and local	(4) Households	(5) Non- financial business	(6) Total
1952	61.5	8.7	26.0	31.6	127.8
1962	43.6	14.5	44.7	40.5	143.4
1972	27.6	14.7	47.9	50.1	140.3
1973	25.4	14.1	48.7	51.3	139.4
1974	24.5	14.2	49.1	54.3	142.1
1975	27.5	13.7	47.9	52.0	141.0
1976	29.1	13.4	48.9	51.5	142.9
1977	28.8	12.7	50.5	51.5	143.5
1978	27.4	12.0	51.4	50.3	141.0
1979	26.5	11.7	53.9	51.9	144.0
1980	27.1	11.5	53.7	52.0	144.3
1981	27.4	10.7	52.6	52.0	142.6
1982	31.9	11.6	53.8	54.2	151.5
1983	34.3	10.8	55.0	53.0	153.1
1984	36.6	10.8	56.4	55.1	159.0

Source: Flow of Funds Accounts, Summary of Credit Market Debt Outstanding and Credit Market Debt Owed by Nonfinancial Sectors, Board of Governors of the Federal Reserve System. Years through 1982 taken from Albert M. Wojnilower, 'Discussion,' Table 1, p. 105, in Conference Series No. 27, *The Economics of Large Government Deficits: Proceedings of the Conference held at Melvin Village, New Hampshire* (Federal Reserve Bank of Boston, Oct. 1983).

In fact, business debt has been increasing much more rapidly than federal debt. At the end of 1952, gross federal debt held by the public was 62 percent of GNP, while the debt of nonfinancial business came to 32 percent, as shown in table 7.4. By 1979, the federal debt ratio had *fallen* by more than half, to 26 percent, but the business debt figure had risen to double that, or 52 percent. By 1984 the federal debt held by the public had risen to almost 37 percent, but business debt was then 55 percent of GNP.

But investors or others trying to evaluate the fortunes of a corporation hardly look only at gross debt figures. Clearly, they must also concern themselves with assets.

Thus for example, while General Motors' liabilities grew, so did its assets and net worth. From 1970 to 1984, assets increased from $14.2 billion to $52.1 billion, and net worth, the difference between assets and liabilities, rose from $9.9 billion to $24.2 billion. In the case of IBM, from

1970 to 1984, assets increased from $8.5 billion to $42.8 billion, while net worth rose from $5.9 billion to $26.5 billion.

But then, with all the talk about government debt, and the deficits which contribute to it, what about looking also at *government* assets and *government* net worth? We are accustomed to thinking of the government taking our money and squandering it. There may of course be some truth to that. But after all, the government does own some roads and some buildings. It has some equipment, non-military as well as military. And it retains title to a great deal of land.

Thanks to my collaboration with Paul Pieper, I am able to present government balance sheets which show the market values (or estimated replacement costs) of all tangible and financial assets as well as liabilities. They indicate that the federal debt has indeed grown, like that of General Motors and IBM, but so have federal assets. The increase in financial assets, as noted earlier, damps the growth in net debt.

It is the growth in value of federal tangible assets, however, which deserves particular attention. In the decade of the 1970s, the value of federally owned structures, on the basis of BEA figures, increased from $106 billion to $284 billion, as may be noted in table 7.5. Some outside estimates put the numbers considerably higher. The value of federal-owned equipment rose from $95 billion to $229 billion. Inventories went from $59 billion to $136 billion. And the (almost certainly under) estimates of the value of federal land increased from $45 billion to $175 billion.

Dramatic evidence of the extent of these underestimates may be seen in Department of the Interior figures on federally owned reserves of oil, gas and coal. Multiplying the estimated quantities of these reserves by current market prices, we estimate the *value* of the government oil reserves at $177 billion, gas at $169 billion, and coal at $264 billion. That gives a total of $611 billion in federally owned, offshore and onshore minerals to be added to our estimates of the value of "land," or separately categorized among assets. There alone is "backing" for more than half of the net debt. And Michael Boskin and associates offer still higher estimates of the value of federal minerals, setting the 1982 value of oil and natural gas rights alone at $817 billion.[1]

Thus, from 1970 to 1980, total liabilities grew what seems an enormous amount, from $484 billion to $1,162 billion, and net debt from $252 billion to $441 billion. But that is only part of the picture. With tangible and financial federal assets each rising by half a trillion dollars, the growth in total assets considerably exceeded the growth in liabilities.

So, yes, the federal debt did grow as deficit followed deficit. But there was something to show for it. And with all that increase in debt, as with General Motors and IBM, the federal net worth also increased. It rose, according to our conservative estimates, from a modest $53 billion in

Table 7.5 Federal government net debt and net worth, billions of dollars

	1945	1950	1960	1970	1980	1984
Assets						
Tangible	186.2	111.7	205.8	304.6	822.5	1,118.0
Reproducible assets	179.3	102.2	187.4	259.8	648.1	915.2
Residential structures	2.2	2.2	3.2	5.7	20.9	24.5
Non-residential structures	28.9	39.1	60.8	100.2	262.9	299.6
Equipment	88.3	34.4	65.6	95.3	228.6	395.6
Inventories	59.9	26.5	57.7	58.6	135.7	195.5
Land	6.8	9.5	18.4	44.8	174.4	202.8
Financial	102.8	98.7	124.7	232.8	720.9	887.4
Currency, demand + time deposits	31.3	9.7	12.8	17.6	31.3	40.7
Gold	20.1	22.8	17.8	12.0	155.9	81.0
US government securities	31.5	26.2	35.2	77.5	129.8	172.2
Treasury issues	31.5	26.2	35.2	77.4	120.6	162.7
Agency issues	0.0	0.0	0.0	0.2	9.2	9.6
Mortgages	2.5	2.8	11.2	32.6	132.3	202.6
Other loans	4.7	16.0	25.1	65.2	201.5	288.1
Taxes receivable	9.6	16.5	12.7	5.7	7.1	−16.2
Miscellaneous assets	3.1	3.2	8.4	18.9	47.3	94.9
Total assets	289.0	210.4	330.4	537.4	1,543.4	2,005.4

Liabilities

Treasury currency + SDR certificates	2.3	2.4	2.7	6.0	13.6	17.5
Demand deposits + currency	31.1	28.2	30.6	52.0	121.5	171.4
Bank reserves + vault cash	19.0	19.9	20.4	31.2	47.3	40.5
Credit market instruments	264.5	224.5	246.7	338.5	841.9	1,613.7
Saving bonds	43.2	49.5	46.5	53.1	68.4	76.1
Other Treasury issues	220.4	173.1	192.5	246.1	625.1	1,296.8
Agency issues	0.9	1.8	7.8	39.3	148.4	240.8
Insurance, retirement reserves	6.5	12.7	20.5	34.9	85.5	139.8
Miscellaneous liabilities	9.2	7.4	10.9	21.8	51.8	80.4
Total liabilities	332.6	295.0	331.8	484.3	1,161.6	2,063.3
Net debt[a]	229.8	196.3	207.1	251.5	440.7	1,175.9
Net worth	−43.7	−84.6	−1.3	53.1	381.8	−57.9

[a] Total liabilities minus financial assets.

1970 to a 1980 figure of $382 billion, and clearly would be shown to have risen much more with proper accounting for federally owned mineral reserves.

Despite this substantial increase in federal net worth in the 1970s (not repeated in the following decade, it must be acknowledged), we kept referring to federal deficits. When private businesses had similar increases in debt, assets and net worth we did not think of them as suffering losses or having "deficits." What is the difference?

A significant part of the answer lies in the fact that the federal government, unlike private business and state and local government, keeps no separate capital budget. When American businesses spend $354 billion on new plant and equipment, as they did in 1984, they do not charge that as a current expense. Profits, or "surplus" are reduced only by depreciation or "capital consumption." But when the federal government makes similar capital expenditures of $77 billion, as it did in (fiscal year) 1984, that goes right into the deficit.

In the great majority of firms where capital expenditures are increasing, whether because of real growth or inflation or both, the current depreciation, which is based essentially on previous capital expenditures, is less than current capital spending. For General Motors in 1984, depreciation on old plant and equipment was $2.7 billion while new capital spending was $6.0 billion. For IBM, depreciation was $3.0 billion and capital spending $4.6 billion. Since federal capital expenditures have been increasing too, federal depreciation charges similarly calculated would also be less than federal spending.

If the federal government were to keep separate current and capital accounts as does private business, and were also to adjust its depreciation for inflation, the budget picture would look considerably different. In

Table 7.6 Current and capital federal accounts, 1984

(1) Account	(2) Credits	(3) Debits	(4) Deficit[a]	(5) Deficit ÷ GNP
	Billions of dollars			%
Current	704.7	860.9[b]	156.2	4.3
Capital	53.6[c]	73.2[d]	19.6	0.5
NIPA	704.7	880.5	175.8	4.8

   [a] Col. 4 is col. 3 minus col. 2.
   [b] Includes capital consumption allowances of $53.6 billion and current outlays of $807.3 billion.
   [c] Capital consumption allowances.
   [d] Capital expenditures.

1984, for example, as shown in table 7.6, the total national income account federal sector budget deficit of $176 billion would be decomposed into a capital account deficit of $20 billion and a current account deficit of $156 billion. The difference, though significant, is not overwhelming. But there is more to be said.

First, the $20 billion deficit on capital account in 1984 and the total of $73 billion of federal investment related only to assets acquired by the federal government. But in fiscal 1984, for example, that would omit another $26 billion of federal grants to state and local governments for physical capital investment – for highways, for urban mass transportation and airports, for community and regional development and for pollution control facilities.

Second, as the Office of Management and Budget points out, a reasonable definition of the category of federal investment is outlays "which yield long-term benefits." The OMB therefore includes among "federal investment-type outlays" $41 billion for research and development and $22 billion for education and training. Total federal investment, excluding loans and financial investment, thus came to $171 billion in fiscal 1984, almost identical, we might point out, to the national income account deficit of $170 billion. The OMB's estimates of non-financial federal investment for 1985 and 1986 are $195 billion and $215 billion, respectively.

It is thus clear that all of the federal budget deficit, and more, is accounted for by investment. We should, it is true, make some allowance for depreciation or capital consumption. Thus, if we were to put together separate current and capital accounts, with all federal investment-type outlays in the capital account but depreciation as an added current account charge, the current account budget would still not be in balance.

But the figures for the current account deficit would be far less than those with which we have become familiar. When we add the inflation adjustments discussed earlier and relate all this to the growth of population and the economy we may easily have no deficit left at all.

The federal budget, by official measure, has been in deficit in all but eight of the 55 years from 1931 through 1985. In fact, in the 25 years since 1960 only one, 1969 had no deficit. The last 16 years have presented an unbroken picture of deficits.

World War II saw what were then huge deficits, totaling $170 billion for the years 1942 through 1945. The total gross federal debt over that period rose by $203 billion.

From 1946 through 1984, budget deficits, net of surpluses, totaled $988 billion and, including off-budget outlays, totaled $1,112 billion. And over that period, the gross federal public debt increased by $1,317 billion. This is a history, which in at least general terms, is well etched in the public consciousness. It has been the stuff of many sober pronouncements and warnings and has frequently agitated political debate. A number of additional items of information, however, complicate the picture, and also put it in better perspective.

First, when numbers are changing rapidly over time, particularly with economic growth and inflation, it is important to put the figures in some kind of relative terms. The gross federal debt held by the public, for example, grew from $235 billion at the end of the 1945 fiscal year to $1,313 billion by the end of the 1984 fiscal year. But our national income and gross national product grew relatively more over these years. Thus, as may be seen in table 7.7, while the gross federal debt held by the public was 108.4 percent of gross national product at end of the fiscal 1945, despite

Table 7.7 Federal budget surpluses and deficits and gross federal debt, selected fiscal years, 1941–1984

(1)	(2)	(3)	(4)	(5)	(6)
	Surplus or deficit (−)		Gross federal debt (end of period)		
Fiscal year	On budget	Including off-budget outlays	Total	Held by the public	
	Billions of dollars		Billions of dollars		% of GNP
1941	−5.0	−5.0	57.5	48.2	44.2
1945	−47.5	−47.5	260.1	235.2	108.4
1946	−15.9	−15.9	271.0	241.9	119.8
1960	0.3	0.3	290.0	237.2	47.6
1970	−2.8	−2.8	382.6	284.9	29.4
1975	−45.2	−53.2	544.1	396.9	26.8
1980	−59.6	−73.8	914.3	715.1	27.8
1984	175.3	−185.3	1,576.7	1,312.6	36.7
Sum, 1942–45 or change 1945–45	−170.1	−170.1	202.6	187.0	64.2
Sum, 1946–84 or change 1945–84	−987.6	−1,112.6	1,316.6	1,077.4	−71.7
Sum, 1946–80 or change 1945–80	−448.4	−512.3	654.2	479.9	−80.6
Sum, 1981–84 or change 1980–84	−539.2	−599.9	662.4	597.5	8.9

the very large dollar growth in that debt over the following years, it had fallen, as a proportion of gross national product, to 27.8 percent by the end of the 1980 fiscal year. With all the subsequent red ink and increase in the debt, at the end of the 1984 fiscal year the debt as a ratio of GNP had risen to only 36.7 percent, still well below the 108.4 percent figure of 1945 (and the 119.8 percent figure of 1946).

There are some analogous observations to make with regard to our annual budget deficits. They surged during the years of World War II, but then were generally modest until they rose toward the end of the Vietnam War, and surged again after 1981. Over all these years federal outlays and receipts have been fluctuating – generally growing – and gross national product has increased enormously. How can we get an appropriate view of the *relative* size of the deficit?

One way of securing a broader perspective is to note what has happened to the deficit as a percentage of outlays. We see in table 7.8 that, while the proportion of federal outlays which is deficit-financed stood at a substantial 21.8 percent in fiscal 1984, this was far from a record. During the depression fiscal year of 1932 (from July 1, 1931 through June 30, 1932), although the deficit was "only" $2.7 billion, 58.7 percent of federal outlays were deficit-financed. And during the war years, that proportion soared, rising to 70 percent in 1943. In the presumably fiscally responsible Administration of Dwight Eisenhower, in fiscal 1959, the ratio rose to 13.96 percent. During the peak-deficit, Vietnam fiscal year of 1968, the ratio was slightly higher, some 14.3 percent.

The size of the deficit relative to the economy as a whole may be reasonably captured by the ratio of the deficit to gross national product. That ratio was also relatively high in depression and war years but fairly small over the rest of the period until the years from 1982 on.

But how can we measure the effects of deficits on the economy? Do they cause inflation or recession? Do they reduce unemployment or crowd out investment? Do they stifle economic growth or stimulate it? Do they increase our foreign debt and wreck our balance of trade, or do they contribute to world prosperity?

A simple, naive approach would be to relate the federal deficit to some of the broad aggregates in which we are interested. We might check the correlations among deficits and gross national product, business investment, or the rates of unemployment or inflation. The difficulty, a common one in economics, is especially serious here: we cannot distinguish between cause and effect.

The problem is that the economy affects the deficit, perhaps as much as or more than the deficit can be expected to affect the economy. When economic conditions are good, incomes, profits and employment are high. Treasury receipts, tied as they are to individual and business income taxes and payroll taxes on employment, are hence high. Further, government

Table 7.8 Federal receipts and outlays, and surplus or deficit as percentage of outlays and GNP, fiscal years 1929–1984

(1) Fiscal year	(2) Receipts – billions of dollars	(3) Outlays (including off-budget outlays) Billions of dollars	(4) As percent of GNP	(5) Billions of dollars	(6) Surplus or deficit (−) As percent of outlays	(7) As percent of GNP
1929	3.9	3.1	3.03	0.7	23.47	0.71
1932	1.9	4.7	6.96	−2.7	−58.70	−4.09
1943	23.6	78.5	44.37	−54.9	−69.89	−31.01
1945	45.2	92.7	42.71	−47.5	−51.22	−21.88
1946	39.3	55.2	27.32	−15.9	−28.73	−7.85
1959	79.2	92.1	19.41	−12.9	−13.96	−2.71
1960	92.5	92.2	18.52	0.3	0.29	0.05
1965	116.8	118.2	17.92	−1.6	−1.35	−0.24
1966	130.8	134.5	18.57	−3.8	−2.82	−0.52

1967	148.3	157.5	20.26	-8.7	-5.53	-1.12
1968	153.0	178.1	21.42	-25.2	-14.13	-3.03
1969	186.9	183.6	20.16	3.2	1.76	0.36
1970	192.8	195.6	20.19	-2.8	1.45	-0.29
1971	187.1	210.2	20.38	-23.0	-10.96	-2.23
1972	207.3	230.7	20.44	-23.4	-10.13	-2.07
1973	230.8	245.7	19.62	-14.9	-6.06	-1.19
1974	263.2	269.4	19.53	-6.1	-2.26	-0.44
1975	279.1	332.3	22.45	-53.2	-16.01	-3.59
1976	298.1	371.8	22.67	-73.7	-19.82	-4.49
1976TQ	81.2	96.0	22.21	-14.7	-15.31	-3.40
1977	355.6	409.2	21.97	-53.6	-13.10	-2.88
1978	399.7	458.7	21.93	-59.0	-12.86	-2.82
1979	463.3	503.5	21.36	-40.2	-7.98	-1.71
1980	517.1	590.9	22.94	-73.8	-12.49	-2.87
1981	599.3	678.2	23.50	-78.9	-11.63	-2.73
1982	617.8	745.7	24.48	-127.9	-17.15	-4.20
1983	600.6	808.3	25.09	-207.8	-25.71	-6.45
1984	666.5	851.8	23.79	-185.3	-21.75	-5.17

Fiscal years until 1976 ran from July 1 of the preceding calendar year to June 30. From 1977 on, the fiscal years began on October 1. TQ denotes the transition quarter, July 1 to September 30, 1976.

expenditures for unemployment benefits and welfare payments will be less when the economy is prosperous.

The combination of higher tax receipts and lower expenditures means a lower deficit. But it is clearly the high GNP, income, profits and employment that have caused the low deficit, and not the reverse. Since high rates of saving and investment generally accompany high GNP, income and profits, they too would the associated with smaller deficits. The inference that the smaller deficits brought on the higher saving and investment would be similarly unwarranted.

The inverse relation between deficits and inflation is somewhat more complex. At first blush it might appear that inflation would be neutral in its effects on the deficit. While higher prices would mean larger nominal incomes and hence greater tax payments to the Treasury, the government would also have to pay more for what it buys. If federal salaries and social security benefits are indexed to the cost of living, we might conclude that expenditures and receipts would both be increased by inflation and the deficit therefore not changed.

There are, however, a number of complications. First, income taxes have historically risen more than in proportion to the increases in income brought on by inflation. This has happened because of the notorious "bracket creep" – inflation has pushed more of income into taxable brackets and into higher brackets with higher tax rates.

While indexing of exemptions and tax brackets to the price level has now essentially ended that contribution of inflation to a more than proportional enhancing of individual income tax payments, the effect of inflation in bringing more than proportional increases in business tax payments remains. This stems from the failure of original cost depreciation deductions to rise with inflation, as well as swollen inventory profits of firms which use FIFO ("first-in, first-out") accounting. For revenues reflect current higher prices while accounting costs of materials and fixed capital are based on the lower prices of bygone days.

Inflation also brings about more than proportionate increases on the expenditure side. These stem from the higher interest rates and hence greater Treasury interest payments as inflation expectations take hold.

In the past, bracket-creep effects of higher prices were such that inflation tended on balance to reduce deficits. But such an association of higher inflation with lower deficits *cannot* then warrant the inference of the inverse relation – that *deficits* reduce *inflation*.

Actual budget deficits are therefore not a good measure of fiscal policy. The Administration and the Congress might be following a tight fiscal policy, keeping discretionary expenditure down and tax rates up, and yet a recession would create a substantial deficit. Indeed the tight fiscal policy, by depressing aggregate demand, might bring on such a recession.

To ascertain what deficits do to the economy, we need a measure that is uncontaminated by what the economy does to deficits. Economists have been able to develop a measure that removes some of the contamination, that brought on by cyclical fluctuations in income and employment. It has been variously called the full employment, high-employment, and standardized employment budget, and the cyclically adjusted budget and the structural budget.

Whatever its name, the important thing about this budget is that it presents estimates of what expenditures and receipts, and hence the deficit, *would be* if the economy were at a level of activity independent of cyclical variations in employment, output and incomes. Since the cyclical variations in output and income are closely associated with those of employment and unemployment, the budget has usually been defined for a constant rate of unemployment.

The Bureau of Economic Analysis of the Department of Commerce has in fact constructed a series of high-employment budget surpluses and deficits beginning in 1955. "High" employment was initially taken to mean 4 percent unemployment; but that figure was raised in several steps in later years, apparently on the assumption that structural or demographic change in the economy was increasing the amount of unemployment – unfortunately frequently called the "natural" rate of unemployment – which should be accepted as consistent with high employment. It was argued, particularly, that the population contained increasing proportions of youths and urban Blacks, with high rates of even non-cyclical unemployment, and these increasing proportions were forcing up the national average of unemployment which was attainable.

The comparison of actual and high employment budgets is intriguing. From 1955 to 1965, as shown in table 7.9, the actual budget was in deficit five times and in surplus six. The high-employment budget was never in deficit. When the actual budget was in surplus the high-employment budget was more so. All this reflected the fact that actual unemployment was more than the high-employment rate over this period. Hence actual tax revenues were less while government expenditures were more.

From 1966 to 1969, with the boom aggregate demand produced by the Vietnam War, actual unemployment was less than 4 percent high-employment rate. (That is an interesting commentary on our view of "high-employment" even then. Quite ignoring the Humphrey-Hawkins Full Employment and Balanced Growth Act, we now cheerfully project unemployment in the 6 and 7 percent range.) The low unemployment of those years caused the three actual deficits to be *less* than the high-employment deficit, and the 1969 surplus to be greater.

The 1970s ushered in the era of unrelenting federal deficits. For none of the last sixteen years has the budget been balanced, let alone in surplus. Those who saw deficits as evidence of unbridled government spending contributing to inflation seemed to have some support for their views.

Table 7.9 Actual and high-employment federal budget surpluses and deficits on national income account, 1955–1984

(1)	(2) Actual	(3) High-employment	(4) Actual	(5) High-employment
	Billions of dollars		Percent of GNP	
1955	4.4	5.2	1.10	1.30
1956	6.1	7.9	1.44	1.87
1957	2.3	6.1	0.51	1.37
1958	−10.3	0.0	−2.28	0.00
1959	−1.1	5.4	−0.23	1.11
1960	3.0	12.1	0.60	2.39
1961	−3.9	7.1	−0.74	1.35
1962	−4.2	3.0	−0.75	0.53
1963	0.3	7.4	0.04	1.24
1964	−3.3	1.1	−0.51	0.17
1965	0.5	0.9	0.03	0.13
1966	−1.8	−5.6	−0.24	−0.74
1967	−13.2	−15.1	−1.65	−1.89
1968	−6.0	−11.0	−0.69	−1.26
1969	8.4	4.9	0.89	0.52
1970	−12.4	−4.6	−1.25	−0.46
1971	−22.0	−11.3	−2.04	−1.05
1972	−16.8	−12.1	−1.42	−1.02
1973	−5.5	−9.5	−0.42	−0.72
1974	−11.5	−0.3	−0.80	−0.02
1975	−69.3	−29.1	−4.47	−1.88
1976	−53.1	−17.4	−3.09	−1.01
1977	−45.9	−20.4	−2.39	−1.06
1978	−29.5	−15.9	−1.36	−0.73
1979	−16.1	−2.0	−0.67	−0.08
1980	−61.2	−17.1	−2.33	−0.65
1981	−64.3	−3.2	−2.17	−0.11
1982	−148.2	−32.6	−4.83	−1.06
1983	−178.6	−59.7	−5.40	−1.81
1984	−175.8	−108.6	−4.80	−2.96

Inflation rose through most of the decade of the seventies, peaking in 1981. But then, as deficits soared to unprecedented heights in 1982, inflation rates dropped precipitously.

The deficits were widely interpreted, nevertheless, as evidence of expansionist fiscal policy. Richard Nixon had said in 1972, "We are all

Keynesians now." If the Keynesian analysis which had presumably come to dominate policymaking were correct, should not unemployment have been low and the economy sizzling? In fact, unemployment was inching up and the economy was sluggish. What was wrong?

One try at an answer was that it was the actual budget that showed the repeated and generally growing deficits. As we have observed, these deficits may have been essentially the product of poor economic conditions, rather than their cause. We may point, for example, to the then record deficit of $69 billion in 1975. Clearly that was largely the result of the sharp 1974–75 recession. Unemployment after all averaged 8.5 percent in 1975. If we had looked at the high-employment budget might we have had a different picture?

But now comes the shocker. The high-employment budget deficit was less than the actual deficit throughout the 1970s and into the 1980s, but it, too, was never quite balanced, coming close only in 1974. Indeed, in 1975 the high-employment deficits seemed generally to be getting larger, not smaller.

It might be said that with growth in the economy and inflation everything was getting larger. The deficit figures would be more comparable over time if they were adjusted for this growth. A simple way to do this is to present the deficit figures as percentages of GNP. As we can also see in table 7.9, however, this does not change the basic picture. Actual deficits as a percentage of GNP set post-World War II records. But high-employment budgets also showed an unmistakable trend to deficit.

Indeed, the high-employment budget was never in deficit and was usually substantially in surplus until the Vietnam War. By 1966, however, the high-employment budget moved to deficit and remained in deficit thereafter, with the solitary exception of the tax-surcharge year of 1969. It would thus appear that the original charge that fiscal policy had been overly expansive is supported – or at least not contradicted – by the history of the high-employment budget deficit.

We come now to our critical departure. We must adjust deficits for inflation. The *real*, actual surplus or deficit may be viewed as essentially the sum of three components: (1) the nominal surplus or deficit as currently measured; (2) an adjustment for changes in the market value of government financial assets and liabilities due to changes in interest rates; and (3) an adjustment for changes in real value due to changing general price levels incident to inflation. An identical or analogous set of adjustments is appropriate for the high-employment budget surplus or deficit.

We can then calculate the adjusted high-employment budgets which, by correcting for these inflation effects, come closer to measuring real surpluses or deficits and the consequent thrust of fiscal policy on aggregate demand. Applying our calculations of net revaluations on actual

Table 7.10 High-employment surplus as percent of GNP, 1955–1984

(1)	(2)	(3)	(4)	(5)	(6)
	Surplus or deficit (−)		On national income accounts		
Year	Official	Adjusted for price effects	Adjusted for interest effects	Adjusted for price and interest effects	Percent change in GNP
1955	1.30	2.81	2.26	3.77	6.72
1956	1.87	3.83	2.79	4.74	2.14
1957	1.37	2.46	0.11	1.20	1.82
1958	0.00	0.93	1.32	2.24	−0.42
1959	1.11	2.09	1.96	2.94	5.99
1960	2.39	2.83	0.45	0.89	2.15
1961	1.35	1.99	1.81	2.45	2.63
1962	0.53	1.28	0.12	0.87	5.78
1963	1.24	1.79	1.70	2.25	4.02
1964	0.17	0.78	0.12	0.72	5.27
1965	0.13	0.98	0.58	1.43	6.04
1966	−0.74	0.33	−0.97	0.11	5.97
1967	−1.89	−0.89	−1.33	−0.34	2.70
1968	−1.26	0.06	−1.14	0.18	4.62
1969	0.52	1.94	1.32	2.74	2.79
1970	−0.46	0.77	−1.87	−0.64	−0.18
1971	−1.05	0.11	−1.41	−0.25	3.39
1972	−1.02	0.02	−0.66	0.39	5.66
1973	−0.72	0.89	−0.46	1.14	5.77
1974	−0.02	2.15	−0.16	2.01	−0.64
1975	−1.88	−0.38	−2.04	−0.54	−1.18
1976	−1.01	0.22	−1.75	−0.52	5.41
1977	−1.06	0.46	−0.23	1.30	5.51
1978	−0.73	1.26	0.15	2.15	5.03
1979	−0.08	1.72	0.11	1.91	2.84
1980	−0.65	1.45	−0.13	1.97	−0.30
1981	−0.11	1.57	−0.23	1.45	2.52
1982	−1.06	0.02	−3.10	−2.01	−2.13
1983	−1.81	−0.75	−0.53	0.54	3.70
1984	−2.96	−1.81	−3.53	−2.37	6.78

net federal debt, we originally adjusted the official high-employment budget surplus series for the years 1955 through 1981. Maintaining the 5.1 percent unemployment benchmark for high employment in effect in the official series since 1975, we have now extended our calculations to 1984.

The results, shown in table 7.10, are dramatic. Inflation and rates of interest were low and relatively steady in the early 1960s prior to escalation of our military involvement in Vietnam. Corrections to the official high-employment budget surplus are hence generally small in those early years.

But in later, more inflationary years, when the official high-employment budget as well as the actual budget moved substantially to deficit, the corrections are striking. *In the 1970s, the entire perceived trend in the direction of fiscal ease or expansion is eliminated or reversed*. The high-employment budget surplus, fully adjusted for price and interest effects, was higher as a percent of GNP for every year from 1977 through 1981 than the surplus of all but two of the years from 1966 through 1976. The only exceptions were the tax-surcharge year of 1969 and the oil-price-shock year of 1974. With similar exceptions, the surplus adjusted only for price (and not interest) effects was higher in every year from 1978 to 1981 than in any other year back to 1963. And since we have accepted Bureau of Economic Analysis increases in the "high-employment" bench mark from 4.0 percent to 5.1 percent unemployment over the period of its "official" series, we may well understate the move to fiscal tightness. The high-employment surpluses would have been even greater in later years if calculated at 4.0 percent unemployment.

So some significant rewriting of recent economic history is in order. Inflation could hardly be ascribed to excess demand associated with increasing fiscal ease and stimulus if, at least by the appropriately corrected high-employment budget measure, there was no such movement to fiscal ease. Some explanation of sluggishness in the economy, climaxed by the severe 1981–82 recession, might then be found in a relatively tight fiscal policy, as measured by the adjusted high-employment budget surplus, as well as in the widely blamed (or credited) role of monetary policy.

The record of deficits from 1982 on is another matter. We shall come to that later. For now we want to show the relation of budget deficits to the economy. And we will find that prevailing views reflect the distortions of improper measures, the most important of which, again, are those tricks played by the effects of inflation.

A few charts can begin to set the record straight, and tell a dramatic new story. First, figure 7.1 shows the widening gap between official and price-adjusted high-employment budget surpluses or deficits as inflation began to heat up in the late 1960s. The two measures moved up and down in

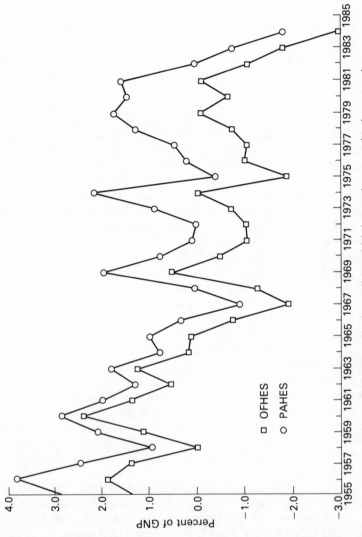

Figure 7.1. Official and price-adjusted high-employment budget surplus

broadly similar fashion. But by the mid-1970s the inflation-adjusted budgets were some 1.5 to 2 percentage points more in surplus or less in deficit than the unadjusted, official high-employment budgets.

What about the relation between budget deficits and the economy? In table 7.11 we relate annual changes in real gross national product for the years 1967 to 1984 to previous high-employment surpluses or deficits. GNP change is tabulated as greater or less than the median growth of 3 percent over this period.

In the upper left-hand panel we see again that the official high-employment budget was in deficit in 17 years, in nine of which GNP growth was more than 3 percent and in eight of which it was less. For the one year of surplus (1969), subsequent growth was less than 3 percent (in fact, virtually zero), but one year does not offer very much evidence. In the lower left-hand panel, however, we observe that the *adjusted* budget was in surplus in 12 of the years. *For the years that it was in surplus, subsequent GNP growth was more than 3 percent only three times, and less than 3 percent nine times. For all of the six years that it was in deficit, subsequent GNP growth was more than 3 percent.*

The official high-employment budget surplus or deficit is in fact also closely related to subsequent growth in GNP. This relation becomes clear when we recognize that inflation makes a true surplus appear as a deficit in the official accounts, and recategorize our official budgets accordingly. Thus, in the upper right-hand panel of table 7.11, we divide the period into years when the previous official high-employment deficit was less than 1 percent of GNP and years when it was more than 1 percent. We find that for the nine years when the deficit was less than 1 percent, subsequent GNP growth was greater than 3 percent in only one case. For the nine years where the deficit was more than 1 percent, subsequent GNP growth was more than 3 percent in eight cases.

Recategorization of the price- and interest-adjusted high-employment budget as in *surplus* by more or less than 1 percent (or in deficit) shows similar results. For the eight years in which the surplus was more than 1 percent, subsequent GNP growth was greater than 3 percent in only one. For the ten years when the adjusted budget was in surplus by less than 1 percent or was in deficit, subsequent GNP growth was greater than 3 percent eight times.

But a single picture may be worth a thousand words, or as many statistics. Figure 7.2 juxtaposes the percentage change in real gross national product and the previous year's price-adjusted high-employment deficit as a percent of real gross national product.

The two curves, it must be conceded, show a remarkable fit. *The greater the deficit, the greater the next year's increase in GNP. The less the deficit, the less the increase or the greater the decline in the next year's GNP.*

Changes in real GNP, as is well known, are closely but inversely related

Table 7.11 High employment surpluses and deficits and growth in GNP, 1967–1984

1. Official budget

Previous high-employment budget	ΔGNP ≷ 3 percent			Previous high-employment budget	ΔGNP ≷ 3 percent		
	Greater (+)	Less (−)	Total (T)		Greater (+)	Less (−)	Total (T)
Surplus (+)	0	1	1	Deficit > 1%	1	8	9
Deficit (−)	9	8	17	Deficit < 1%	8	1	9
Total (T)	9	9	18	Total (T)	9	9	18

2. Price- and interest-adjusted budget

Previous high-employment budget	ΔGNP ≷ 3 percent			Previous high-employment budget	ΔGNP ≷ 3 percent		
	Greater (+)	Less (−)	Total (T)		Greater (+)	Less (−)	Total (T)
Surplus (+)	3	9	12	Surplus > 1%	1	7	8
Deficit (-)	6	0	6	Surplus < 1% or deficit	8	2	10
Total (T)	9	9	18	Total (T)	9	9	18

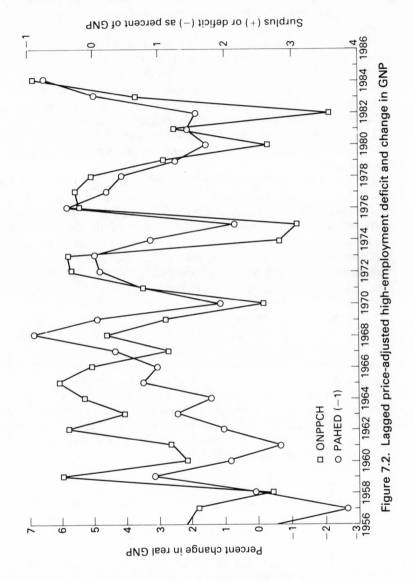

Figure 7.2. Lagged price-adjusted high-employment deficit and change in GNP

to changes in unemployment. Production requires labor and the more people that are working the greater is output. When unemployment goes up, real GNP growth slackens or actually becomes negative. When unemployment goes down, GNP goes up. And the faster unemployment goes down, the faster GNP rises.

In view of the relation between the deficit and GNP, we should thus expect a similar close, but inverse, relation between the deficit and changes in unemployment. Figure 7.3 confirms this. Converting the inverse relation with the deficit into a direct one, it plots the percentage point change in unemployment and the previous year's ratio of the price-adjusted high-employment *surplus* (the negative of the deficit).

The close fit of the two curves is again outstanding. *Higher surpluses – or lesser deficits – are associated with greater increases or lesser decreases in unemployment.*

This relation indicating the stimulative effect of budget deficits has held up under a substantial amount of more vigorous statistical analysis, reported upon in my forthcoming book, *How Real Is the Federal Deficit?* That analysis indicates that monetary policy, as measured by changes in the monetary base, also affects rates of growth of gross national product and unemployment. The independent effect of budget deficits remains substantial, however, probably greater, when the deficit is adjusted for inflation, than effects of changes in the monetary base.

Budget deficits are found to be positively associated not only with increases in consumption but also with increases in investment. Deficits in the past have generally "crowded in" investment, not crowded it out. There is evidence as well, however, that budget deficits have contributed to increasing our trade deficit, particularly in their association with substantial increases in imports. It should be added that these increases in our imports have in turn stimulated growth in output in our OECD partners. And it may be added, that after adjustment for inflation, it turns out that Japan had the greatest deficits in recent years along with the fastest growth. And the very slow-growing United Kingdom has substantial budget surpluses after inflation adjustment.

Where does all this leave us? The officially reported federal debt has been growing at astronomical rates. Since President Reagan took office in 1981 the gross public debt has more than doubled, from $930 billion to $1.9 trillion. The increase has reflected huge and repeated annual deficits, reaching $212 billion in fiscal 1985.

But this has not been all bad! Indeed, given the economic collapse of 1981–82, lesser deficits would have made the deep recession worse. Unemployment would have risen above the official 10.7 percent figure, which was already the highest since the Great Depression of the 1930s. Total production and business profits would have been less. Without the

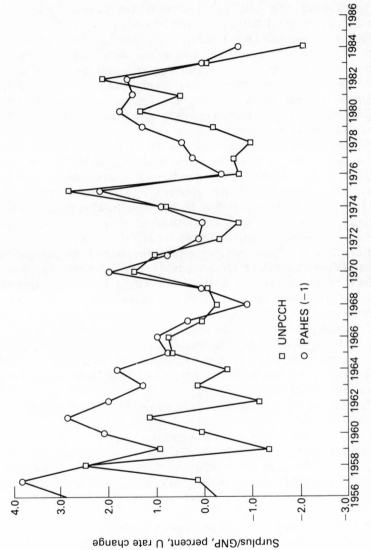

Figure 7.3. Lagged price-adjusted high-employment surplus and change in unemployment

□ UNPCCH

○ PAHES (−1)

Surplus/GNP, percent, U rate change

huge deficits, we would not have had the brisk recovery of 1983 and 1984. And the 1984 election results – whether regarded as good or bad – might well have been quite different.

Up to about 1966, when inflation was relatively minor, budget deficits were really budget deficits. In the period from 1966 on, however, when inflation became substantial, the officially balanced budget turned into one of surplus after inflation corrections were made. A balanced, inflation-adjusted high-employment budget would have been substantially expansionary, producing high rates of growth of GNP and declines in unemployment. As late as 1981, however, we had a roughly balanced *official* high-employment budget, while the budget adjusted for inflation was substantially in surplus.

The Carter Administration, along with most outside critics, ignoring indications of sluggishness in the economy, interpreted the combination of apparent deficits and inflation as indicating excess demand. It initiated moves to combat the inflation by encouraging a tight money policy and, in its final years, striving to reduce budget deficits. This policy continued through the first year of the Reagan Administration as domestic spending was further restrained and more taxes rose than declined.

But in fact, fiscal policy was not stimulative. The high inflation and rising interest rates meant that budgets seemingly in deficit were actually in substantial surplus. Our statistical relations indicate strongly that these inflation-adjusted surpluses contributed significantly to the 1981–83 recession.

This suggests two important correctives to widespread views of fiscal and monetary policy. First, that recession cannot properly be interpreted as a triumph of all-powerful monetary constraints over relatively ineffective fiscal ease. Tight monetary policy *and* tight fiscal policy were its proximate causes.

Thus, those who acquiesced in tight money as "the only game in town" to slow a presumedly overheated, inflationary economy were wrong on two counts. First, the inflation had come from supply shocks, with critical energy prices up some 500 percent in a decade, rather than excess demand, an inference reinforced by the absence of real increases in fiscal thrust. And second, a strong-willed rejection of accommodative monetary policy, rather than balancing budget excesses, offered a near lethal combination of monetary and fiscal contraction.

But fiscal policy moved in a monumentally different direction in 1982. A combination of major tax cuts and increases in military expenditures with a fall in inflation and interest rates converted the *adjusted* high-employment budget from a very high surplus to a very high deficit. Indeed, the change of 3.46 percentage points, from a surplus of 1.45 percent of GNP in 1981 to a deficit of 2.01 percent in 1982, was one of the greatest such swings to expansion on the record. Our estimated relations between budget deficits and changes in GNP and unemployment predicted a major swing to economic recovery and lower unemployment in 1983 and on into 1984, and that is of course precisely what occurred.

Prior to both the Fiscal 1986 Congressional Budget Resolution and the Gramm–Rudman program to "balance the budget" by 1991, CBO estimates included very large and increasing deficits in the years ahead. August 1985 projections of the official *high-employment* ("standardized-employment") budget, reduced to a 5.1 percent unemployment rate, showed a deficit of $225 billion by 1990. This corresponds to an actual projected national income account deficit of $258 billion for that year.

Adjustment for price effects, however, brings the high-employment deficit down substantially, to $58 billion in 1986, but shows it rising to $119 billion by 1990. The price- and interest-adjusted deficit in 1990 is projected at $116 billion.

We thus had projections of substantial high-employment deficits over the rest of this decade. The adjustments for anticipated inflation reduced those projected deficits but still left them high. The projected adjusted deficits, therefore, while initially less than their 1982–84 peaks, were substantial, and turning higher.

Indeed, make no mistake about it. From a historical perspective, these deficits are enormous. From 1986 to 1990 they would *average* 2.15 percent of GNP, while up to 1982 the largest inflation-adjusted deficit we had ever had, in any year since the high-employment series began in 1955, was 0.64 percent. From 1955 to 1981, the adjusted high-employment budget was, on the average, in *surplus* by 1.35 percent of GNP.

Deficits this large, according to my equations – and probably those of any major econometric model – imply a considerable excess demand. Unchecked, they would be pushing the economy toward rates of growth of GNP and declines of unemployment – the latter to negative figures! – which are clearly unattainable.

Initially, however, it should be recognized that the large deficits would be expected to contribute to a reduction of our 7 percent overall unemployment rate. Once unemployment is driven as low as possible with aggressive measures, further fiscal stimulus would generate inflation. The Federal Reserve would then be expected to tighten the money supply, and interest rates, both nominal and real, would rise.

The curious consequence is that associated declining real market values of the public holdings of government debt would mean that the *real* federal deficit would be reduced. It would have been reduced, however, by an inflation tax rather than explicit tax increases or reductions in government expenditures.

The deficit reductions envisaged in the Congressional Budget Resolution for fiscal 1986 were in fact substantial. With adjustment for inflation, the *high-employment budget*, calculated at an unemployment rate of 5.1

Table 7.12 Projected high-employment budget surplus or deficit and GNP, on basis of Fiscal 1986 Congressional Budget Resolution[a]

(1)	(2)	(3)	(4)	(5)	(6)
			Budget surplus or deficit (−)		
				High-employment	
	GNP	Actual (National income accounts)	Official	Adjusted for price effects	Adjusted for price and interest effects
A. Billions of dollars					
1985	3,906	−161.3	−95.9	−36.8	−62.7
1986	4,217	−138.3	−80.6	−15.6	−25.8
1987	4,548	−125.5	−72.3	−0.2	−1.8
1988	4,905	−104.0	−57.6	17.5	15.9
1989	5,289	−96.8	−57.2	24.1	13.9
1990	5,704	−84.6	−51.7	33.7	19.7
B. As percent of GNP					
1985	100.0	−4.13	−2.43	−0.94	−1.60
1986	100.0	−3.29	−1.91	−0.37	−0.61
1987	100.0	−2.76	−1.59	0.00	−0.04
1988	100.0	−2.12	−1.18	0.36	0.32
1989	100.0	−1.83	−1.08	0.46	0.26
1990	100.0	−1.48	−0.91	0.59	0.34

[a] GNP, national income account surplus, and "official" high-employment surplus from Congressional Budget Office projections in *The Economic and Budget Outlook: An Update* (1985). High-employment surpluses have been recalculated at 5.1 percent unemployment. Adjustments have been made on the basis of CBO projections of future prices and Treasury bill rates, and net debt consistent with actual deficits.

percent, would be brought into balance by 1987, as shown in table 7.12, and would be in some surplus in subsequent years. While none of this can be predicted with great accuracy or confidence, it would appear that such a path for the high-employment budget, and the associated relatively moderate actual budget deficits that implies, would be consistent with relatively low unemployment and reasonably non-inflationary economic growth.

The Gramm–Rudman program, on the other hand, envisages from 1987 on, very drastic deficit reduction. As shown in table 7.13, by bringing the actual budget to balance by 1991, it would create a surplus in the official high-employment budget and, most important, very substantial

Table 7.13 Projected future high-employment budget surplus or deficit and GNP, on basis of Gramm–Rudman[a]

(1)	(2)	(3)	(4)	(5)	(6)
				Budget surplus or deficit (−)	
				High-employment	
	GNP	Actual (National income accounts)	Official	Adjusted for price effects	Adjusted for price and interest effects
A. Billions of dollars					
1985	3,906	−161.9	−95.7	−37.5	−63.4
1986	4,217	−138.2	−79.5	−14.5	−24.6
1987	4,548	−102.7	−49.3	−22.3	23.8
1988	4,905	−63.2	−16.0	57.3	60.8
1989	5,289	−31.2	9.1	86.1	84.2
1990	5,704	6.2	39.0	116.6	114.4
B. As percent of GNP					
1985	100.0	−4.14	−2.45	−0.96	−1.62
1986	100.0	−3.28	−1.89	−0.34	−0.58
1987	100.0	−2.26	−1.08	0.49	0.52
1988	100.0	−1.29	−0.33	1.17	1.24
1989	100.0	−0.59	0.17	1.63	1.59
1990	100.0	0.11	0.68	2.04	2.01

[a] GNP from Congressional Budget Office projections in *The Economic and Budget Outlook: An Update* (1985). High-employment surpluses have been recalculated at 5.1 percent unemployment. Adjustments have been made on the basis of CBO projections of future prices and Treasury bill rates, and net debt consistent with actual deficits.

surpluses in the high-employment budget adjusted to include the inflation tax. Gramm–Rudman would, in a real sense, give us high-employment budget surpluses, when adjusted for inflation, comparable to those which have been usually associated in the past with a sluggish economy or sharp recessions.

Once we get over the notion that deficits are automatically a sin, and once we learn to measure them correctly, a lot of the easy answers have to be rejected. It is not true that deficits must always be reduced. The current mix of fiscal and monetary policy, with high real interest rates and a huge trade imbalance accountable to an expensive dollar is far from ideal. Our budget priorities may be all wrong. But the knee-jerk reaction that wiping out all of the overall official deficit will solve our problems is hard to sustain.

The federal budget deficit has become in some circles the hottest political issue since Vietnam. Democrats and Republicans echo each other's proclamations of disaster and largely restrict their differences to their proposed remedies, and the casting of blame. Scoring political points has replaced almost all efforts at sober economic analysis.

Deficits do matter but to know how and how much you have to measure them correctly. And deficits can be good as well as bad.

The public has feared that budget deficits add to their own debt burden and that of future generations. What we really bequeath to the future, however, is our physical and human capital. A "deficit" which finances construction and maintenance of our roads, bridges, harbors and airports is an investment in the future. So are expenditures to preserve and enhance our natural resources or to educate our people and keep them healthy. Federal budgets which are balanced by running down our country's capital or mindlessly selling public assets to private exploiters are real national deficits.

As for that bottom line on what to do about the current federal deficit, it depends. If we were to realize the projection of the fiscal 1986 Joint Congressional Budget Resolution, and we are seriously committed to a high-employment economy, we would probably have gone far enough in overall budget cutting. The increase in debt for the last five years has been such that even our slower rate of inflation generates a substantial inflation tax. The inflation tax rate is less, but the public debt on which it is paid is more.

Inflation-adjusted budget deficits, on the basis of the budget resolution projection, did not promise to be unduly large. For those that highly prize economic growth and low unemployment, the risk of insufficient fiscal stimulus must be weighted heavily. One cannot properly counsel budget-balancing in an economy with unemployment still at 7 percent and real economic growth well below its potential. A budget balanced by current federal rules of accounting is an invitation to the worst economic downturn in half a century.

The budget mix is another matter. We may wish to spend more on investment in our public infrastructure and human capital and less on subsidies and support to those with the most political clout. We may also wish to devote more to our nation's welfare and less to welfare. And we may wish to finance our expenditures with a more equitable tax system.

With a sound and balanced fiscal policy, we should look all the more to a monetary policy which permits the economy to move at full speed. No artificial shortage of money should be allowed to drag down private investment or so distort the value of the dollar as to cripple the significant sectors of the American economy which do and should compete in world markets.

A competitive, market-oriented economy is capable of stunning successes. But there remains a major role for government policy to insure the aggregate demand necessary for full employment and maximum growth. With correct measures, the macroeconomic theory of the past half century can continue to point the path.

Note

1. See M. J. Boskin, M. S. Robinson, T. O'Reilly and P. Kumar, 'The new estimates of the value of federal mineral rights and land,' *American Economic Review*, 75 (1985), Dec.

PART III

Opportunity and the American Dream

Introduction

The success of an economy is best measured by how it meets the needs and values of its people. The American commitment to opportunity and equality runs deep in our political culture and greatly influences how we judge our economy. Our founding document, the Declaration of Independence, tell us that "all men are created equal" and that all have inalienable rights to "life, liberty and the pursuit of happiness." To most Americans, the equal right to pursue happiness has meant that no American shall be prevented by accidents of birth – whether religion, race, gender or family status – from developing his or her talent to the fullest. To this end, our Founding Fathers sought to make cheap land available to as many as possible; in the middle nineteenth century we began to build a system of free public education; and during the Civil War we took the first halting steps toward affordable public-supported State universities. Subsequent generations created VA and FHA loan programs to promote the opportunity to own homes, the National Defense Education Act, Guaranteed Student Loans and many other programs designed to help Americans help themselves. In general, we are a richer nation and a stronger economy because we have increased the opportunity of so many of our citizens.

Yet recent generations of Americans are fearful that the same opportunity for growth and development will not be available for them. Median family income is lower today than in 1973. Young workers have not seen the same growth in their wages as their parents saw a generation ago. Buying a house, the primary financial asset for most Americans, is more difficult today than in any recent period. Poverty has increased significantly in the 1980s and, perhaps most disconcerting, the segment of our population most commonly living in poverty is now children – the group whose future opportunity is most threatened by their present condition. In short, for many Americans opportunity now seems to be fading rather than beckoning.

Bennett Harrison, Chris Tilly and Barry Bluestone (chapter 8) note that the United States has been successful in creating large numbers of jobs in the last decade, but they also demonstrate that we are not producing large enough numbers of jobs that promise higher wages and a ladder to future opportunity. Robert Kuttner (chapter 9) discusses various public policies which he believes can enhance individual opportunities. Kuttner suggests that recent public policy has concentrated too much on "static" income support for the unemployed or poor, and not enough on "dynamic" approaches that expand individual opportunity. Similarly, Bernard Anderson concentrates on the need to improve the skills of unskilled and displaced workers. Anderson argues that the private sector inevitably under-invests in "human capital" and that government must pick up the slack. This is especially true for youths from economically disadvantaged backgrounds. Anderson argues forcefully that we need the developed talents of unskilled youths and outlines successful programs whose benefits have outweighed their costs.

Michael Piore (chapter 10) ends this section on a slightly different note. Future growth in income and opportunity depends strongly on productivity growth. Piore believes that the American workplace has become rigid and hierarchical. Workers do not get the opportunity to exercise much creativity and thus do not fully contribute all that they can to the productive process. In the end they, their firms and the economy at large do not realize their fullest potential.

The future of the American economy depends upon the performance of its people as well as its machines. If our economy is to continue to grow, we must develop new avenues of opportunity that are appropriate to our own era as the Homestead Act, the Land Grant College and the GI Bill of Rights were for theirs. The authors in this section offer us this challenge.

8

Rising Inequality

BENNETT HARRISON, CHRIS TILLY, and BARRY BLUESTONE

Inequality among American workers in their annual wage and salary incomes declined steadily throughout the 1960s, and well into the decade of the 1970s. Then, somewhere between 1975 and 1978, the distribution of wages and salaries took a sharp U-turn. This was before the election of Ronald Reagan, before the passage of the sharply regressive tax act of 1981, and even before the official commencement of the monetarist experiment in 1979. Income inequality has been increasing ever since.

What is causing increasing polarization of wage incomes among American workers? At this point, we do not know for certain. The factors most commonly suggested in recent years by Washington-based researchers, columnists, and politicians – the business cycle, the entrance of the baby boom generation into the work force, and fluctuations after 1973 in the exchange value of the American dollar in international trade – explain at most a third of the variation in wage and salary inequality since the Great Society officially left town in January, 1969. That these conventional wisdoms explain so little suggests the need to probe much more deeply into the changes that have taken place in the deep structure of the American economy over the past 15 years, and how corporations and governments have responded to those changes. It is in that direction that our future research lies.

We hear much talk these days about the need for greater wage "flexibility," in order to achieve enhanced "competitiveness" with foreign business. All of the mechanisms now being proposed or already in place – the substitution of wage bonuses for fixed, contractural rises of pay, two-tiered company wage systems and the creation of a sub-minimum wage for younger people – would almost certainly have the effect of exacerbating wage inequality among workers, regardless of their particular skills and contributions to overall productivity.

As we will show in this chapter, the trend of wage inequality had already turned upward even before these new schemes were introduced into the workplace (and into official discourse in Washington). To make the situation even worse through deliberate public policy (or by public sanctioning of private business policy) could return to haunt us in the future. If it turns out that we are indeed facing a long-term tendency toward increasingly unequal wage incomes, work incentives (and conceivably even long-run economic growth) could be threatened. Perhaps even more disturbing is the fear – expressed by a growing number of journalists and political analysts – that the frustrated expectations of significant numbers of younger workers unable to attain the living standards of their own parents could lead to potentially serious social unrest.[1]

If market forces (and past public policies) are indeed giving us an increasingly polarized distribution of income, it is only a matter of time before a large (and probably increasingly diverse) mass of citizens are going to begin pressing the federal government to correct these inequalities. At a time when everyone in Washington is trying desperately to fashion ways to *reduce* the federal budget deficit, what the country surely does not need is yet another source of pressure on an already fragile public sector.

The Revival of Concern with Income Inequality

The past year (1985) has seen an extraordinary revival of public interest in the problem of income inequality. So far, this interest has focused almost entirely on what is happening to the distribution of *family* incomes. There has been a flood of academic papers, reports written for congressional committees, and an important new book.[2] Taken together with the earliest statements on this subject in the current period[3] all of this work indicates (to varying degrees, depending on the specific definitions in use) a rise in family income inequality in the United States since at least the middle of the last decade.

All sorts of explanations have been offered for this "stylized fact." Some suggest that it is only a temporary phenomenon, an artifact created by such transitional developments as the movement of the business cycle, fluctuations in the exchange value of the dollar against foreign currencies, and the entry of the "baby boom" generation into the workforce. Consider the latter hypothesis. The crowding of the labor market for young adults would (it has been suggested) depress the wages and family incomes of that age cohort, thereby increasing income dispersion between younger and older workers (and probably among the younger workers, as well). As the baby-boomers mature, this age-based source of inequality will (it is predicted) dissipate.

By contrast, others have identified more long-term, structural shifts in economic and demographic relationships as likely causes of growing inequality. Thus, for example, two of us have argued elsewhere that

American workers have become increasingly exposed to competition from much lower-paid (but, in some industries, nearly equally productive) workers in other countries. Moreover, so long as this competition from offshore labor is even potentially present, American corporations are able (and, it would seem, increasingly willing) to invoke it as a lever in the struggle over the distribution of income between wages and profits at the level of the firm. The effects of this new international wage competition, being highly uneven across industries, occupations, and regions, could well be responsible for the growing inequality in domestic labor incomes.[4]

Similarly, demographic theories suggest that rising income inequality mainly reflects growing disparities in family structure. Proponents of this explanation cite the confluence of the growth of two-earner families at one end of the income distribution, and single-parent families at the other.[5] Some feminist authors explain the latter by rising divorce rates (made affordable by increasing female labor force participation) and – for black women – increasing rates of incarceration of young black men.[6]

In a new book, we will explore the origins, magnitudes, and possible political consequences of the growing polarization of incomes and communities in "post-industrial" America. Our review of the evidence will of course begin with this question of what has been happening to family incomes. But probably the most important part of our work is addressed to a question that seems not to have yet made the transition from the technical journals to the congressional hearing rooms: to what extent is the apparent trend toward growing income inequality grounded in the labor market? At the very least, we should want to know whether the distribution of wages and salaries of individual workers is itself becoming more unequal.[7]

To the extent that the income from working – wages, salaries and cash benefits – is becoming distributed more unequally among employees, the potentially destabilizing consequences go far beyond social unrest *per se*. For example, consider the problem of *work incentives*. In a capitalist economy, some degree of wage inequality is unquestionably functional to the efficient operation of labor markets. Wage differentials signal occupational shortages and surpluses. Higher than average wages constitute a payoff to experience in many work settings, and can therefore be expected to induce a higher degree of job-attachment than might otherwise be forthcoming. However, beyond a certain point, wage differentials can become counterproductive. Albert Hirschman has suggested that the perception that a person is receiving unequal treatment can lead her or him (or an entire class of people) either to readjust expectations *or* to withdraw from full participation in some social process ("exit"). The danger in the present context is that *rising* inequality – a *growing* gap between rich and poor – will be perceived as unbridgeable. That could undermine work incentives and thereby further erode already lagging productivity growth.[8]

In this chapter, we offer some preliminary findings on trends in inequality in individual workers' wage and salary incomes since the 1960s. Our objectives are twofold. First, we will demonstrate that, after a long period of decline, inequality underwent a remarkably abrupt "U-turn" in the latter half of the 1970s. Second, we will test several of the most popular conventional hypotheses about rising income inequality. These concern the business cycle, the baby-boom and the exchange value of the dollar. We will show that, taken together, these three factors explain only a small part of the growing inequality in individual wages and salaries (about one-third, to be precise). In our opinion, these findings invite a reopening of the search for deeper, more fundamental explanations for what appears to be a secular worsening of the distribution of labor income in the United States.

Inequality in Wages and Salaries[9]

There are any number of ways to characterize "inequality." In this paper, we employ the economist's most standard indicator: the variance of the natural logarithm. By concentrating on *annual* labor incomes, we are including in our measure both fully employed workers and those who are able (or choose) to work for only a portion of the year. At this point in our research, we deliberately did not want to truncate the samples to year-round employees (or to study, say, hourly wage rates). We believe that variation in the hours and weeks of employment available to a person in the jobs (s)he holds constitutes fully as important a criterion for evaluating the quality or adequacy of that person's work situation as does the hourly rate of pay.

During the long macroeconomic expansion of the mid 1960s, wage and salary inequality fell dramatically (figure 8.1). The decline continued (albeit at a slower rate) until 1978. In that year, the pattern of inequality in annual labor income underwent an abrupt U-turn, rising rapidly thereafter (figure 8.2). By 1983, what we'll abbreviate as "wage inequality" was considerably above the level of the late 1960s. This is a robust finding. To at least some extent, the U-turn appears in every series we studied: year-round, full-time workers, men and women, youth and middle-aged persons. Certainly *every* subgroup shows a sharp increase in inequality after the middle of the decade (appendix figures 8.A3–A8).[10, 11]

The first of three "conventional wisdoms" about wage inequality that we have been able to subject to rigorous econometric scrutiny concerns the business cycle. It is widely held that wage differentials contract during periods of macroeconomic expansion and widen during recessions. The reason conventionally offered by labor economists is that high wages tend to be relatively "stickier," i.e. more well-protected by explicit or implicit

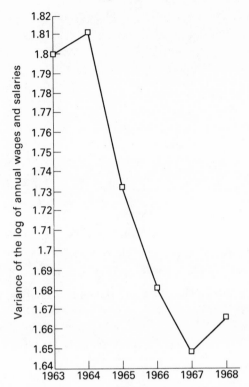

Figure 8.1. Inequality in annual wages and salaries, 1963–1968

contracts, than low wages (middle-level wages have their own forms of protection, such as unionization and civil service status). Low-wage jobs are far less likely to be protected. In recessions, it is therefore the low wages which tend to be eroded *vis-à-vis* the rest, while during recoveries, employers are relatively freer to augment low wages if temporary shortages appear. The policy implication is that "sound" macroeconomic policy can smooth the path of aggregate economic growth and, in that process, promote a continued tendency toward income equality.

There is certainly no doubt that the seventies was a rocky decade for the US economy, with three recessions between 1970 and 1980 (figure 8.3). Yet, when we statistically control for the effect of year-to-year variations in the cycle – whether the latter is measured by the aggregate rate of unemployment or by the Federal Reserve Board's index of capacity utilization – the U-shaped pattern of inequality in individual wage and salary incomes becomes, if anything, even more pronounced (figure 8.4).[12] The movements of the business cycle are simply not a statistically

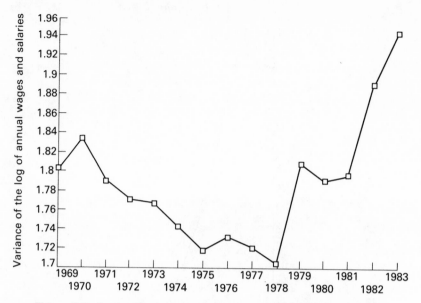

Figure 8.2. Inequality in annual wages and salaries, 1969–1983

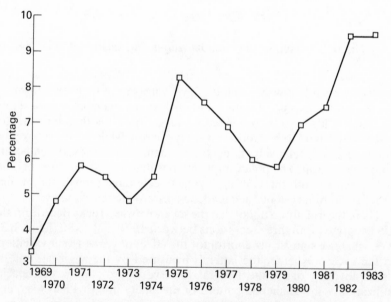

Figure 8.3. National unemployment rate, 1969–1983

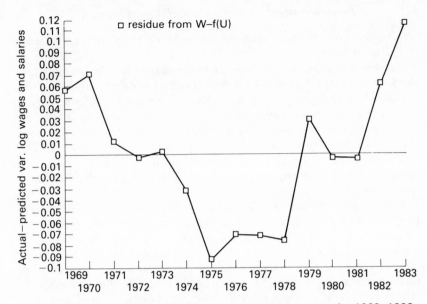

Figure 8.4. Wage inequality after removing business cycle, 1969–1983

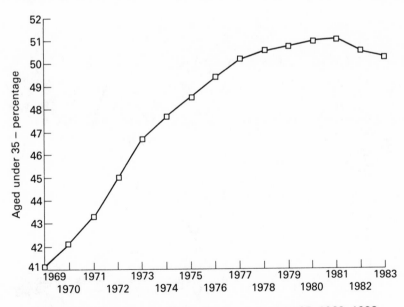

Figure 8.5. Percentage of labor force under age 35, 1969–1983

significant cause of the variations since 1969 in the degree of wage inequality in the US.

Another explanation of aggregate income inequality is the entrance into the workforce of the post-World War II baby-boom generation. As was explained in the first part of this chapter, standard economic theory clearly leads to the inference that an excess supply of labor offered by younger workers will, holding other things constant, depress the wage of that cohort, thereby increasing inter-generational wage variations.[13] The policy implication seems to be that we need do nothing about any apparent trend in growing inequality: it will disappear by itself as the baby-boomers mature.

That the baby-boomer's entry into the world of work probably created precisely such conditions of excess supply is strongly hinted at by the numbers in figure 8.5. The share of the civilian labor force made up of workers under the age of 35 rose from 41 percent in 1969 to 51 percent only ten years later. And yet once again the conventional wisdom turns out to be empirically difficult to support. After statistically removing the effects of both the business cycle and the baby boom, we see a pattern of wage inequality which is fundamentally unchanged (figure 8.6). The great U-turn of the late 1970s is still apparent.[14]

Still another widely held view is that the 38 percent increase in the

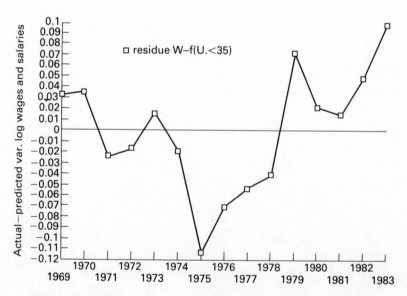

Figure 8.6. Wage inequality after removing business cycle and baby boom, 1969–1983

exchange value of the American dollar between 1980 and 1983, weighed against the currencies of our nine major trading partners, has so damaged American export industries as to dislocate factory workers who are predominantly "middle-level" wage earners. The implication seems to be that a policy of judiciously managed trade, combined with reduced federal deficits to bring down interest rates and therefore the foreign demand for dollars), can substantially eliminate this dollar-based source of trading disadvantage, thereby restoring the vitality of US export industries and the concomitant expansion of "good" jobs.

Since the exchange rate did not begin to rise until 1980, we already know that this factor cannot possibly explain the timing of the U-turn in wage inequality, which occurred at least two years earlier (figure 8.7). Certainly the rapid increases in exchange rates is correlated with the rise in inequality. To find out how correlated, we again ran multiple regressions, this time to remove statistically the joint effects of all three explanatory variables: the business cycle (measured by the unemployment rate), the baby-boom (measured by the share of the workforce in each year under the age of 35), and the trade-weighted exchange value of the dollar. As the regression parameters in Appendix table 8.A1 reveal, this model explains only about one-third of the year-to-year variation in wage inequality. Figure 8.8 confirms that, while the three predictors do have some impact on the dependent variable, the underlying parabolic time path of our indicator of wage inequality is still clearly discernible in the data.[15]

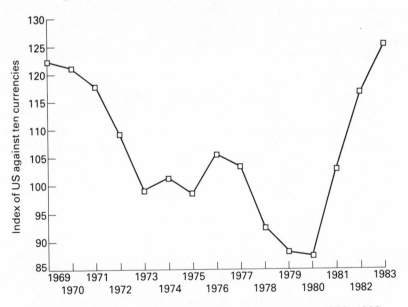

Figure 8.7. Trade-weighted US dollar exchange rate, 1969–1983

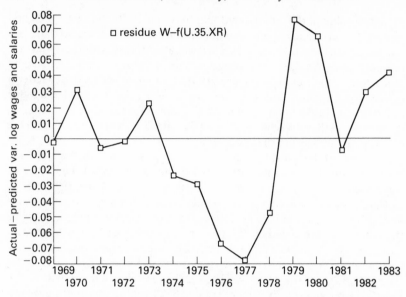

Figure 8.8. Wage inequality given cycle, age, exchange rate, 1969–1983

A Research Agenda on Wage Inequality

Our research into the origins, magnitudes and potential political and economic consequences of the tendency toward increasing income inequality in the US has only begun. There is still much to learn. Five questions, in particular, will dominate our efforts in the spring and summer of 1986.

How many people are earning high, middle, and low wages?

First, the finding of growing inequality, as measured by the variance of the wage and salary income distribution, is consistent with many different sorts of changes in the shape of that distribution over time. For example, is it the case that the increasing inequality is attributable mainly to growth of the upper end? (this might be called the "rich are getting richer" hypothesis). Or perhaps the situation is the opposite, and it is the lower end of the distribution which is growing ("the poor are getting poorer"). It is even conceivable that *both* things are happening simultaneously, with a proportionate decline in the number of people earning middle-level wages ("the declining middle class" hypothesis that has been so much debated in the press since Robert Kuttner first broached the subject in 1983).

Virtually all of the critics of Kuttner have tried to answer these questions by examining changes in the shares of total income (or wages, or

earnings) going to the highest-paid 20 percent of the workforce or population, the next highest-paid 20 percent, etc. On this basis, there seems to
have been very little change since the end of World War II in the relative
sizes of the top, middle, and bottom of the income distribution.[16] But how
the shares of total income are being distributed is really *not* what most of
us want to know. Rather, we want to know *how many* people have been
earning "high," "middle" and "low" wages in each year, and how that has
been changing over time. To do that, we need to analyze the shape of each
year's income distribution against some *outside* standard of what constitutes high, middle, and low-wage income.

For that purpose, we are presently experimenting with the use of
multiples of the official government poverty line for an unrelated individual under the age of 65, as the nearest approximation to an estimate of
minimal income needs for individual workers. Thus, for example, in 1982
a person whose annual wages and salaries placed her or him in a range
between twice the poverty line and seven times that benchmark would
have been earning between $10,000 and $35,000 a year. The mean,
median and mode of the distribution of wage and salary incomes all fall
within the $10,000–20,000 range in 1982, so our standard for defining
adequate incomes seems quite suitable. At the upper end, with current
costs of living and popular expectations about consumption, it would be
difficult to consider wages below something like $35,000 to be indicative
of great privilege.

We are therefore preparing tables on the number of workers falling
below, within and above this poverty-line-based definition of "middle-
income persons." Of course, for all of our estimates of the share of the
workforce made up of high-wage, middle-wage and low-wage workers, we
will test their sensitivity to these choices of exogenous income standards.
In other words, how much difference would it make if the cutoffs were
(say) twice and *six* times the poverty line? (roughly $10,000–$30,000 in
1982 dollars).

*How much of the intertemporal dispersion in annual wages and salaries is
variation among workers in the hourly or weekly wage rates of their jobs,
and how much is variation in the number of hours or weeks they work each
year?*

A number of labor economists, most notably James Medoff, have
argued that the personal distribution of hourly wage *rates* has remained
virtually unchanged since the late 1960s, implying that there has been little
or no change in the job structure. Instead, it is suggested, virtually all of the
year-to-year variation in annual wages (or earnings) is attributable to
differences among people in work experience: hours and weeks of paid
employment over the course of the year. This may well be so – although no

one to our knowledge has conclusively proven it by formally decomposing variance in annual labor income into variance in weeks or hours of work, on the one hand, and variance in weekly or hourly wage rates, on the other. This is an analysis we intend to perform this Spring.

But even if the assertion were correct, this need not imply that the job structure has remained unchanged. Under the pressure to show higher short-term profits, some personnel managers may be deliberately trans-forming jobs with full-time work schedules into positions that are staffed on a part-time basis, at more-or-less unchanging hourly wage rates (pos-sibly in order to economize on fringe benefits). Alternatively, the out-sourcing of tasks that used to be performed by unionized workers in large firms (whether auto plants or big-city hospitals) may plausibly be resulting in the relative growth of less-than-year-round work – even if the hourly rate of pay hasn't changed much. In any case, even in the absence of such practices, since different industries are characterized by a different mix of full- and part-time (or part-year) jobs (e.g. department stores vs. steel mills), any significant shift in industry mix over time could produce an aggregate change in the ratio of full- to part-time (or part-year) work opportunities. All of this needs to be explored.

To what extent are income inequalities appearing within the Black com-munity that mirror those which we find for the population as a whole?

Under the theme of "the declining significance of race," such prominent Black social scientists as William Julius Wilson have argued that racial discrimination *per se* has become less consequential for the Black experi-ence in contemporary America than growing class disparities within the community itself. Certainly much public policy over the last 15 years has been explicitly devoted to encouraging the development of a Black bour-geoisie in the US. At the same time, there has been a significant growth in the proportion of all Black children growing up in poor, fatherless house-holds. While there are competing explanations for (and heated debates about the causes and implications of) this phenomenon, no one denies its importance as a major social issue.

And yet no one seems to have subjected the hypothesis of growing intraracial income polarization to rigorous quantitative scrutiny. We strongly suspect that the alleged growth of a Black middle class has been greatly exaggerated, and that Black people in this country continue to share much more in common with one another in relation to the principal institutions of the society – work, government entitlements and treatment under the law – than is true for whites.

What are the implications of growing wage inequality (and especially of the hypothesized relative increase in the supply of low-wage jobs) for family work effort? That is, are more family members having to work more hours or weeks in order to achieve the same level of real family income from labor as before the great U-turn?

Among which industries and sectors (such as high-tech) is the tendency toward increasing wage inequality visible? On the other hand, which industries and sectors show declining inequality over time, even into the 1980s?

Once we have answered these questions, we should have a rather complete description of the anatomy of contemporary wage inequality. We will then be in a position to explore alternative explanations for why progress toward greater income equality among American workers has been so dramatically arrested within the last ten years.

Postscript

It now seems fairly clear that both family incomes and individual wages and salaries are being distributed more and more unequally among the working people of the United States. There is still much to learn about the causes, precise magnitudes and possible political-economic consequences of this development. Nevertheless, even with what we already know, two striking ironies become apparent.

Since the 1960s, the very mention of the word "inequality" has tended to raise images of the Black inner city ghetto (or of the desperately poor rural hollow). In both the popular media and political forums "inequality" has for all practical purposes been the study of the poor. The new research on inequality suggests that this comfortable notion has become outmoded. The sense of relative deprivation, of frustrated expectations, of falling behind, of being badly-paid – this is becoming the common experience of a growing number of Americans. They are white as well as persons of color. They are men as well as women. Having a full-time, year-round job is no longer a guarantee of being sheltered from this experience.

The second irony has even more far-reaching implications. It was in 1954 that Nobel laureate Simon Kuznets first proposed that income inequality tends to increase during the early stages of economic development, then levels off and diminishes as development proceeds. Economic historians and other social scientists have for a generation taken the "Kuznets curve" as an article of faith. The long gradual movement toward greater equality within the developed industrial countries has been held out to the workers and farmers of the Third World as the eventual payoff to current sacrifices in the process of transcending "underdevelopment." Surely the perception that the long-run tendency toward greater equality in the United States may have been arrested can be expected to undermine the legitimacy of existing strategies of economic development throughout the developing world.

Notes

1. A bevy of prominent national economic journalists – Peter Behr, Thomas Edsall, James Fellows, Jeff Greenfield, Robert Kuttner, Jane Seabury, Robert Samuelson, Victor Zonana, to name only a few from the print media – certainly seem to take this matter seriously (although they are far from agreed on the probability of its occurrence). Edsall is using the apparent fact of this economic class polarization to fashion a political theory about voting patterns. See Thomas B. Edsall, More than ever, the electorate is polarised on economic lines', *Washington Post National Weekly Edition*, Jan. 6, 1986, p. 23; idem, *The New Policies of Inequality* (W. W. Norton, New York, 1984).

2. See, for example, Richard S. Belous, Linda H. LeGrande and Brian W. Cashell, *Middle Class Erosion and Growing Income Inequality: Fact or Fiction?* (Congressional Research Service, US Library of Congress, Report No. 85–203E, Nov. 1985); McKinley L. Blackburn and David E. Bloom, 'What is happening to the middle class', *Demography* (1985), Jan.; Sheldon Danziger and Peter Gottschalk, *How Have Families with Children been Fairing?* (US Congressional Joint Economic Committee, Washington DC, Dec. 1985); idem, 'A framework for evaluating the effects of economic growth and transfers on poverty', *American Economic Review* (1985), March; Frank Levy and Richard Michel, *The Economic Future of the Baby Boom* (US Congressional Joint Economic Committee, Washington DC, Dec. 1985); Lester B. Thurow, *The Zero-Sum Solution* (Simon and Schuster, New York, 1985).

3. See Frank Levy and Richard Michel, 'The Way We'll Be in 1984: Recent Changes in the Level and Distribution of Disposable Income', The Urban Institute, Washington DC, Nov. 1983; Stephen J. Rose, *Social Stratification in The U.S.* (Social Graphics Co., Baltimore, 1983); Lester B. Thurow, 'The disappearance of the middle class: it's not just demographics', *New York Times*, Feb. 5, 1984, p. F3.

4. See Barry A. Bluestone and Bennett Harrison, *The Deindustrialization of America* (Basic Books, New York, 1982). The mechanisms that mediate the relationship between the new global competition and the domestic distributions of employment and income include greatly increased import penetration of the domestic market of the US, but also the expanded capacity of American companies to produce (or to "source" from) foreign locations – or to credibly *threaten* to do so. Similarly, firms are under some pressure to automate their domestic operations in order to make their unit labor costs more internationally competitive. One effect of these developments has been to force many (especially blue-collar) workers in depressed export-oriented industries to "skid" down into lower wage, typically service sector jobs (Gordon, Schervish, and Bluestone; Flaim and Sehgel). This would also increase the dispersion of labor incomes. Even those mainly middle-level wage-earners who do *not* actually lose their jobs may still be forced to accept declines in their relative wages as a result of concession bargaining impelled by that same threat of

international competition (Slaughter). Finally, the flight of American capital into financial speculation (especially the rash of highly leveraged mergers and acquisitions) – activities which arguably create a more unequal mix of jobs than would the rebuilding of the nation's physical infrastructure, or the revitalization of the machine-tool industry – might also be interpreted at least in part as an attempt to restore short-run profits that had been eroded during the 1970s by foreign competition. See Avery Gordon, Paul Schervish and Barry A. Bluestone, 'The Unemployment and Re-employment Experiences of Michigan Auto Workers', Social Welfare Research Institute, Boston College, Chestnut Hill, Ma., Aug, 1985; Paul Flaim and Ellen Sehgel, 'Displaced workers of 1979–83: how well have they fared?', *Monthly Labor Review* (1985), June; Jane Slaughter, *Concessions – and How to Beat Them* (Labor Education Project, Detroit, 1983).

5. Blackburn and Bloom, 'What is happening to the middle class?'
6. William B. Dainty, Jr, 'The managerial class and industrial policy,' *Industrial Relations* (1986), Spring.
7. For other research on the subject of inequality in labor incomes see Linda A. Bell and Richard B. Freeman, 'The Rising Dispersion in Industrial Wages in the U.S.: Efficient vs Inefficient Wage Flexibility', National Bureau of Economic Research, Cambridge, Ma., Sept. 1985, MSS; Barry A. Bluestone, Bennett Harrison and Lucy Gorham, 'Storm Clouds on the Horizon', Economic Education Project, Brookline, Ma., May 1984; Martin D. Dooley and Peter Gottschalk, 'Does a younger male labour force mean greater earnings inequality?', *Monthly Labor Review* (1982), Nov.; idem, 'Earnings inequality among males in the United States: trends and the effect of labor force growth', *Journal of Political Economy* 1984), Feb.; idem, 'The increasing proportion of men with low earnings in the United States', *Demography* (1985), Feb.; Peter Henle, 'Exploring the distribution of earned income', *Monthly Labor Review* (1972), Dec.; idem and Paul Ryscavage, 'The distribution of earned income among men and women, 1958–77', *Monthly Labor Review* (1980), April; Robert Z. Lawrence, 'Sectoral Shifts and the Size of the Middle Class', *The Brookings Review* (1984), Fall; Sar A. Levitan and Peter E. Carlson, 'Middle class shrinkage?', *Across the Board* [Journal of the Conference Board] (1984), Oct.; James L. Medoff, 'The Structure of Hourly Earnings Among U.S. Private Sector Employees: 1973–1984', National Bureau of Economic Research, Cambridge, Ma., Dec. 1984; Thierry Noyelle and Thomas Stanback, *The Economic Transformation of American Cities* (Rowman and Allanheld, Totowa, NJ, 1984); Neal H. Rosenthal, 'The shrinking middle class: myth or reality?', *Monthly Labor Review* (1985), March; Saskia Sassen-Koob, 'The new labor demand in global cities', in *Cities in Transformation*, ed. Michael P. Smith (Sage, Beverly Hills, Ca., 1984).
8. A parallel macroeconomic danger is the threat to the aggregate rate of economic growth. "Underconsumptionism" – according to which a tendency toward income inequality may depress consumption spending and, on balance, retard short-run cyclical recoveries and possibly even promote recessions – is an old debate, not to be settled here (the subject is comprehensively reviewed in Gottfried Habeler, *Prosperity and Depression* (Harvard University Press, Cambridge, Ma., 1960).

In this era of almost obsessive concern for increasing the national rate of savings, John Maynard Keynes' endorsement of the basic underconsumptionist thesis of Hobson has been all but forgotten: "It is the first explicit statement of the fact that capital is brought into existence not by the propensity to save but in response to the demand resulting from actual and prospective consumption" John Maynard Keynes, *The General Theory of Employment, Interest and Money* (Harcourt, Brace/Harbinger, New York, 1964), p. 368.

In any case, whether the marginal propensity to consume is or is not inversely related to the level of income, such that regressive redistribution from lower to higher income classes could be expected to lower the size of the multiplier and thereby retard economic growth, is an empirical question which is completely ignored in the contemporary macroeconomic literature, where the consumption function is simply assumed to be linear in current (or lagged) income. Perhaps the recent discoveries of growing income inequality in the US will stimulate new empirical research in this area.

9. Our data for this analysis were drawn from a special version of the computer tapes containing the US Census Bureau's March *Current Population Survey*. This file was generously provided to us by Professor Robert Mare of the Department of Sociology, University of Wisconsin. The sample size of workers who had at least some annual wages or salaries ranges between 27,241 and 74,319 individuals across the twenty-one years in Mare's file. The March interviews were conducted in the years 1964–1984. However, the "annual wage and salary income" variable refers to the previous calendar year. Hence we refer to our observations as occurring in 1963–83. Apparently there were significant definitional and/or coverage changes after March 1969 – at least in the Mare file – which resulted in sharp discontinuities between the (calendar) 1968 and 1969 estimates of virtually all the variables of interest to us. It therefore seemed advisable to treat the data as two discrete time series: 1963–68 and 1969–83. In the present paper, we focus on the latter period.

10. Although we think that wages and salaries is the preferred indicator of labor income, many economists and sociologists choose to study "earnings" (which includes the incomes of independent consultants, small business owners, self-employed farmers, etc.). Our data on earnings also show a U-turn, although the trough occurs somewhat earlier in the decade (Appendix figures 8.A1, 8.A2).

11. The discovery of the U-turn is especially interesting in shedding light on the findings of other researchers. Thus, for example, by looking at only two years – 1969 and 1983 – Robert Lawrence of the Brookings Institution completely missed the dramatic switch in the direction of change in inequality, which did not occur until after the mid-1970s. As a result, his own estimates of polarization, while obviously correct on their own terms, give a misleading picture of the extent of the changes over the more recent past.

Analogously, by studying patterns of wage dispersion only among men, Peter Gottschalk and Martin Dooley missed an important difference in inequality by gender. Their path-breaking research demonstrated that male earnings inequality had been increasing since the mid-1960s (their time series terminates in 1977). Appendix figure A6 reveals that wage and salary inequality among women was actually falling throughout that same period. Together with the fact that the mean of women's wage and salary income was (slowly) approaching that of men throughout these years, this was sufficient to pull the aggregate distribution in the direction of greater equality, up until 1978. Both groups then experience a roughly similar degree of rising inequality beyond that point.

12. These and all other multiple regression results are given in Appendix tables 8.A1 and 8.A2.

13. This of course assumes that newly minted 23-year-old college graduates are not generally considered by companies to be close substitutes for 46-year-old experienced workers – an assumption we would not challenge for the purposes of this inquiry.

14. The baby-boom hypothesis held that the phenomenon of increasing wage inequality (or, in some arguments, bi-polarization) was primarily a problem for younger workers and a temporary problem, at that (cf. Lawrence, 'Sectoral shifts and the size of the middle class').

    In fact, when we break out the two prime age groups 25–34 and 35–54, we discover that the facts are exactly the opposite of the conventional wisdom (figures 8.A7 and 8.A8). The younger group actually experiences *declining* inequality well into the decade, while inequality begins rising for the older cohort as far back as 1972.

15. The results are virtually identical when the Federal Reserve Board's capacity utilization index is used instead of unemployment to measure the business cycle. We also tried a first difference model, regressing the change in wage inequality on year-to-year changes in unemployment, age mix and exchange rates. In these regressions, the predictive power of the three variables disappeared entirely! Finally, to be even more certain about our conclusions, we fit a second-degree spline regression to the residuals displayed in figure 8.8 with a knot at 1977. The results, displayed in appendix table 8.A2, confirm a highly statistically significant change of sign in the time path of wage inequality (after controlling for cycle, age, and exchange rates) from negative (indicating declining inequality) between 1969 and 1977 to positive thereafter.

16. Belous, LeGrande and Carhell, *Middle Class Erosion and Growing Income Inequality*.

Appendix to Chapter 8

Table 8.A1 Regressions of variance of log real annual wages and salaries (t-statistics in parentheses)

Equation no.	(1)	(2)	(3)	(4)
Constant	1.699	2.094	0.690	0.829
Unemployment rate	0.014	0.028	−0.005	
	(1.39)	(2.12)	(0.26)	
FRB capacity utilization index				−0.002
				(0.01)
% of labor force under age 35		−1.020	1.207	0.954
		(1.54)	(1.13)	(1.52)
Trade-weighted exchange rate index (1973=100)			0.005	0.005
			(2.44)	(2.73)
$\bar{R}^2$	0.063	0.152	0.340	0.342
N	15	15	15	15

Table 8.A2 Spline regression of residuals from the equation 'var log real W&8 = f(Urate, % <35, Xchange)' (t-statistics in parentheses)

Equation	(1)	(2)
Constant	−0.018	0.027
Time	0.002	−0.008
	(0.82)	(1.79)
Spline (1978=1)		0.025
		(2.71)
Sum of squared residuals	0.027	0.017
N	15	15

Rate of change for 1969–77 = −.008.
Rate of change for 1978–83 = +.025.
$H_0 1$ [(SSR (1) − SSR (2))/[SSR (2)/12] < F(1, 12).
F (1, 12) at the .05 level = 4.54.
7.33 > 4.54.
Therefore the knot at 1977 is statistically significant at a 95% level of confidence.

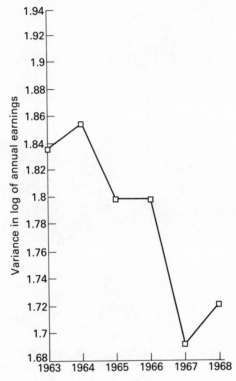

Figure 8.A1. Earnings inequality (includes self-employed income),
1963–1968

Figure 8.A2. Earnings inequality (includes self-employed income),
1969–1983

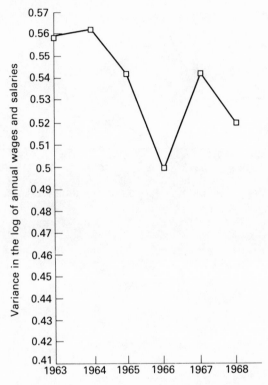

Figure 8.A3. Wage inequality, year-round, full-time workers, 1963–1968

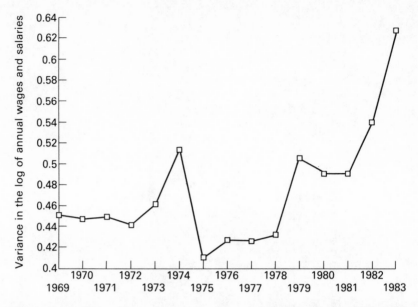

Figure 8.A4. Wage inequality, year-round, full-time workers, 1969–1983

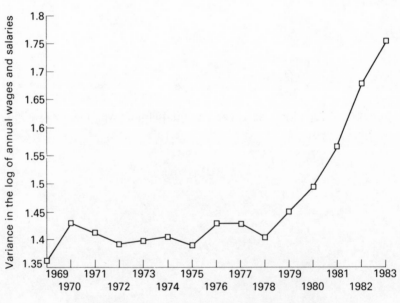

Figure 8.A5. Wage inequality – men, 1969–1983

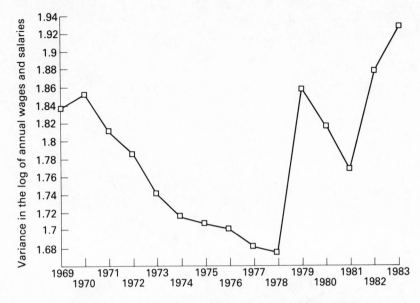

Figure 8.A6. Wage inequality – women, 1969–1983

Figure 8.A7. Wage inequality – people aged 25–34, 1969–1983

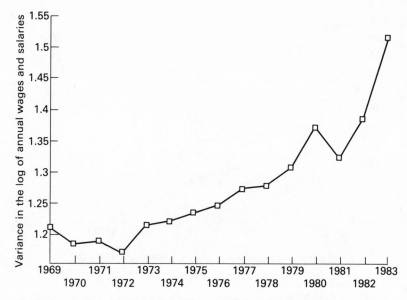

Figure 8.A8. Wage inequality – people aged 35–54, 1969–1983

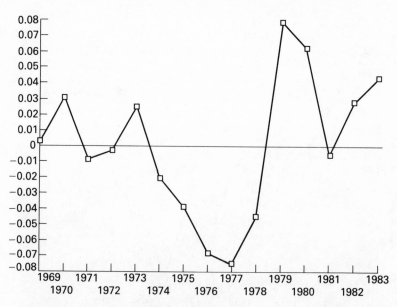

Figure 8.A9. Residues, using capuix instead of U-rate, 1969–1983

9

Renewing Opportunity

ROBERT KUTTNER

The Employment Act of 1946 grew out of a national commitment, late in the war, to put government on the side of economic security and opportunity. President Roosevelt's State of the Union Address of 1944 had outlined an "Economic Bill of Rights," including the right to a useful job, a decent home, adequate medical care, and a good education. Opportunity – the prospect of bettering one's economic condition – has always been at the center of the American experiment. Countless millions of Americans have advanced economically through their own hard work, and often with a boost from public programs.

Lately, the concept of opportunity has been appropriated by opponents of a constructive government role in the social economy. The newly fashionable premise is the ancient one of *laissez-faire*: remove the fetters on personal creativity – get the government out of the way – and let individual opportunity flourish. This view reflects both a theory of economics and a philosophy of politics. Economically, it is in keeping with the premise that public programs are necessarily a drag both on overall economic performance and on individual initiative; politically, it suggests a radically libertarian civic philosophy: that "the government" is something on our backs, rather than on our side, and that in any case the debate seems mooted fiscally because deficit politics suggest that we can't afford new government programs.

In this paper, I want to recall the venerable history of public programs intended to enhance individual opportunity, and to suggest a theme for future uses of affirmative government. Although opportunity programs have often required a substantial government role and sizeable public outlays, they have been both popular and on the whole effective.

In recent decades the emphasis of government social expenditure has shifted from opportunity programs to programs of security and redistribution. Public security programs such as Medicare, unemployment compensation or retirement pensions, and redistributive programs such as food stamps and AFDC can certainly be defended as a necessary "safety net," but they do not directly serve the bulk of the working age population.

Thus, they represent a somewhat different philosophy and certainly a different politics. At present, the economic security programs consume the overwhelming share of the government's social outlays. While programs like social security and Medicare remain broadly popular, younger age groups are increasingly skeptical about the return that they are likely to get from their social security taxes. It may well be that we need to refocus the role of social programs from security and redistribution to opportunity.

Antecedents

Although we typically think of government social programs as something invented only in the Great Depression, it is worth recalling that the American experience has used public outlays in the service of individual opportunity since before the American revolution. Free public education, invented in the seventeenth century in the Massachusetts Bay Colony, was a very radical idea. That citizens have an entitlement to education, independent of the size of their parents' purse, is still a radically egalitarian notion.

Similarly, in the nineteenth century, the Homestead Acts of the Civil War era, the Morrill Act which established the first land grant colleges, the concept of agricultural extension, and even the public subsidy of the railroads, used the power of the state to enhance the economic opportunity of individuals.

The American conceptions of equality and of the role of government in promoting equality are well represented in these early opportunity programs. Politically, the American Republic was predicated on the inherently egalitarian principle of one man, one vote. Socially, at least among the white population, there was no great problem of inequality of wealth undermining the egalitarian political principle, for the vast bulk of Americans were small freeholders. Nineteenth-century America was therefore spared a conflict that afflicted most European nations, namely the conflict between a political democracy and a class-ridden economy.

Economically – and this is the crux of the matter – most Americans saw opportunity as individual rather than social. They understood equality as equality of opportunity, not as the struggle of an entire class to win basic economic and political rights, as was the case in Europe of a century ago. In the American experience, therefore, the appropriate role of government was not to take from the haves and give to the have-nots, but to expand the horizons of the have-nots by facilitating their education, their access to credit, and to land.

In retrospect, the egalitarians of the early nineteenth-century had it easy; they could have their equality and their individualism too. Land could be taken from the Indians, who did not vote and who were conveniently outside the egalitarian social contract; the concentration of industrial wealth was not yet a threat to a society where nobody was very rich or very poor. Philosophically, despite the Jeffersonian maxim "that government which governs best governs least," it troubled few people that government played a major role in these opportunity programs, because government was serving individual aspirations.

With the industrial revolution, the end of cheap empty land, the rise of robber barons, and the growth of urban poverty, the conception of equality and the issue of the appropriate role of government in enhancing opportunity became rather more complex and divisive. In place of the innocent, homely functions of providing free education and farmsteads to aspiring pioneers, government was called upon to tax the rich, to subsidize the poor, to manage the economy, to regulate capital markets, to provide retirement security, to underwrite medical care, to create jobs, and so on. Equality, which had once meant nothing more than an equal opportunity for individual advancement, had become a social question. Despite the egalitarian rhetoric of the American constitution and the dream of a broadly middle class society, plainly, the life chances of an unemployed urban school dropout were radically different from those of an industrialist's son. The consensus of the early nineteenth-century about the American conception of equality and the appropriate role of the state, never even then quite as unanimous or simple as it now seems, was shattered.

And yet, even in the twentieth century, as government has taken on broader social functions, it has continued to enhance individual opportunities in ways that resonate with its older role. The government no longer gives away homesteads, but it sometimes helps to provide education and job training, which in an industrial economy are the economic equivalent of 160 acres.

Consider the GI Bill. In June 1944, President Roosevelt signed the "Servicemen's Readjustment Act," popularly known as the GI Bill of Rights. The original bill provided tuition payments up to $500 a year, and subsistence payments of up to $50 a month, which was increased to $75 a month in 1948. During the 12-year existence of the original program, 7.8 million World War II veterans received subsidies for education and training: 3.5 million of them in vocational and technical schools, 1.4 million on the job, almost 700,000 in agricultural courses, and 2.2 million in colleges and universities. Although many prominent educators of the time opposed the virtual open enrollment of veterans, the typical supposedly underqualified veteran actually outperformed the average younger college student. The total cost of education and training under the original GI Bill was $14.5 billion, or something like $55 billion in current dollars. Another 2.4 million Korean War vets received training and education under successor legislation, at a cost of $4.5 billion.

The GI Bill of Rights had almost universal support, despite the fact that it represented a very sizeable government intervention into a largely private arena, higher education, and a very sizeable outlay of public funds. The reasons are not hard to discern. It was widely agreed that veterans had earned the benefits, by serving their country in wartime. The outlay was not considered a giveaway program, since it was serving the eventual self-sufficiency of the recipients. Thus, in both senses, the beneficiaries were considered "deserving." The program, significantly, was not income-tested. It was what we would now call an entitlement; to qualify, one only had to have served in wartime for at least 90 days.

In the same manner, the two notable housing programs of the era, VA-guaranteed home loans and FHA-insured loans, were almost universally supported. VA mortgages, initially at an interest rate of 4 percent, eventually served more than 11 million veterans and their families. FHA loans served another 15 million families. Unlike the education grants under the GI Bill, these programs were mainly loan guarantees, not subsidies, and they were also in the service of individual economic opportunity and advancement.

Higher education subsidies, which began in the Great Society era, can be considered part of the same tradition – public outlays to promote individual advancement. Under the present program of so called Pell grants, named for Senator Claiborne Pell, students from low or moderate income families can get grants of up to $2,100 per academic year, up to 50 percent of their total educational costs. Last year, some 2.6 million students benefitted from this program. Like the GI Bill and the guaranteed housing loans of the 1940s and 1950s, this program also enjoys wide support. The purpose is to promote individual advancement; the program is not criticized as a handout, for the recipients are deemed deserving. It is not a safety net, but a ladder of opportunity.

However, as federal social spending has come under increased budgetary pressures, Congress has de-emphasized student grants, and put greater reliance on student loans. A decade ago, in the academic year 1975–76, funding for grants and loans was about equal. By 1984–85, reliance on guaranteed student loans was about three times that of grants. As tuition expenses have outstripped family incomes, and as the minimum wage typically available to part-time student jobs has lagged behind inflation, millions of young college graduates now enter the world of work saddled by educational debts. In the case of a graduate of a law school, or a medical school, the financial need to pay off a debt that can exceed $100,000 reinforces the tendency to look to high personal income rather than service to society.

Generational Perspectives

Life chances, and the view of government as an ally of opportunity, can be strikingly different for different generations. Compare the perspectives of a man born in 1921, and one born in 1961. A person born in 1921, who is just at retirement age today, was a teen-ager in the Great Depression. He probably had the unsettling experience of expectations lowered as a young boy in the early 1930s. An early memory may be that of a father bringing home a paycheck from a public works job. He probably fought in World War II, and quite possibly got educated on the GI Bill and bought a house with a GI loan. As he matured into midlife, and raised a family, he almost surely participated in the remarkable rise in real incomes between 1945 and 1973. During that period, he watched government provide tangible, useful things – new public schools, an interstate highway system. And on reaching age 65, he will enjoy the benefits of Medicare and an inflation-indexed social security pension far in excess of his lifetime social security tax contributions.

The opportunity horizons, and the role of government in promoting opportunity, seem radically different for the man born in 1961. Paradoxically, he was born into a far more affluent world than the older man; his family, in all likelihood, never experienced the steep reverses in economic status of the older man's family during the Depression.

But as the younger man enters the world of work, government as provider looms much smaller, and government as taxer looms much larger. Since 1973, real disposable income has not kept pace with inflation. As Frank Levy and Richard C. Michel documented in a recent paper for the Joint Economic Committee, prior to 1973 the average man passing from age 40 to age 50 saw his real earnings increase by 30 percent. A man passing from 40 to 50 after 1973 saw his disposable income drop by 14 percent. Although overall taxation as a fraction of GNP increased only slightly between 1953 and 1960, the burden of those taxes changed dramatically – from corporate to personal, and from upper income to middle income. In 1953, the average-income family paid just 8.7 percent of its income in federal income and payroll taxes. By 1980, that had grown to 16.2 percent.

As the younger man looks at what he buys for those taxes, he doesn't see very much that benefits him directly. There is unemployment insurance, if he finds a job and loses it, but there is not entitlement to job training; there are very high taxes to finance social security and Medicare – 14.1 percent of payroll compared to 3 percent in 1944 – but social security retirement is forty-some years off and Medicare does not cover the working population. All told, over 70 percent of the entire federal budget is now in just four categories – defense, social security, Medicare, and interest on the public debt.

If the man is a college graduate, government may have helped with the tuition payments, but the help was more likely to have been a loan than a grant, and the loan payments are now due. On the housing front, there are no more cheap government loans, and virtually no more government subsidy of moderately priced houses. Even after the recent drop in mortgage interest rates, an FHA or VA loan is in the 10–11 percent range. In the 1940s, a VA loan carried an interest rate of 4 percent, with no money down. Levy and Michel calculated that an average-income 30-year-old could buy a median-priced house on just 14 percent of his income in 1949; by 1985, it took an astonishing 44 percent.

There are still the safety net programs – AFDC if the young man fathers an illegitimate child; food stamps and Medicaid if he finds himself in sudden poverty; short-term unemployment compensation if he has a work history, but no entitlement to a job or to job training. And most of the working-age of the population does not receive safety net benefits. So it is not surprising that the present mood of the young is self-directed, and skeptical about government. A new political action group called Americans for Generational Equality – "AGE" – is founded on the belief that young, working Americans are getting a raw deal from government.

Our hypothetical young man born in the idealistic year of 1961 may well decide to join the parade of voters who are increasingly cynical about government's ability to deliver much of anything besides bills from the tax collector. He may vote for the politician who favors IRAs over social security, because IRAs at least promise a tax deduction now, while social security may never deliver. He may well agree that safety net outlays should be cut back further, since welfare is something for "them," not for "us," and welfare often goes to people who don't deserve it.

But it is questionable whether generational equity and opportunity would be served by further cutbacks in public outlays. The trouble is that a market economy presents opportunities very unevenly. If the young man has an entrepreneurial bent, or inherited money, was lucky enough to have gotten an advanced degree in law, or medicine, or engineering, individual initiative will in all likelihood serve him fine. But if he is just an ordinary working American, without elite education, or family advantages, he may experience great difficulty finding a good job, good housing, and a rewarding career.

Government performs best when it serves opportunity. I suggest that government needs to be redirected, not for the sake of restoring faith in government, but in order to use government as the engine of opportunity that it has so often been in the American experience. What, then, are the needs of the 1980s and 1990s, in the great tradition of opportunity programs stretching back through Pell Grants, FHA loans and GI education, all the way to the Homestead Acts and the Massachusetts free common school? Consider three basic areas: post-secondary education, employment and training, and housing.

Education

As noted, the emphasis of federal aid to higher education had gradually shifted from grants to loans. This has occurred during a period when tuition costs have risen faster than disposable family income. In turn, it has left a generation of students burdened with debt, and more concerned about short-term financial prospects than about service to society.

Last year, Dr. Frank Newman, President of the Education Commission of the States, wrote a fine report entitled "Higher Education and the American Resurgence," published by the Carnegie Foundation for the Advancement of Teaching. Taking note of the abrupt shift from grants to loans, Dr. Newman wrote: "The tradition of this country has been that the colleges and universities are the gateway to a student's future, that a determined and hard-working graduate from a poor family starts out on an equal footing with other graduates. Today, not only is that student less likely to graduate, but if he does he is more likely to start out owing tens of thousands of dollars. That is hardly starting even."

Dr. Newman proposed a simple, egalitarian concept. College students would accept an obligation to perform two or three years service, post graduation, and in exchange would receive grants of $3,000 per year toward higher education. High school graduates who did not attend college could perform civilian or military service, and receive tuition credits to go back to school, on the model of the GI Bill.

Dr. Newman's specific proposal was for public service teaching fellowships. The required community service would be teaching in urban public schools. But the program could also reach a wider range of community needs. The value of this approach is that it leaves the new college graduate unburdened with debt, and thinking about how he or she can serve, rather than how much he or she can make. As part of the bargain, the student gets a college education, and the government gets needed community workers, in teaching, public health, and other difficult-to-fill fields. The young graduate also gets useful work experience, and a sense of service.

Employment

A second area where government has emphasized security to the exclusion of opportunity is job training and unemployment compensation. And lately, even the promise of security has fallen well short of the mark. Since 1935, we have spent close to two hundred billion dollars paying unemployment insurance claims, nearly $30 billion of it in the recession year 1982 alone. We have done little to assure jobs; and as budgets have tightened and eligibility has been cut back, needy people are left with neither employment nor income security. In 1985, less than 30 percent of unemployed people received unemployment benefits.

When unemployment insurance began in the 1930s, the idea was to provide a 16-week bridge between the job that the worker lost, and some new job, either in the private sector or in the New Deal "work relief" project. Unemployment insurance was never intended to be a long-term dole. By the same token, Aid to Families with Dependent Children, a creation of the same 1935 Social Security Act that gave us unemployment insurance, was intended as a program for people in exceptional circumstances. In the 1930s, the female-headed household was a rarity. The "normal" family included a breadwinning father, and a mother who stayed home with the children. Dependent Children – the DC in AFDC – were seen as the consequence of unusual personal calamities, such as the untimely death of a father.

But during the postwar years, both of these programs evolved into grudging, long-term sources of subsistence for large segments of the population. AFDC, however unintentionally, used income-support formulas that encouraged women, once on welfare, to stay on. The gradual cutback, in Medicaid, from a program that served the working poor to one that served only the welfare population, created yet another obstacle to moving from welfare to work. Large numbers of women bore children out of wedlock, and stayed on welfare as long as their children were at home, even though many wanted to work as soon as the children were in school. But the formulas and guidelines made it very difficult to improve one's final income position by forsaking welfare for work, and no transitional machinery existed.

By the same token, unemployment insurance grew from a short-term "bridge" to an income support mechanism that provided income for as long as 65 weeks during recessions, and even longer for some classes of workers deemed idled by foreign competition. In a society that supposedly prizes the work ethic, the policymakers never got around to devising the other two legs of the labor market tripod – a comprehensive approach to training, and a guarantee that jobs would be available. The manpower programs of the 1960s and 1970s had confused, diverse goals, and although some of them did train people, they were never part of a coherent system or strategy. A labor market approach that stressed jobs and job training would be far better for the citizenry, and far more defensible politically and as public policy.

Despite the present fiscal climate, one can identify the beginnings of a more dynamic labor market strategy aimed at re-employment rather than relief. In several states, including Massachusetts and Ohio, the state welfare program permits grant diversions to finance supported work. During a transitional period on a new job, a former AFDC recipient receives both a paycheck and a series of support services ranging from counselling to training to transportation to daycare. Transitional employment partnerships help convert a welfare check into a paycheck, and allow a transfer payment to be used dynamically, as a bridge off welfare and into a job.

In two states, California and Delaware, there are pilot efforts to do something similar with unemployment compensation. Federal law at present does not permit using unemployment insurance trust funds directly to subsidize employment or even transitional training, but California, for example, peeled off a separate payroll tax equal to 0.1 percent, and created a separate fund to finance an "Employment and Training Panel."

The California Panel works with employers to subsidize retraining of workers who have been laid off and who have run out of unemployment benefits, or workers who would be idled by technological changes unless retrained. The Panel has also helped subsidize efforts of employers to raise the quality of an entire workforce. One major retailer decided it needed a higher quality sales force. It upgraded pay levels from minimum wage to over $5 an hour, and used a short-term subsidy from the Panel to pay for the training. An aerospace company used Panel training subsidies to upgrade machinists to technicians qualified to program advanced, numerically controlled machining centers.

Most economists agree that this kind of subsidy makes economic sense because the failure of private employers to invest sufficiently in training is a classic case of "market failure." From the perspective of an individual employer, it is a waste to put money into training an employee, because the employee is then free to take his newly learned skills and go to work for somebody else. But if society pays some of the cost, everybody gains. The employee gets higher skills and better pay, and the employer gets a more productive workforce.

Another state, Minnesota, has used public funds to subsidize the costs of employment directly, through a program called MEED. During a transitional six-month period, the state will pay up to $5.00 an hour of the wage and fringe benefit costs of all newly hired workers over and above the number of workers that were on an employer's payroll the previous year. The results have been very impressive. The retention rates exceed 60 percent – that is, employers keep most of their new workers on the job even after the subsidy expires; and in the first two years the program produced 27,720 new jobs, returning to the state treasury $37.1 million that would have been lost if these tax-paying citizens had remained idle.

These new labor-market approaches have two interesting characteristics in common. First, they use public income-support dollars *dynamically*, to get people into permanent jobs. Second, most of these jobs are in the private sector. Surprisingly, this approach was pioneered in Sweden.

Most Americans think of Sweden as a fairly socialistic country best known for its comprehensive welfare state. But it is no accident that the welfare state has such broad public support in Sweden, for the Swedes don't think of "welfare" as a dole, but as the means to a job.

Sweden's National Labor Market Board, the AMS, spends the equivalent of 3 percent of Sweden's entire national income putting people back to work. In America, the equivalent sum would be over $100 billion a year. And the bulk of this money goes not to pay for unemployment checks, or even for CETA-style public works jobs, but to provide retraining and to subsidize the creation of new jobs in the private sector. This is the microeconomic counterpart of a macroeconomic commitment to full employment.

This use of labor market funds to subsidize retraining and re-employment is a vast improvement over the two extreme alternatives of either guaranteeing a dole to idle people, or trusting to the harsh discipline and the uncertain outcomes of *laissez-faire*. In recent years, public policy has cut back unemployment insurance benefits, and has continued to limit their use to subsidizing idleness. We should do the opposite, on both counts. Outlays need to be increased, and they need to be used flexibly, to subsidize retraining and re-employment.

Housing

Housing is a third area in which government once served to advance individual opportunity and mobility, but now public policy serves to widen the chasm between haves and have-nots. Under the current administration, direct subsidy of new low and moderate income housing construction has all but disappeared.

Instead, the principal public subsidy for housing is a tax subsidy, the unlimited mortgage interest deduction, which will cost other taxpayers an estimated $40 billion by 1988. This, too, is distributively and generationally perverse. An upper-middle-income family, which bought a large house a decade ago, enjoys a substantial tax subsidy, as well as an inflation-proof investment that is largely exempt from capital gains, and an out-of-pocket cost of housing well below that which could be purchased currently on the open market. Even worse, the subsidy is in direct proportion to the affluence of the taxpayer: the more lavish the house, and the higher the tax bracket, the steeper the subsidy.

A young family looking to buy a first home may well find itself paying 30 or 40 percent of total income, while the family that bought years ago enjoys more house for far less outlay. We ought to be subsidizing the have-nots, not the haves. Here, intelligent public policy would cap the mortgage interest deduction at an amount reasonable to buy a basic "starter house" – say the interest on a loan of $50,000. Taxpayers could continue to deduct that amount from their taxable income, but if they chose a more expensive home the additional mortgage interest would not be a tax deduction. This would save the Treasury some $7–8 billion. That money, in turn, could be used to subsidize a first-time mortgage of, say 7 percent, for every new homebuyer. The below-rate mortgage would be a one-time entitlement, good for the first five years of homeownership. This policy-shift would produce no net cost to the Treasury. But it would put government on the side of the family looking to buy its first house, rather than giving subsidies to the already well-off.

Similarly, in the area of moderate income rental housing, public policy has swung from doing nothing, to making extravagant commitments and expensive mistakes, and back to doing nothing again. Traditional public housing, with more than a million units built, is often unattractive, yet affordable housing is in such short supply that public housing continues to have long waiting lists. The subsidized for-profit low-income housing built in the 1960s and 1970s has been plagued by a very high failure rate. Local rent control, where it exists, is a very imperfect way of keeping an affordable housing stock, at the expense of private investors and often at the expense of new housing construction. Condominium conversion continues to deplete the supply of rental housing.

One alternative, which has been used very widely abroad, but scarcely at all in the United States, is called mutual housing. A mutual housing association is a kind of cooperative apartment complex owned by the residents, but insulated from ordinary market forces. A member of a mutual housing association is assured a decent housing unit at a moderate cost, secure from eviction or condominium conversion, but foregoes the opportunity to make a large capital gain if he chooses to cash out and move elsewhere. Membership in the association is kept at a very nominal cost, for the next member. Mutual housing is a hybrid between owning and renting; it offers the security of owning, but not the capital investment potential; it offers the low cost of rental, without the insecurity. Socially, it provides the benefits of rent control, without the adversary relationship between landlord and tenant. Economically, it "de-commodifies" a portion of the housing supply – that is, it removes it from the inflationary pressure of market forces, but without the inefficiencies of bureaucratic ownership and management.

Mutual housing has provided approximately one housing unit in three in postwar Germany. It also provides million of homes in Scandinavia and in Canada. Recently, the Neighborhood Reinvestment Corporation, a non-profit public corporation chartered by the Congress, which sponsors Neighborhood Housing Services for single-family homes, has begun assisting mutual housing associations. This approach is well worth expanding.

I have proposed to put government outlays back on the side of expanding individual opportunities. In some areas, as in the tax treatment of mortgage interest, this might be accomplished by changing the pattern of present subsidies. But in other areas, such as the national service education idea, or the proposal to expand and redirect labor market outlays, this will require additional public expenditure.

This may seem implausible, at a historical period when the main pre-occupation of both parties and both the executive and legislative branches of government is cutting the federal deficit and reducing public spending. Yet if we fail to enlist government or promote economic opportunity, we will increasingly have a government whose main constituency is the old, the sick, the isolated poor and the military; we will have a truncated party system where both parties are the party of anti-government, and an electorate that has forgotten what affirmative government can accomplish.

Although that seems to be the current course, I doubt it will remain the case for very long. For government has proven itself time and again to be a very useful ally of economic opportunity. The trick is to align the functions of government with the contemporary aspirations and needs of the broad public. That is what must be done before the voters will entrust government to undertake opportunity ventures as bold as the GI Bill, the FHA, the nineteenth-century homesteads and the colonial common schools.

10

Developing Talent

BERNARD ANDERSON

The laudable and ambitious goals of the Employment Act of 1946 are as compelling today as they were when the Act was passed, but the difficulties in achieving maximum employment with price stability continue to challenge policymakers in both the legislative and executive branches of our government. One aspect of that goal, namely the achievement of equity in the distribution of economic opportunity in an environment of growth, is an especially important challenge.

US Performance in Job Creation

The American economy has been highly successful in creating new jobs during the last two decades. Between 1965 and 1985, employment grew by 36 million, or about 50 percent. During the same time, the US labor force surged from 74 million to 115 million, an increase of about 55 percent. Because the labor force grew more rapidly than employment, both the number of unemployed, and the number of persons not in the labor force have increased since 1965. The unemployment rate was less than 5 percent in the mid-1960s, and averaged 6.1 percent during the 1970s, and has remained above 7.0 percent since 1982.

The vigorous job creation economy has been amply demonstrated during the recovery from the 1981–82 recession. During the past three years, about 7.7 million people have found work. The percentage of working-age population in the labor market grew from 57.2 percent in 1982 to 64.9 percent in 1985, and the number of unemployed dropped from 10.7 million to 8.0 million.

Uneven Growth

The pattern of job growth, however, has been uneven. For some time, most new jobs have been in the services sector, reflecting a long-term

This is a revised version of a paper presented before the JEC symposium in January 1986.

trend in the economy. Employment in the goods-producing sector rose by only 5.6 percent, while service sector jobs grew by 46.4 percent since 1970.

The imbalance in job growth has been associated with a tendency toward the erosion of the wage level among previously high-wage earners, the development of pockets of unemployment in some geographical locations, and the increase in pre-employment hiring standards in many occupations.

An especially troublesome feature of the current economic expansion is the unequal labor market experience of different population groups. For example, minority-group workers have not enjoyed economic gains comparable to those experienced by other groups. Between November 1982, when the recovery began, and December 1985, the black unemployment rate fell from 20.2 percent to 14.9 percent, a decline of about one-fourth. In contrast, the non-minority unemployment rate dropped from 9.6 percent to 5.9 percent, nearly two-fifths. Thus, the gap between the unemployment rates of minority and other workers, widened despite the strong expansion since 1982. Unemployment among black youth remains above 40 percent, and the proportion of such youth with jobs is at an all-time low.

Persistent Economic Inequality

Many of those concerned about inequality in American life often look at the income and employment experience of minorities during economic growth as a barometer of progress toward greater equal opportunity.

Between 1965 and 1980, the median income of black families increased fourfold, from $3800 to $12,600, but the ratio of black family income to that of white families increased from only 0.56 to 0.58 over the 15-year period.

Similarly, Black employment rose from 14.5 million to 17.8 million between 1970 and 1980, but because of job losses sustained during the 1980 and 1981–82 recessions, black workers held only 10.5 million jobs in 1985. Black workers showed occupational advancement during the years since 1965, but by the early 1980s, half were still concentrated heavily in the low and semiskilled blue collar and service jobs.

Numerous studies of change in the economic status of black Americans attempt to explain the rate and determinants of progress achieved during the past two decades. Although there are still debates among economists on these matters (economists rarely agree, no matter how conclusive the evidence) the consensus is that much of the improvement in black family income was generated by the long, uninterrupted period of economic growth between 1965 and 1969, and much of the occupational advancement was influenced by greater protection against employment discrimination. It is not possible (or necessary) to assign precise values to the relative importance of economic growth and anti-discrimination efforts as determinants of change in the economic status of black Americans during the past two decades. It is sufficient to recognize that both factors played an important role in generating wider opportunities to participate in American economic life.

Decline of the Family

Stable family life has been a major casualty of economic hardship in the Black community. A disproportionate number of black families are headed by women, many of whom work at low-wage jobs out of sheer economic necessity. For example, 64 percent of black mothers with children under the age of one were working in 1985, 15 percentage points higher than the rate for whites. Black wives have a long history of participating in the labor market at rates exceeding their white counterparts mainly because of labor force difficulties of black men. In March 1985, for example, the unemployment rate for black fathers with pre-school children was 10.2 percent, compared with 5 percent for white fathers. Moreover, median weekly earnings of black husbands who worked full time in the third quarter of 1985 were $353, or fully 30 percent below comparable earnings for white husbands.[1]

The Underclass

During the past few years, many of those concerned about continuing progress in civil rights have focused increasingly on a segment of the black community whose social and economic status has been unresponsive to the wider opportunities generated by economic growth and greater protection of equal job opportunity. This group is often called "the underclass," a commonly used, but unfortunate term because it suggests that those within the group are there because of perverse values and anti-social behavior. Many of those in the "underclass" are unprepared to fill available jobs, and live in depressed communities where few jobs exist. Economic growth brings little progress to such areas.

The conditions faced by the social and economically disadvantaged within the black community are not attributable to values and behavior, but rather to widespread institutional barriers to their full participation in our society. When viewed in this way, the problems of the group seem more amenable to public policy intervention.

Nature of Structural Unemployment

Structural unemployment is still a serious problem in American labor markets, and will require continued attention if the benefits of economic growth are to be distributed equitably throughout the population. There are several definitions of structural unemployment but, in brief, it means there are job vacancies the unemployed cannot fill. This may be due to the unemployed being in the wrong place, demanding wages that are too high, or having inadequate education, training or work experience.

There are many determinants of structural unemployment, including the loss of jobs due to competition from foreign imports, shifts in labor requirements due to technological change, rules on eligibility for welfare payments that raise family income above wage earnings in the job market. Whatever its cause, structural unemployment reflects a variety of labor market problems that are unlikely to respond effectively to fiscal and monetary policies. Special targeted labor market measures are required to get at the root cause of joblessness, and to deal with the social and psychological factors, as well as the economic causes for unemployment.

It is fashionable today to say that social policies designed to deal with structural unemployment and other problems of economic inequality don't work and only represent wasteful public spending. This argument is not new, but it has taken on new life and is shared more widely now than ever before. Many of those who make the argument that government has no useful role to play in promoting greater economic equality often call upon the private sector to replace social policy in this field.

Indeed, every 20 years, we seem to rediscover structural unemployment; every 15 years we rediscover the underclass; and every ten years, we rediscover the private sector. In keeping with the periodicity of such concerns, some now suggest that we tackle structural unemployment in order to arrest the growth of the underclass, and that we call upon the private sector to play the major role. There is no question that the private sector must be involved in any effort to improve the distribution of economic opportunity, but there continues to be a major and often initiating role, for public policy.

Policy Choices for Reducing Economic Inequality

There are two key policy options for addressing the problems of income inequality among those who do not share fully in economic growth: income transfers and human resource development. Under the first type of policy, the goal is to provide an income sufficient to allow families to maintain a minimum acceptable standard of living. Under the second, the

goal is to raise the individual's productivity in order to improve employment and earnings through labor market participation.

Of the two policies, the more advisable, and politically feasible
approach at this time, is the human resource development strategy. If the
national goal is simply to reduce poverty, and to equalize income, then
human resource development policies are likely to be less effective than
income transfer programs. According to a study by Peter Gottschalk and
Sheldon Danziger at the University of Wisconsin,[2] the dramatic reduction
in poverty during the 1960s and early 1970s resulted from a combination
of rapid economic growth and increased transfer payments. Although
such benefits contributed most to the reduction of poverty among the
elderly, the relative incomes of other age groups also showed improvement as a result of income transfers.

But despite the fact that the reason people are poor is that they don't
have money, there is no public sentiment for large and continued transfer
of unearned income as the main strategy for reducing poverty. Even more,
there is a deeper reason to question a policy emphasizing larger transfer
payments: labor is not only a factor of production; work is an essential
human value. The best long-term solution to the problem of inadequate
family income is policies designed to expand opportunities for low-
income workers and the unemployed to participate more fully in the labor
market.

Employment and Training Policy: the Record

Much has been written about the failure of job training programs to
improve employment and earnings among disadvantaged populations.
Unquestionably, many mistakes were made and many dollars were wasted
in some of the employment and training programs of the past two decades.
But a careful consideration of the daunting problems such programs tried
to address, and the recognition of institutional change required to deliver
education and training services to the structurally unemployed suggests
that jobs programs achieved some success.

The best way to determine whether job training programs are effective
is to measure the change in earnings received by participants after leaving
the program, compared with the earnings of socioeconomically similar
persons who did not receive training. Not all employment and training
programs developed during the past decade were subjected to this test, but
some were, and the results are instructive.

For example, after an exhaustive review of major studies conducted
between 1971 and 1980, Prof. Michael Borus concluded that institutional
vocational training increased the earnings of participants by about $300 to
$400 in the year following the program.[3] On-the-job training increased

earnings by about $600, and work experience programs raised the earnings of their male participants by nearly $600, and had positive, but lower earnings effects for women participants.

A similar study of the evaluative literature focusing on minorities and youth concluded that while such groups did not register greater gains than others from programs participation, minorities and youth who completed the programs achieved positive economic benefits. Especially important to these groups were direct job creation programs, and those that emphasized the acquisition of marketable job skills.[4]

Evidence of positive earnings gain for program participants is important for justifying public support of job training programs, but social scientists sometimes place an unreasonable burden of proof on policies to help the poor and disadvantaged. The tendency toward unrealistic expectation is reflected in a recently published National Academy of Science study of youth employment and training programs in operation between 1977 and 1981.[5] The NAS verdict is that such programs were a failure because they did not reduce the youth unemployment rate appreciably. Quite apart from the fact that the authors of the study failed to recognize the complexity of the youth employment problem, they virtually ignored the difficulties policy administrators faced in launching a multi-million dollar program, in a short period of time, when the service delivery system was changing rapidly to absorb new funds.

The record of success of youth employment programs is greater than the NAS study implies. For example, the favorable record of the Youth Incentive Entitlement Pilot Projects was revealed in a study of Manpower Demonstration Research Corporation, a New York-based research and evaluation firm.[6] The Entitlement Program was authorized by Congress in 1977 to test the link between schooling and employment for disadvantaged youth. The program was targeted to low income teenagers in 17 communities. A guaranteed job at the federal minimum wage was provided so long as the youth remained in (or returned to) school, and achieved satisfactory performance in both school and work.

During the two and one half years the program was in operation, 76,000 youths worked in program jobs. Most were young minority group members enrolled in school, and members of welfare-dependent families. Few had ever held an unsubsidized job, and most had never participated in other federally assisted jobs programs. There were major gains for program participants: more than half of the eligible youths in each area participated in the program, and the communities showed they could deliver on a job guarantee. Most important, school year employment more than doubled for black youths, reversing the 25 year gap between black and white employment rates. The study showed major weekly earnings gains for participants, especially during the school year.

Programs for the Hard to Employ

Other labor market programs also have shown promising results. One especially interesting example was the Supported Work project, a major experiment to test the potential of specially designed work experience for long-term welfare recipients, ex-addicts, ex-offenders and high school dropouts.[7] Some 6,500 persons participated in the program at some time during its seven-year duration. The program participants were among the most difficult to attract into job training programs, and to serve effectively. They were given a variety of training and work experience opportunities, tailored to their capacity and willingness to advance toward preparation to enter the job market.

The Supported Work project showed small, but reasonable gains for the welfare group; less for the ex-addicts; but little benefit for the ex-offenders and young dropouts. As long as two years after entering the program, the welfare recipients averaged $243 in monthly earnings, and $498 in total monthly income (reflecting the continuation of partial welfare payments for some women). These earnings were nearly one-third more than those of similar welfare recipients who did not participate in the program.

Work/Welfare Programs

A new attempt to bring welfare recipients into the job market was begun with the work/welfare initiatives authorized by Congress as part of the omnibus Budget Reconciliation Act of 1981. Under this policy, several states have launched pilot projects designed to encourage welfare recipients to work. Various measures are being tested, including the diversion of the cash grant to wages for public-service work, the provision of job search assistance, and in some cases, occupational training.

MDRC studies of projects in California, Virginia, West Virginia, Maryland, Illinois, Arkansas, New Jersey and Maine show modest, but perceptible reductions in welfare dependency among program participants.[8]

The combination of job search assistance, work experience, and other services helps many welfare recipients get into the job market, even in areas where unemployment is higher than the national average.

Similar results are shown in work/welfare projects in Massachusetts and New York. Although those projects have not been evaluated to compare program participants with similar welfare recipients who did not participate, the job placement rates (85 percent in Massachusetts) are very favorable. Undoubtedly, a strong labor market helps explain the favorable results, but it is unlikely that the welfare-dependent population would benefit as much from rapid job growth in the absence of the state-assisted job program.

Another successful example of a youth employment program is Jobs for America's Graduates. After more than a decade of experimentation with school-to-work transition programs, a pilot project was designed and tested in Delaware. Organized with the initiative of Gov. Pierre DuPont, the project brought representatives of the school system together with business, labor, and community leaders. Under the project, high school seniors, mainly enrolled in general education and without clear career goals, were selected for a series of counseling, job-preparation and job-placement sessions during the regular school day. The tutoring sessions were led by specially recruited job counselors who were assigned to the high schools. The job counselors, most of whom had private sector rather than professional education experience, taught students the rudiments of job search, and also beat the bushes among local employers to identify jobs for high school graduates. As an added incentive to spur staff productivity, each job counselor's salary increase (and employment retention) was tied to success in placing youth in jobs and keeping them there for a reasonable time after placement. The Delaware project was remarkably successful in its first year, and showed an 80 percent placement rate for high school graduates within three months. Based on this success, the program was expanded to more than 100 high schools in eight states; more than 25,000 students have participated during the last five years.

Overall, JAG shows a 70 percent placement for participants within three months of high school graduation. The benefits from program participation seem greatest for minority youths, especially those with prior marginal academic records. Again, this evidence suggests the important linkage between school performance and job prospects.

Finally, after 20 years of controversy, the Job Corps has recently received a favorable evaluation of its impact on the disadvantaged unemployed. The Job Corps serves 60,000 youths, two-thirds of them minorities, and all of them high school dropouts. Program participants receive help in basic skills, occupational training, job finding skills, and placement assistance. Over half of those who complete the program get jobs, and their earnings increase significantly more than similar youth who did not participate in the program. A Princeton-based firm, Mathematica Policy Research, evaluated the impact of the Job Corps and in 1984 reported that the program pays for itself in three years, despite the relatively high cost of $6,244 per member.

Economic Growth with Equity

The job programs briefly noted above demonstrate the feasibility of labor market policy designed to achieve full employment with equity. Even in an environment of rapid job growth, some members of the population will be left behind. No amount of economic growth alone will help them gain a foothold in the economy. As we move forward to improve productive capacity, to achieve maximum use of resources, to keep control over inflation, and to improve our position in the world economy, it is important to remember the national commitment to full participation of all segments of the population in our economy.

To assure that commitment, it will be necessary to support labor market policies aimed at structural unemployment. We cannot assume that the market alone will solve the problem of structural unemployment; it never has, and it never will.

Notes

1. Howard Hayghe, 'Rise in mothers' labor force activity,' *Monthly Labor Review* (1986), Feb., pp. 43–5.
2. Peter Gottschalk and Sheldon Danziger, 'Macroeconomic conditions, income transfers, and the trend in poverty', in *An Assessment of Reagan Social Welfare Policy*, ed. Lee, Bawden, (Urban Institute, Washington, 1984).
3. Michael E. Borus, 'Assessing the impact of training programs,' in *Employing the Unemployed*, ed. Eli Ginzberg, (Basic Books, New York, 1980), pp. 25–40.
4. Bernard E. Anderson, 'How Much Did the Programs Help Minorities and Youth?,' in Ginzberg, ibid., pp. 41–59.
5. National Academy of Sciences, *Youth Employment Programs: The YEDPA Years*, (National Academy Press, Washington, DC, 1985).
6. Judith M. Gueron, *Lessons from a Job Guarantee: The Youth Entitlement Pilot Projects* (Manpower Demonstration Research Corporation, New York, 1984).
7. Judith M. Gueron, 'The Supported-Work Experiment,' in Ginzberg, *Employing the Unemployed*, pp. 73–93.
8. A series of reports on State Work/Welfare Initiatives are now available at the Manpower Demonstration Research Corporation. Listed by state, they are:

   Arkansas: Janet Quint *et al.*, *Interim Findings*, 1984; Daniel Fredlander, *et al.*, *Arkansas Final Report*, 1985.

   Arizona: Kay Sherwood, *Management Lessons from Arizona WIN Demonstration*, 1984.

   California: Barbara Goldman *et al.*, *Preliminary Findings from the San Diego Demonstration*, 1984; Barbara Goldman, *et al.*, *Final Report*, 1986.

   Illinois: *Interim Report*, 1986; *Final Report*, 1987.

   Maine: Patricia Auspos *et al.*, *Interim Findings*, 1985; *Final Report*, 1986.

   Maryland: Janet Quint *et al.*, *Interim Findings*, 1984; Daniel Fredlander *et al.*, *Maryland: Final Report*, 1985.

   New Jersey: *Final Report*, 1986.

   Virginia: Marilyn Price *et al.*, *Interim Findings from Virginia Employment Service Program*, 1985; *Final Report*, 1986.

   West Virginia: Joseph Ball *et al.*, *West Virginia: Interim Findings on the CWE Demonstrations*, 1984; *Final Report*, 1986.

11

Beyond Social Anarchy

MICHAEL PIORE

The hallmark of labor policy in the Reagan Administration has been the pursuit of what is called, somewhat euphemistically, "flexibility." The policy seeks to give much greater power to management to adjust the terms and conditions of employment to what managers perceive to be the requirements of the production process and the conditions of the market place. Its major thrust is to weaken, and ultimately eliminate, institutional restraints upon managerial policy imposed either by trade unions or by governmental regulations. The debate which this policy has engendered has, however, tended to confuse particular restrictions upon managerial freedom with the issue of regulation in general. This essay attempts to draw a sharp distinction between the two. It argues that while a number of changes are indeed required to adjust effectively to current economic conditions those changes will only be viable in the long run if they are accomplished through negotiated changes in government regulations and collectively bargained rules.

As background for this discussion, it is useful to recognize that we in the United States have a somewhat peculiar set of restrictions upon managerial freedom in the deployment of labor, particularly in blue-collar manufacturing jobs. In essence, our regulatory system leaves management free to vary the level of employment by hires and lay-offs but the allocation of jobs among whatever *numbers* of workers the employer chooses to have is tightly constrained by a set of collectively bargained rules and government regulations known as the seniority system. These rules and regulations determine which members of the labor force will be laid off and how the remaining jobs will be allocated among those who are still employed. They also govern promotion and recall and have been extended in the pursuit of equal employment opportunity to new hires.

The operation of these rules requires that job assignments be unambiguously defined and this requirement in turn limits managerial freedom to allocate workers to the tasks at hand in response to the momentary requirements of the production process. We also tend to attach wages to job assignments; this means that wages of individuals move up and down flexibly when jobs are reallocated in cases of lay-off or technological change but it also puts further pressure on management to preserve the integrity of job definitions.

In most other industrial countries, managers have much greater freedom to assign work to individual employers as they deem necessary and to vary those work assignments to fit the requirements of the production process. But they do not have this freedom because they are *un*restrained. Rather, the freedom exists because the nature of the restraints is *different*. In general, managers abroad are not free to lay-off workers in response to changing market conditions, and they must guarantee the worker a fixed wage rate whatever his or her current job assignment. American managers often admire foreign managerial rights because they see only the freedom without recognizing the restrictions with which that "freedom" is purchased. None the less, it is true that many managers believe that even with the "hidden" restrictions, the European and Japanese systems are more effective; that the US system places us at a competitive disadvantage and has now become intolerably burdensome and must be eliminated.

In evaluating these claims two historical facts must be kept in mind. First, the particular structure of labor market regulation which is now being dismantled because it appears burdensome and restrictive, was deemed compatible with, even conducive to, economic growth and prosperity for the first three decades of the postwar period. If the structure is burdensome now, it is not because of the regulations *per se* but because the economic environment in which the structure operates has changed. Second, the existence of *some* structure of regulation is not peculiar to industrial societies at this particular historical juncture, but is indeed an almost universal and continuing feature of human existence. Historical instances of a completely unregulated labor market in which the wage and the level of employment varied freely in response to market conditions as in an abstract model of a competitive commodity market are rare or non-existent. The closest the US economy ever came to a labor market of this kind was from 1931 through 1933. That labor market was created by the wholesale abandonment, under pressure of the Great Depression, of the structure of employment and wage regulation which had existed in the 1920s. The structure which is under pressure for change today grew out of the spontaneous industrial union movement which sprang up in the late 1930s in reaction to what was widely viewed as the anarchy of the 1931–33 period. If that structure is, relative to others in the world, peculiarly inefficient it is because alternative institutional arrangements, much closer to those of present day Europe and Japan, which existed in the United States in the 1920s, were discredited by the fact that management abandoned them unilaterally in 1931 when workers were poorly organized and unemployment was high.

The experience of the Great Depression should lead us to ask whether

158 *Michael Piore*

what is viewed as flexibility by policymakers and managers will not come to be perceived by the labor force as a kind of social anarchy and, if it does, whether it will prove to be a stable base upon which to build the nation's economic revival. Indeed, it leads me to wonder whether the practices and procedures which business needs to compete effectively in emergent world markets and which in and of themselves may be conducive to a healthy, productive, and even humane work environment, may not come to be foreclosed in the future because to the climate in which they are being introduced today – a climate which, I want to underscore, is being created and maintained deliberately and consciously by the social policy of this administration.

This is the background against which the reality of labor market and industrial relations policy must be judged. I would like to discuss the implications of that reality in terms of two specific problems; one is the problem of wage inflation, the other is the problem of the productive efficiency of American industry. These are the two major problems which have concerned economic policymakers in the last decade. They are the problems which the policy of flexibility – or as it may come to be viewed as anarchy – was designed to solve and, at least as far as wage inflation is concerned, apparently did solve.

Wage Determination and Inflation

The immediate cause of the wage inflation of the 1970s was the continued application of a series of wage setting rules embedded in established collective bargaining relationships and in non-union employment practices by the threat of union organization. The rules were to a large extent implicit, and that and their immense complexity make it very difficult to spell them out in limited space, but their essence is conveyed by the formula which prevailed in the automobile industry. The automobile formula linked wage increases to an improvement factor of 3 per cent per annum plus a cost of living allowance. That formula was compatible with price stability in the 1950s and 1960s when 3 percent represented roughly the long-run rate of productivity increase for the economy as a whole. It was inflationary in the 1970s when productivity gains were closer to 1 percent and the cost of living escalator had the effect of compounding the shortfall of productivity. Prices in the American economy have stabilized in the last five years in very large measure because that formula has been suspended. The prospects for price stability in the future depend on the likelihood that the formula or something like it will be reinstated.

Conventional economic analysts ignore this formula. They do so for two rather different reasons. One group believes that the formula, and others like it, is imposed artificially by trade union and/or government regulation. If one can eliminate that regulation, wages will respond freely to market forces and the wage rate will automatically be non-inflationary. This is presumably the rationale, at least in wage policy, of Reagan's effort to weaken the institutions of union and government regulation. The other view is that wages have always been responsive to market conditions and that what is lowering wage inflation now is the much higher levels of unemployment at which the economy is currently – and is expected in the future to be – operating. This latter view does not seem to have much to do with deregulation since it implies that the regulations were never very effective in the first place. The first view thus seems to dominate Administration policy. Of the two, it is clearly the more optimistic because it implies that once the perverse institutions have been eliminated, the economy will once again be able to operate at low levels of unemployment.

But one must ask whether Reagan will be successful in eliminating unions as the key wage setting institutions and if so whether the market will replace them. There are few large companies in the United States today where the question about union survival is not the subject of an active internal managerial debate, and even in strongly unionized companies there are now important managerial functions arguing for non-union strategy. But I do not know of any manager who seriously believes that the alternative to a collectively bargained wage policy is a free response to the market. Most companies of any size believe that if they are to remain non-union over the long run, they must have a reasoned set of wage setting rules to which they adhere faithfully and which they can explain and justify to their employees. If those rules are not the annual improvement factor plus the cost of living, one must ask what the alternative rules are going to be, because those rules, whatever they are, are going to determine the prospects for price stability.

From this point of view, what is disturbing is that the automobile rule has not gone away, nor have the wage setting structures linked indirectly to the automobile rule. And we have not generated a widely accepted alternative set of wage setting principles. Because the administration has pursued the notion of unrestrained managerial freedom in setting the wage rate, there has been no dialogue at all about what ought to govern wage movements. As a result, instead of being abandoned, the old principles of wage setting have merely been suspended. And indeed in many cases the gains which they would have yielded continue to be calculated and existing wage settlements compared to those gains with some expectation that the difference will eventually be made up. The old rules thus lurk very much in the background of existing wage setting procedures. To put it bluntly: present wage setting is in violation of a well understood and widely accepted set of social principles. Those principles may not have the status of law, but they command the respect and allegiance of law throughout much of American society.

A second factor, moreover, makes the continued violation of these social principles increasingly problematic. The rules were initially suspended because of a particular diagnosis of the problems of the American economy. That diagnosis was that labor costs in the United States had increased too rapidly in the 1970s and had placed American industry at a serious competitive disadvantage relative to our principal trading partners. First managers and subsequently union leaders came to believe that US industry was no longer "world class" (to borrow a phrase from my colleague, Lester Thurow) and that the basic problem lay in our private labor codes, of which wage setting standards were an important component. With the help of the recession of 1981–82 and the example of the air traffic controllers, union leadership managed finally to convince the rank-and-file that this was the case, and that diagnosis provided the intellectual rationale for concession bargaining and the basic justification for the suspension of the prevailing wage setting rules.

The basic argument, however, is no longer really plausible. The impact of wage setting rules upon the competitive position of American industries has been completely swamped over the last four years by the appreciation of the dollar, and it is increasingly clear to everyone that the fate of American industry in international markets is being determined by whatever factors govern foreign exchange and not by labor costs at all. Moreover – and this is a point to which I will return at some length below – while American managers continue to believe that business practice in the United States are not compatible with a "world class" industry even at exchange rates which reflect something like purchasing power parity, they no longer believe that labor practices are the central, or even *a* central, part of the problem. This view is coming to be shared by union leaders and it too will filter down to the rank-and-file worker, not only in unionized establishments but outside the labor movement as well. As the rationale for suspending the old rules becomes increasingly less plausible, and without alternative standards of equity in wage setting, existing procedures are coming to seem increasingly arbitrary and anarchistic. The *status quo* may nevertheless prevail for a time, enforced by the harsh realities of high unemployment rates and aggressive anti-union management, but history does not suggest that it will go on indefinitely.

I have used the suspension of the automobile formula to illustrate the argument because I believe that it has been the most important institutional factor in the recent stabilization of wages, but I could have equally used two-tier wage structures as an illustration. These structures have been introduced as a way of lowering labor costs in response to competitive pressures, particularly in the airline industry. They violate the deeply held principle of equal pay for equal work, but they have been justified as a necessary transition to a deregulated industrial strcuture, a goal which is, at the moment anyway, widely viewed as desirable. Such structures have also been attractive to newly aggressive managements in the airlines because they tend to divide, and hence to weaken, the labor movement. But the structures also have long-term consequences which have received very little attention in the current policy debate. The lower wages attract a type of worker that is very different from those whom the industry has become accustomed to employ. Because the new wages make it difficult to support a settled family life style, new workers tend to be lured instead by the opportunities for travel and the glamour and excitement of the nomadic lifestyle which travel affords. As these people get older and settle down, they will either have to leave the industry or eliminate the wage differential. In the meantime, one wonders what the effects of workers attracted to such a lifestyle will be upon an industry with the exacting standards upon which safety in airlines seems to depend and what the effects of deteriorating safety are likely to be upon the argument for deregulation upon which the rationale for the two-tier wage structure hinged in the first place. Historically, moreover, two-tier wage structures have served as often to enhance union militancy as to weaken the organization and that effect too will probably eventually come into play. In the meantime, the old wage setting rule in the form of the top wage tier paid the old employees remains as a visible wage setting standard. In this sense, we have an exact parallel to the automobile industry: an old wage setting principle suspended but not abandoned under managerial pressure in a loose labor market but with a strong intellectual justification. As in automobiles, the old rule in airlines remains as standard as the justification for its suspension becomes increasingly less plausible and the balance of power begins to move back toward labor.

The basic lesson is that the discipline of the market is no substitute for a policy which seeks to think through and lay out the standards for an alternative institutional structure; and, in abdicating this responsibility, the Reagan administration has sown the seeds for a renewal of inflationary wage pressures in the future.

The same problem reemerges in examining the productive efficiency of American industry. Here it is potentially more serious, for it affects not simply our perception of economic well-being but the underlying capacity of the economic structure to maintain and expand our standard of living. But an examination of the issue of productive efficiency also suggests what alternative institutional arrangements might look like.

Productive Efficiency

The American economy is undergoing a fundamental transformation in its business structures and managerial practices. Both the issue of productive efficiency and that of institutional structures must, I believe, be understood in terms of this transformation and the forces which are bringing it about. The transformation is a response to what is perceived to be a permanent, long-term shift in the business environment. The business environment earlier in the postwar period was conducive to relatively stable, predictable mass markets: the basic production strategy of American industry was one of long runs by standardized products; the basic marketing strategy was to create and maintain a market for output of this kind. In a sense, Keynesian economic policy could be interpreted as the macroeconomic counterpart of the strategy which businesses were pursuing in their own markets: it essentially validated firms' efforts by maintaining the necessary levels of aggregate demand. In the last decade, however, we seem to have entered a world which is considerably more unstable and uncertain both in individual markets and at the level of national economic activity and, in response, business has evolved an alternative strategy, one which seeks out small, specialized niches in demand and seeks to fill those niches through flexible production techniques. The economic policies of the Reagan administration have contributed significantly to the business environment to which this new strategy is a response, but if the principal economic actors actually believed the new environment were basically a product of policy rather than of deeper and more fundamental forces, they would not, I think, have embarked on the long-term adjustments which they have undertaken. Indeed, administration policy has won widespread acceptance, largely because people believe it is a necessary accommodation to underlying economic changes. In any case, it is widely – and I think correctly – perceived that the ability of the American economy to prosper and compete effectively in the international environment will depend on the success of the institutional transformation now in progress.

I spent much of the latter half of 1985 interviewing managers and engineers in large American corporations, where the institutional transformation is clearly apparent. Most of the companies which I have been looking at were historically organized in terms of a tightly integrated, rigidly hierarchical structure. They are attempting to transform themselves into supple, flexible institutions capable of responding quickly to a shifting, unpredictable market place by generating a continual stream of product innovations. The reforms which they are introducing in order to do this range widely. They include the elimination of in-process inventories; the development of design teams which replace the traditional engineering hierarchy of product, process, and industrial engineering departments; new design procedures replacing sequential engineering, which moves down the old engineering hierarchy, with parallel engineering; systems of matrix management in which individual managers report to more than one boss in such a way as to force lateral communication along lower levels of the corporation as managers attempt to forestall conflicts among their several supervisors by anticipating problems and working out

solutions in advance; and a whole series of new and/or restructured relationships with outside enterprises which range from venture capital div-
isions which foster entrepreneurial relationships (and which parallel the
development internally which the business press has labeled "*in*trepre-
neurship") to new cooperative relationships with parts' producers in
which the number of suppliers is reduced and a more permanent, long-
term and intimate relationship is fostered with those who remain.

These firms are also introducing reforms in labor practices ranging from
quality circles to profit sharing. These reforms, taken in isolation, can be
seen as part of precisely that effort to obtain greater flexibility and
managerial control over the work process which Reagan's policy has
sought to encourage. Certainly managers have taken advantage of their
newly acquired power in the industrial relations sphere to press labor to
accept the concessions in traditional collective bargaining relationships
which the reforms require or to establish "union-free" operations where
they are not already committed to a union contract. But the view that the
basic problem of American management lies in the labor practices which
are being changed – a view which was widespread in the late seventies – is
now considered to be naive. The labor reforms are part and parcel of a
whole package of changes in managerial practice: they parallel reforms
being introduced in the structure and practice of management itself, in the
work organization of non-union professionals such as engineers about
whom management has never had either the fears of union organization
nor the complaints about work attitudes and practices which pervade
discussions of blue-collar labor, and in relations with subcontractors and
other outside organizations. Moreover, these other reforms now seem to
loom much larger in the thinking of corporate strategists than those in
work organization and practice, so much so that one can spend hours talking to corporate leaders in organizations where intensive labor reforms
have been introduced without the latter ever being mentioned. Placed in
the context of the environment in which they are being introduced, the
changes in labor practice thus emerge as one piece, possibly one of the less
important pieces, of a new pattern of business practice.

I am particularly conscious of these changes in large corporate organization because they have been the focus of my research in the last six
months. But it is apparent in reading the business, and even the popular,
press that equally dramatic changes are taking place in other economic
institutions. Small and medium size businesses are developing new relationships among themselves and with large organizations which facilitate
new product development, cooperative research and development,
common projects for education and training, marketing, etc. State and
local governments are extending their economic role into venture capital,
incubators for new firms and entrepreneurs, industrial research and
development, export promotion abroad and the like. Even trade unions

are developing new industrial activities which parallel changes within large corporations, and within associations of small firms, including participation in research and development for their industries and expanded roles in training and in industrial strategy.

The various different reforms are sufficiently widespread and have in many places been carried out to a point where one can begin to discern an institutional model of the new economic order and to compare it to the economic philosophy which the President has articulated. The reforms bear out one of the President's major themes: the importance of entrepreneurship and of individual initiative and creativity. This appears to be the basic explanation for the renaissance of small business. And a major theme in the reforms in large organizations is the attempt to free the individual from the restraints of bureaucratic regulation and engage him or her actively in the operation of the enterprise. This is obvious in the case of profit sharing and quality circles. But even such apparently remote changes as the elimination of in-process inventories are viewed as ways of increasing individual responsibility and calling forth personal initiatives. In a certain sense, the whole thrust of corporate reform is to make the large organization behave as if it consisted of a series of small businesses. But it would be a mistake to take the competitive market place as the alternative model of the world which is being sought, at least if one means by the competitive market place the arm's length, hostile, dog-eat-dog relationship which firms are supposed to have with each other in the conventional, competitive model which economists have used to derive their policy prescriptions for deregulation. The President's vision, and that of economic scholars as well, leaves out a second component of these reforms which is cooperative or, I dare say, social. The individualism which the reforms are seeking to introduce is one tempered by a need for collaboration with other members of the organization, and many aspects of the reforms can only be understood in terms of cooperation and the social structures which are required to insure that the cooperation will take place. Quality circles and profit sharing are both reforms designed to encourage the individual to make his or her contribution through the social group. The corporations with whom I have been talking are not seeking to increase competition among parts producers: they are seeking to reduce competition in order to draw the producers into a more participative relationship. They want more flexibility of internal work assignments for their blue-collar employees but they are willing to provide employment security in return. They see profit sharing not as a means to enhance wage flexibility but rather as an expression of the relationship of participation which they would like to establish with their employees. Similarly the new relationships among small firms that are being established through trade associations, state and municipal government or in cooperation with trade unions all have the effect of strengthening the social structure in which small businesses are embedded and the cooperative relations which temper competition among them.

The reason for these cooperative arrangements is not abstract or humanitarian. Nor is it the natural tendency of businessmen to seek to forestall competitive pressure in order to win monopoly profits against which economists since Adam Smith have warned. The reason is that the kind of dynamic flexibility required to launch and maintain a constantly shifting menu of innovative products in a variable and uncertain market place requires an intimate collaboration among the various people involved in production and marketing. The institutional reforms are designed either to enhance that cooperation or to create mechanisms for pooling risks which would otherwise operate to poison the atmosphere in which that cooperation takes place. Many managers now have an articulated understanding of what kinds of collaboration are necessary and as a result the transformation of existing institutions and business practices is increasingly pointed and deliberate. There is also a growing confidence in the ability of the changes to revitalize the organizations in which they are being introduced. But these developments do not alone constitute grounds for optimism about the position of the American economy as a whole. One cannot be optimistic in part because the very strategy of "nicheism" with which the developments are associated is one in which individual firms, or groups of firms, can prosper by picking off small pieces of an international market irrespective of the prosperity of the larger national economy in which they are located. The success in creating a local community within the corporate organization or within an industrial region frees them from dependency upon the larger national community. In the new world, to put it bluntly, *even* the success of General Motors will not be the success of the American economy. And much the same can be said about the success of Route 128 and Silicon Valley or the much heralded Sunrise Services.

But the other reason why the transformations already in process are not alone grounds for optimism is that they are not the only avenue of adjustment available to American business. An alternative strategy which holds out equal promise of renewed profitability in the short run is simple cost cutting. Firms can maintain their own organizational structures and many of their traditional managerial practices intact and compete by reducing labor costs through wage cuts. And if flexibility in some organizations means the reform package which I have just described for others it means precisely the intensified competition among workers for jobs, suppliers for contracts, and entrepreneurs for innovative opportunities which the President's rhetoric seems to exhort and which his policies encourage. In between the organizations undergoing fundamental transformation on the one hand and those involved in draconian cost cutting on the other, are a variety of firms in which the two alternatives are a matter of continual internal debate. It is, I suppose, presumptuous of me as an outsider to pre-judge these issues when the professional managerial community is itself divided. None the less, I do think it is clear that simple cost cutting is only a short-run strategy which, however appropriate it may be for a particular company at a moment of time, will never serve the interests of a national economic system. It is no accident that our most intense competition in world markets comes from countries that have a strong cooperative tradi-tion: Japan in large scale production and high tech and, in traditional industries like machine tools, shoes and textiles, from central Italy. When one sees how organizations in these countries function, one not only has a much clearer idea how the combination of cooperation and competition which the corporate reformers are seeking might work. One also sees a kind of dynamism in both the process and the product that leads one to believe that simple cost cutting adjustments will only keep firms in business in the long run by new wage cuts each year until the United States reaches the levels pervailing in the underdeveloped world. Long before we reach this level, of course, we will face the kind of spontaneous worker revolt which we saw in the 1930s. And the ultimate critique of the Administration is that instead of creating an environment which encour-ages the search for an alternative set of economic institutions, and encou-raging their development now while we still have the freedom to choose, it is pursuing an economic policy which both in its substance and its rhetoric is encouraging crude "sweating." In itself, this cannot solve our economic problems and is rapidly creating a social climate which may well foreclose those alternatives which would lead us back to a stable long-term prosper-ity. This policy is especially dangerous because, while American firms no longer share a single national market, they do operate together in one social structure, and the social policy which emerges in reaction to the dra-conian cost cutting of the least dynamic of American business is likely to constrain the policies of the most dynamic firms as well, perhaps in ways that will permanently cripple the economy as a whole.

PART IV

Working Together

Introduction

Economists typically think in terms of separate individuals and units –
workers, firms, consumers, investors – operating in free and open
markets. We assume private interest motivates behavior and emphasize
the importance of competition as the force which leads us to the most efficient market outcome. Following along these lines, we tend to view
workers and owners (or managers) as adversaries grappling with each
other towards a market clearing price for labor. The chapters in this final
part of the book take a different tack. They shift the focus from individuals
and individual units toward a look at the shared institutional environments
in which all economic actors operate. In addition, they stress the need for
cooperation as well as competition if we are to achieve our economic
goals.

The success of many of our trading partners, as well as our own dissatis-
faction with recent economic performance, leads the authors of these
essays to conclude that we must re-think our views on labor-management
relations, national savings rates, research and development and training
for workers. This requires a new attention from economists to a variety of
relationships within firms, between firms, and between firms and government. At times we will need a greater sensitivity to market signals which
current institutional arrangements muffle, at times a sensitivity to necessary functions which markets do not perform.

One could argue that many of the greatest economic breakthroughs
have come about because of new discoveries in cooperative techniques –
the assembly line using interchangeable parts might be one example. If we
examine this example closely, we find that cooperation is not always anti-
thetical to competition, but in fact may be required by competitive
demands. The first manufacturer of rifles using interchangeable parts
gained a tremendous advantage over his competitors, as do contemporary
firms that reduce their overhead costs with suggestions made by workers
in quality control circles. Today a firm's competitors may be in Singapore

or Brazil as easily as Peoria or Houston. As a result, the success of specific firms and industries is of national concern. In order for US firms to compete in a global economy, the authors in this section of the book argue, we must improve our ability to cooperate on a number of fronts. Government, labor and business must learn to work toward common goals. This will not always be easy, nor is it as simple as it sounds. Interests do not always coincide. Long-term interests and short-term interests do not always coincide. Groups may share interests but seek ways to avoid sharing the costs necessary to achieve them. Moreover, government may be easily used to promote the interests of some firms or industries to the detriment of others, or the detriment of the public at large. All of these difficulties present problems. However, the success of some of our most serious global competitors in overcoming many of these problems makes this a challenge we cannot ignore.

Lestur Thurow begins his essay with the assumption that Americans must face up to the global competitive challenge. He discusses the limits of Keynesian tools for many of our immediate and long-range problems. Thurow proposes that we take many supply-side questions quite seriously, but urges us to look beyond simple manipulation of the tax code. Ray Marshall analyzes the causes of low productivity growth and argues that future improvement will require public institutions which create a stable environment for investment and trade. He also emphasizes the importance of better labor-management relations and a well-educated, flexible work force. Without those ingredients, productivity growth will continue to limp along and the real wages of US workers will decline. Similarly Sheldon Weinig brings to bear his experience as a businessman in a rapidly changing field to suggest a philosophy of management which better taps the potential of the labor force. In the section's final essay, Kevin Phillips challenges Americans to develop a comprehensive "competitiveness" strategy. Phillips contends that the United States is losing ground to nations that focus their economic policy on their position as global traders. He urges us to think "strategically."

The theme of Part IV is "working together." Yet it is clear from these essays that it is the challenge of global *competition* which drives their analyses. Achieving the appropriate blend of the cooperative and competitive, old and new, market and non-market will not be easy. None the less, policymakers, businessmen, economists, and social scientists in many disciplines – i.e., all those who engage in public economics – must participate in the search for these answers. The consequences are of more than academic interest.

12

Creating a World-Class Team

LESTER THUROW

Sustained Economic Growth

With the advent of Keynesian economics, macroeconomics came to be identified with demand management. The reasons for that identification are not hard to find. In depressions or recessions the economic gains to be made from returning to full employment dwarf all other possible economic gains in magnitude. The Great Depression was clearly a demand management problem that required 100 percent of the policymakers' attention. The same perspective legitimately dominated economic thinking in the first two decades after World War II. Frequent recessions (five in number) were the main enemy of economic growth. Productivity was above trend, growing between 3 and 4 percent per year, and the United States enjoyed across-the-board technological leadership.

In the future, however, it will be important not to identify macroeconomics exclusively with demand management. Macroeconomics will, like binoculars, require both a supply and a demand focus.

The Demand Focus

The demand focus will be as important in the future as it was in the past since it is just as impossible now as it was 40 years ago to have a satifactory growth performance with frequent recessions. But it is important to note that the nature of the anti-recessionary problem has changed. Thirty years ago recessions occurred accidentally and it was the job of the policymaker to prevent those accidents from happening.

The problem of accidental recessions, however, has been cured. There have been no accidental recessions in the US economy since that of 1960–61. Each and every recession since then has been deliberately created to stop inflation. Some of these recessions have occurred later, lasted longer, or been more severe than desired, but none of the last four has been an accident. They have all been deliberately generated by the Federal Reserve Board or the administration in power.

As a result the nature of the anti-recession problem has fundamentally changed. The key to full employment without recessions is not to be found in demand management but in some alternative to negative demand management – be it a share economy, a social contract, or something else – for curing inflation. To make demand management work requires changes in the microeconomic structure of the economy. With the current income setting arrangements, demand management is not a device for achieving full employment, but a device for creating unemployment. If macroeconomics is to accomplish what is supposed to accomplish, it needs different income setting arrangements.

With inflation more or less under control and commodity prices falling inflation is not today's problems, but changes in the microeconomic structure of the economy to make demand management work should be today's problem, for the appropriate time for changing the microeconomic parameters of the wage setting system is when inflation is not a problem. Once inflation has again become a problem it will be too late to make the necessary changes.

There is another respect in which the demand management problem has changed. In a very real sense it is the industrial world's supply of money and the industrial world's tax and expenditure policies and not just the American pieces of that total that matter for the American economy. Today it is not just Americans sitting at the demand management controls of the American economy. When demand management is needed it is going to have to be coordinated with the policies of Germany and Japan if it is to be successful.

This can be clearly seen by thinking about the deficit reduction problem in the United States. If the United States were to cut expenditures or raise taxes to cure its $200 billion deficit without expansionary policies being simultaneously adopted in Germany and Japan, the result would be a massive world-wide recession. Since the world's industrial economies are not now operating at full employment, if $200 billion of American demand were to be subtracted from the system, then $200 billion of extra demand would have to be added to the system somewhere else. Thus even American deficits cannot be reduced without foreign cooperation. Americans now live in a world where they are merely part of a larger world economy; a world where they control less than they used to control.

The Supply Focus

The past 15 years have proved that supply does not take care of itself. No one can be satisfied with the economy's *per capita* growth rate (1.9 percent) or its productivity growth rate (1.5 percent).[1] Such growth rates are unacceptable relative to America's past, relative to the performance of the rest of the industrial world, and more importantly relative to the rate at which Americans would like to see their own standards of living grow.

While there are many places were private markets can be liberated to improve performance, a supply focus is not a synonym for *laissez-faire* or lower taxes. In economy theory one can show that *laissez-faire* economies have some desirable properties (they optimally distribute private goods relatively to the initial distribution of income), but a high rate of growth is not one of them. This is most clearly seen in one of the weak points of the US economy – its low rate of investment and savings.

Given the institutions of the American economy (tax deductibility for consumer and mortgage interest, no low or down payments, long periods for repayment) it may be rational for the average American to take advantage of those institutions and make generous use of consumer and mortgage credit. But if each and every American does so, the net result is a very low aggregate rate of savings. Government at the very least has a responsibility to set the parameters within which people maximize their private utility to yield aggregate results that are consistent with a good long-run economic performance. Free market economies can be organized with or without generous provisions for consumer credit and will have very different performance characteristics depending upon how they are organized. In the end free market economies depend upon the social organization that goes into them.

To accelerate economic growth America needs to make economic growth one of its policy goals. Full employment and low inflation are most often cited as economic goals but it is important to understand that they are only means to an end. The real goal is a high rate of growth in *per capita* income. While American policy makers talk about economic growth, they have not traditionally set growth targets as they have set unemployment or inflation targets. They should start to do so. To set a target is to make something important, but more importantly it is to set a standard of success and failure relative to which the policymakers can and will be judged.

America's growth target should be set relative to the performances of the rest of the industrial world. Basically the United States should have a standard of living that grows in pace with that in the rest of the world. This means that if other leading industrial countries have productivity growth rates in the 3 to 4 percent range the United States should aim for a similar result. Given this goal one can then ask what must be done to achieve it.

Policies for Economic Growth

Growth policies can operate at several levels, but the appropriate place to start is with the quantity and quality of the inputs (capital, labor, technology) going into the economy. In each area the aim should be inputs as good as those going into the economies of the best of our industrial competitors. Everywhere Americans should aim for world-class inputs.

The Quantity of Capital

Unfortunately America does not now have an economy marked by world-class inputs. American investment in plant and equipment is roughly half that going into the Japanese economy and two-thirds that going into the economies of Europe. America should aim to bring investment up to the levels of these competitors. An interim target should be set for bringing investment up to European levels, and once this is achieved the target should be raised to the level that will make the United States competitive with Japan if Japanese investment is still above that in the United States.

In theory, with a world capital market, it is not necessary to have a world-class level of savings to have a world-class level of investment. One simply borrows from the rest of the world what is necessary to make the necessary investments. In fact it does not make sense from a national or a world perspective for the United States to be borrowing much of its capital from the rest of the world. Ultimately interest payments on those foreign debts become a drag on the US economy and the world's surplus capital should more appropriately be invested in the developing world and not in the United States.

This means that higher investment rates will in fact require higher savings rates within the United States. In addition to shifting the federal government from being a net dissaver to being a saver, higher savings rates will require changes in tax laws (eliminating the tax deducitibility of interest payments) and limitations on consumer and mortgage credit to raise initial down payments and to shorten repayment periods. The American political system seems to be in the process of proving that such changes cannot be sold in the guise of tax reform. It also seems to be proving that it cannot raise taxes as a part of federal deficit reduction.

Whether such changes can be sold as necessary for economic growth remains to be seen. If they cannot, the United States is unlikely to enjoy a world-class rate of growth investing much less than the rest of the industrial world.

The Quality of the Work Force

Ultimately the quality and skills of the workforce are a country's only real comparative advantage. As the inventor of mass public education America for many years had the best educated and most skilled work force. But all of the current evidence indicates that the United States now has a work force that does not meet world-class standards when it comes to education and skills.

Eight percent of American youths 14 to 21 years of age test out as functionally illiterate (i.e. they cannot read and write at the fifth grade level).[2] Using slightly tougher definitons of functional illiteracy, as much as 20 percent of the American work force may be functionally illiterate. In contrast less than 1 percent of the Japanese labor force is functionally illiterate.

When 19 different achievement tests were administered to students in different countries, Americans never ranked first or second, and if comparisons are limited to other developed nations only, the US ranked at the bottom seven out of 19 times. Mean scores placed America in the bottom half of the rank-order distribution 13 times and in the top half only six times.[3] In an international study of mathematics ability for eighth and twelfth graders, the eighth graders ranked in the bottom tenth internationally and the twelfth graders were 'markedly lower' than the international average in all seven of the areas tested.[4]

Those are unacceptable results that must be altered. Education may be a state responsibility, but no national government can for long tolerate an education system that is not generating a competitive work force.

If one looks for the reasons for a poor American performance, one factor stands out. The United States has a much shorter school day and school year than most of the rest of the industrial world. Students go to school 240 days in Japan and 220 in Sweden. In contrast, American students are in school only 180 days. Americans cannot learn in 180 days what it takes the rest of the world 220 to 240 days to learn.

To lengthen the school year half of federal educational aid should be conditioned on a longer school year. The other half should be conditioned on a school's achievement test scores relative to what one would have expected from the historical norms for schools with students of the same socioeconomic background. If one does well on performance measures relative to schools with similar student inputs one gets more federal aid than if one does poorly relative to similar schools.

If the federal government can set standards for interstate highways if a state wants federal highway money, it can set standards for educational inputs and outputs if a state wants federal education money. When it comes to that famous bottom line a well educated work force is much more important to national economic success than a good highway system.

If one looks at the US education system there is a major gap. No training system exists for the training of the non-college bound. Germany fills this gap with an elaborate system of publicly financed but privately run apprenticeship training and private firms provide such training in Japan. America has no general system of publicly financed training for the non-college bound and because of high labor force turnover rates, private firms find that it is not in their immediate self-interest to pay for the extensive training of workers who are unlikely to remain on their payrolls.

Such a gap is both inefficient (the economy has a perpetual shortage of skilled non-college workers) and unfair (the average American college student gets a public subsidy of $12,000 over the life of his college career). It is a gap that must be closed. Individual training accounts are one possible answer, but some answer must be adopted if the US is to grow rapidly in the future. In the past the United States could count on immigration (principally from Germany and Austria) to provide skilled blue collar workers but now that real standards of living have essentially reached parity in northern Europe that source of supply has essentially ended.

Maintaining Technological Parity

In the last few decades Americans have relied on superior technology to offset other handicaps. America may not have had the best labor force or the newest capital, but it had the best technology and many goods were only to be had from American sources. But that era is now gone. The rest of the world has caught up with the United States technologically and few if any goods are only to be had from US sources. While it is impossible for the United States to go back to the effortless technological superiority that it had in the 1950s (it was a product of the human and physical destruction of World War II), it is important that the United States maintain civilian technological parity.

While the United States is not yet generally behind technologically, it is clear that there is a technological problem. Process technology is a clear American weakness. In too many leading industries American firms are operating with inferior processes. Foreign firms could pay the same wages and still sell below American costs. Expenditures on civilian R&D as a fraction of the GNP are now below those in Japan, Germany, and France.[5] Both Japan and Germany graduate about 40 percent of their college students in science and technology while less than 10 percent of American students graduate with engineering or science degrees.[6] In addition 40 percent of America's scientific personnel is involved in defense work.[7]

It is interesting to note that in the decade of the man-on-the-moon effort, the United States thought that it was necessary to have programs for augmenting the supply of scientific manpower so that the demands of the space effort did not cripple domestic industries. Yet in the 1980s with a much bigger build-up underway in the defense department no similar efforts are being made to increase the supplies of scientific manpower.

In reality America will need a similar intensification of scientific effort in the 1980s if it is to enjoy a competitive rate of growth. This intensification of effort is not going to occur automatically. In a closed economy a shortage of engineers would lead to higher wages for engineers and in the long run a larger supply of engineers. Given the high costs of scientific education, however, even in a closed economy it should be emphasized that the long run might be very long and that for this reason the man-on-the-moon effort did not rely on automatic market mechanisms to cure potential shortages of scientific personnel.

In an open economy a shortage of engineers need not lead to more engineers even in the long run. Those industries that are engineering intensive simply move to those countries that have an adequate supply of engineers. If one looks at the industries that are now moving abroad (machine tools, electronics) it is perhaps not an accident that these are precisely those industries that are intensive users of technical personnel.

Taxes and High Quality Inputs

In maintaining technological, labor force and capital parity, the main problems are not those of what must be done or how should it be done, but in politically deciding that something must be done if the United States is to enjoy a competitive rate of growth. "Cut taxes" or "do nothing" are the current winners when it comes to public policy prescriptions.

At the moment the federal budget deficit is usually advanced as the main reason why it is impossible for the United States to undertake any new federal expenditure programs. Yet both a skilled labor force and technological parity are realistically going to require some new expenditure programs. Perhaps it is well to point out that with Japan having just passed the United States it is now true that all of the major developed nations pay a larger fraction of their GNP in taxes than the United States. The United States is not an over-taxed society. It is in fact an under-taxed society.

To be a nation with the world's lowest industrial tax rate is not a desirable goal if achieving that goals means an economy that cannot generate a competitive rate of growth. At some point Americans will have to face the fact that higher taxes will be necessary to have a competitive economy.

If the Federal government is to shift from being a net dissaver to being a net saver (and it must if savings rates are to increase), higher taxes will be necessary. If the United States is to have a labor force with skills second to none, higher taxes will be necessary at some level of government to pay for a better education system. If the American economy is to maintain its technological base, it is going to have to pay higher taxes since research and development expenditures are everywhere paid for by government. The externalities are simply too great to rely on private markets to generate adequate research and development efforts.

If higher taxes are politically impossible, then it is impossible for the United States to have a competitive growth rate for it cannot grow at competitive rates investing less, employing a less skilled labor force, and working with inferior technology.

Implicitly Americans are now assuming that if they are willing to play a free market game they will automatically be winners of that game. Yet no such outcome is guaranteed. There will be winners but they need not be American. Economic growth requires social organization. Those economies with rapid rates of growth of productivity are those that pay attention to good social organization.

The Game Plan

The winners in economics as well as in sports are those who play with the best inputs, but what about the game plan – America's economic strategy for success? In the past America has not relied solely on its private firms to guarantee economic success. America's first great process invention, interchangeable parts, was financed with money from the War Department. The railroads were financed with grants and loans from the government. The steel industry developed behind trade barriers that kept cheap British steel out of America during the railroad building era. America's advantage in agricultural productivity can be traced to government programs such as its agricultural colleges, its extension service, its reclamation projects, its electrification programs and a plethora of financial institutions that made it possible for farmers to mechanize. The civilian aviation industry is a by-product of defense spending. Historically the American government has often intervened at strategic points to improve economic performance.

If the managers of any large American company operated without a strategic plan, they would be considered derelict in their duties. Yet because strategic thinking has been equated with economic planning in the socialist sense American policy makers publicly maintain that the American economy does not need a strategy *vis-à-vis* its international competitors. Yet if one looks at America's principal economic competitors – Germany, Japan – they each undertake some form of strategic planning. Outside observers argue as to how much of their success can be traced to their strategic planning and how much can be traced to other factors, but it is interesting to note that both think that such strategic thinking is useful.

In the past these strategies have most often been implemented with government investment banking or with government allocation of scarce foreign exchange, but in the present foreign strategies seem to be operating primarily at the level of research and development. Just as the American government has picked SDI as a target area for defense research so have foreign governments picked various civilian industries (electronics, new materials, biotechnology) as target areas for industrial research.

If one wants to look at the impact of such foreign policies one need only look at the current plight of the American semiconductor industry. Starting first with a governmentally financed research effort to leapfrog American technology and develop large (64K RAM and up) chips but continuing with a designated and limited set of producers, quasi-protected home markets and production loans that did not have to pay interest or principal until and unless profits were earned, Japan has succeeded in capturing more than 90 percent of the market for 256K RAM chips and may have prevented any American firms from attempting to build the megachip (100K RAM). Yet semiconductor chips are the building blocks for the rest of electronics. It is difficult to believe that an industry can ultimately be competitive when it cannot competitively build its own basic ingredients. Consumer electronics has been captured by foreign producers and the same trend is now visible in the rapidly diminishing competitiveness of American industrial electronics products.

Germany has announced similar efforts in the new materials industry (powdered metals, metal ceramics, pressed graphites, etc.) that is now emerging. It is too early to say whether they will be as successful in materials as the Japanese have been in semiconductor chips, but no one should discount their effort.

If one looks at America's mounting trade deficit in research-and-development-intensive products, one has to be a little concerned whether the United States is going to be able to maintain its traditional position in leading edge new industries. Current trends are not running in the American direction.

Japanese strategic planning is coordinated by a government agency (MITI) while German strategic planning is coordinated by the large private investment banks, but in both countries government and industry meet to formulate a strategy to increase economic growth and to maximize international competitiveness. America need not organize itself as either Germany or Japan is organized, but it needs some forum for doing what is being done abroad.

Americans often think that private American firms will do whatever strategic planning is necessary for the American economy to be successful and that, as a result, government has no role to play. Private firms simply will not do what is necessary. In a very real sense there are no private American firms. There are firms legally headquartered in America but they can locate their research and development, office or production facilities anywhere in the world. *Per se* they have no direct company interest in the success or failure of the US economy. They have a direct interest only in their own success or failure. Often it is cheaper for an American-based company simply to move production or engineering abroad than it is for it to make its American operations competitive. Yet foreign production is not a solution to American growth problems even if it is a solution to the competitive problems of American-based companies. If economic strategies are necessary for the United States to be successful in world markets they are going to have to be developed with the impetus of government leadership or they will not be developed.

While government has to be an organization catalyst for strategic planning, the plans have to be developed and implemented with the cooperation of private industry and labor. Only they know what must be known to chart the correct directions of movement. Once plans are formulated only they can implement. But to bring the interested parties together in a serious way some locus of decision-making authority must exist. Historically government investment banking has played this role. A key missing ingredient has often been capital, and industry automatically takes a potential source of funds seriously. Bankers, government or private, can demand information before making loans.

Since such a government banking vehicle raises political hackles and may in any case not be the currently appropriate vehicle for strategic planning, let me suggest that American strategic planning should take place in a government funding institution for industrial research. The federal government should set up a research and development institution for industry similar to the National Science Foundation that now exists for basic (mostly university based) research and development. Just for the sake of a title let me call the agency the National Industrial Research Foundation or NIRF.

This institution should be separate from the NSF since stimulating industrial research is fundamentally different from paying for basic research and development. In all cases firms would be expected to play a leading role in formulating the target areas for research, always be expected to contribute part of the funds and help organize cooperative efforts with other firms, and have priority rights to the products and processes that were developed. Since the agency must have an interest in process research (making old products cheaper) and since process research can only be developed and tested in the context of actual production the agency will be interested in a level of research and development that is now far outside of the scope or expertise of the NSF. With government funds involved, the government would also insist that technologies developed in cooperation with the agency could only be used in the United States for some period of time, say 5 years. Government would also expect to earn its share of the profits on products and processes that were successful. Government money is not a grant but a contingent investment that will be repaid with a share of the profits if the investment is successful. In many ways NIRF would be doing for civilian industry what the Defense Department now does for defense industries.

Of necessity an industrial research agenda can only be formulated in the context of information on a more general set of economic parameters. As a result the need to formulate an industrial research strategy would automatically lead to discussions on more general economic strategies.

Conclusion

To maximize the macroeconomic parameter of economic growth requires changes in the microeconomic structure of the American economy on both the demand and supply sides of the equation. Frequent recessions can only be avoided if alternative means of fighting inflation are developed and if the principal industrial governments can coordinate their demand management policies, be they fiscal or monetary.

On the supply side of the equation the general quantity and quality of the fundamental inputs going into the economy have to be of national concern. Local school districts are not going to solve the aggregate problem of creating a world-class labor force. Since each district's contribution to that result is vanishingly small and each district can imagine itself hiring skilled personnel from elsewhere in the economy, every local district has an incentive to under-invest in education. Yet if each district does so the end result is an American disaster. Similarly each individual find its rational to take full advantage of the current generous provisions for consumer and mortgage lending and each company finds it rational to cut back on general research and development expenditures. Yet if each does what it is individually rational to do the general result is social irrationality and an economy that does not perform as it should perform.

In economics, social organization matters and government has to take responsibility for insuring that America's social organization is second to none. If it is to do its thing free enterprise needs the right operating context. Without that context it can only fail.

Notes

1. Council of Economic Advisers, *Economic Report of the President, 1985*, pp. 234 and 278; Council of Economic Advisers, *Economic Indicators*, 1985 (Nov.), pp. 2 and 16.
2. Gene Maeroff, 'Task force reports 8 percent of city youths are illiterate', *New York Times*, April 7, 1982.
3. Barbara Lerner, 'American Education: How are we doing?', *Public Interest*, 69 (1982), Fall, 64.
4. Edward B. Fiske, 'American students score average or below in international math exams', *New York Times*, Sept. 23, 1984, p. 30.
5. National Science Foundation, *National Patterns of Science and Technological Resources, 1982*, p. 33, IP no. 12.
6. National Science Board, *Science Indicators, 1982*, 1983, p. 22.
7. Charles L. Schultze, 'Economic effects of the defense budget', *Brookings Bulletin*, (1982) Fall.

13

Working Smarter

RAY MARSHALL

Introduction

There is no more important indicator of an economy's performance than trends in real wages and incomes. Nor is there a clearer sign that the American economy is losing its competitiveness than the inability of its enterprises to operate in international and domestic markets on terms that will make it possible to maintain or improve real wages and profitability. We should therefore be very concerned about the 20-year trend decline in real wages for American workers.

The main purpose of this paper is to outline some of the main obstacles to increases in real wages. This is not an easy assignment because real wages are important consequences of complex economic processes. I begin with a discussion of productivity, because it is fairly well established that in market economies the main room for improvement in real wages is provided by productivity growth. But other forces are involved because productivity itself is a complex process and the relative weight to be assigned to its components is not very well understood by economists. There is agreement, however, that productivity is heavily dependent on the nature and quality of human resources, technology, management, industrial relations systems, the economic environment and public policy.

Industrial competitiveness is important because of internationalization. The American economy has subjected high-wage American workers to world-wide competition and therefore has changed the basic nature of the domestic economy and the influence of public policy. Internationalization requires all major economic institutions to meet the viability conditions of international competition. These conditions depend much more on productivity and flexibility than was true of earlier, more self-contained economies.

In my view, public policy failures are the main reason for our failure to use American resources more efficiently, to improve productivity and international competitiveness, to stabilize the economy and to eliminate the material and human waste from unemployment and slow growth. Our policies are too fragmented, ideological, adversarial and shortsighted to create the conditions to make it possible for workers and employers to improve real wages and profitability as rapidly as our resources would permit. This is not to deny, of course, that market systems and individual performance are mainly responsible for economic outcomes. But individuals and markets must operate within the framework of *public* policies, institutions, and infrastructures. Relative to our more successful international competitors, our most debilitating shortcomings are in public, not private, systems. Indeed, in a more competitive environment, noncompetitive private systems tend to disappear, but there is no such mechanism to cause the elimination of unwise public policies. Public policy failures can therefore cause or allow competitiveness to erode over a long period of time, as is currently happening to the American economy. Gross weekly earnings in constant (1977) dollars of all workers in private, non-agricultural employment in the United States declined from $187 in 1980 to $170 in 1981. Real wages in manufacturing have been relatively flat since 1973, after increasing at an annual rate of 2.6 percent a year between 1960 and 1973 – peaking around 1970. Gross weekly earnings of manufacturing workers (in 1977 dollars) were $227 in 1983, $231 in 1979, and $208 in June 1982. Median family incomes declined from $23,111 in 1970 to $22,388 in 1981, again in constant 1977 dollars.

The 1985 Joint Economic Committee (JEC) study of income changes of families with children found similar results. The real median pre-tax income of families with children (measured in constant 1984 dollars) declined by over 6 percent a year between 1973 and 1984 after having grown by 4 percent a year between 1947 and 1973. Median real pre-tax incomes of such families were $28,989 in 1973 and $26,836 in 1984.[1] Family incomes would have declined more except for the increased labor force participation of women – a process that is self-limiting because there are not many families with another wife to put into the work force. If we are unable to reverse the decline in real wages, it therefore will be difficult to reverse the decline in family incomes.

That these changes are due to broad economic trends is suggested by the fact that profit rates also have been declining. Indeed, profit rates actually fell below bond yields in the 1970s and 1980s (see figure 13.1). The composite index of profitability based on 1967 as 100 fell to 85.2 in 1974, and was only 93.9 in 1982.[2]

Why Have Real Wages Declined?

The *slowdown in productivity growth* has been a major factor in the decline in real wages for American workers. Although productivity and wage changes are not highly correlated between industries at any given

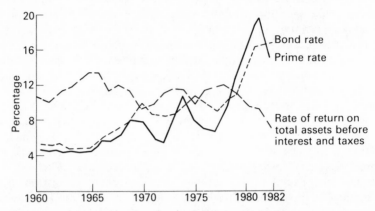

Figure 13.1. Rate of return on total assets in manufacturing, corporate
bond rate and prime rate, 1960–1982
Source: Bruce Scott and George Lodge, *U.S. Competitiveness in the World
Economy* (Harvard Business School Press, Boston, Ma, 1985), p. 31

time, the ability to promote the growth in both real wages and total
economic output depends heavily on productivity. That is why we must be
concerned that productivity growth in the US private business sector
declined from 3.1 percent between 1948 and 1967 to 2.3 percent between
1967 and 1973 and has been less than 1 percent since 1973.

As can be seen from table 13.1, manufacturing productivity growth also
has declined, whether measured in output per hour of employment or per
unit of capital. Indeed, output per unit of capital actually was negative for
1973–83 and very small for 1950–73, and in all cases was lower than
output per unit of labor. Table 13.2 compares manufacturing productivity
in the US and other countries between 1973 and 1981. The US and
Canada have the lowest rates of growth of manufacturing productivity for
1973–83, but all of these countries experienced slowdowns in productivity growth.

Through its influence on unit costs, productivity influences the competitiveness of American industries. Table 13.3 demonstrates that relationship. The best performances in both productivity and unit labor costs
between 1980 and 1982 measured in yen. Note, however, that Germany
and France benefited more from the appreciation of the dollar, which
worsened the cost disadvantage of American enterprises.

Table 13.4 shows the influences of the overvalued dollar on relative
wage rates between 1981 and 1984. Note that no country had hourly
compensation levels of over 75 percent of the average for the United
States in 1984; hourly compensation gaps narrowed during the 1970s – in

Table 13.1 Output per hour, capital effects, and multifactor productivity in manufacturing, 1950–1973 and 1973–1983 (average annual percent change)

	Productivity				Inputs			
	Output per hour of all persons	Output per unit of capital	Multi-factor productivity[a]	Output[b]	Hours of all persons[c]	Capital services[d]	Combined units of labor and capital inputs[e]	Capital per hour of all persons
1950–83	2.5	−0.2	1.7	3.1	0.5	3.3	1.3	2.7
1950–73	2.8	0.8	2.1	4.0	1.2	3.4	1.9	2.2
1973–83	1.8	−2.1	0.8	0.9	−1.0	3.0	0.0	4.0

[a] Output per unit of combined labor and capital inputs.
[b] Gross domestic product originating in manufacturing constant dollars.
[c] Paid hours of all employees plus the hours of proprietors and unpaid family workers engaged in manufacturing.
[d] A measure of the flow of capital services used in manufacturing.
[e] Hours of all persons combined with capital input, using labor and capital shares of output as weights.

Table 13.2 Manufacturing productivity changes,
selected countries 1950–1973 and 1973–1983
(average rates of change)

	Productivity in manufacturing 1950–1973	1973–1983
US	2.8	1.8
Canada	4.3	1.8
France	5.8	4.6
Germany	6.5	3.7
Japan	10.0	6.8
UK	3.3	2.4

Source: *Economic Indicators*, Jan. 1984.

fact, Germany's compensation level actually was 125 percent of that of the US during the late 1970s.[3]

Some analysts believe that the trend of decline in productivity growth has been reversed since the 1981–82 recession, which troughed in November 1982. This is, however, a highly questionable conclusion. US productivity growth at the *peak* of recovery from the 1981–82 recession remained below that of all other OECD countries, whose recovery lagged ours. Moreover, the growth of productivity since November 1982 has been only about half as large as needed to restore the trend rate of productivity growth. As the following BLS data show (table 13.5), recovery from the 1981–82 recession was smaller than for any nine-month recovery period since 1949.

These data suggest that lower productivity was associated with a relatively rapid rate of employment growth. Employment growth, in turn, was associated both with the depth of the 1981–82 recession and the relatively small growth in unit labor costs. As can be seen from figure 13.2, there seems to be a rough inverse relationship between changes in employment and changes in real wages, with the exception of Japan, which, during the 1970s, had employment growth rates second only to the US and Canada, but had the highest real wage growth of any country. The United States has had higher employment growth than most major European countries, at least in part because policy makers in the US were less concerned about the *quality* of jobs and income support systems for the unemployed. Relative to the Europeans, we were more willing to accept lower real wages and relied more on market forces to fix wages within the framework established by economic and labor market policies that provided less support for workers who were unemployed – as illustrated by figure 13.3. The Europeans also had slower labor force growth because they accepted many fewer immigrants and refugees and their post-war

Table 13.3 Unit labour costs in manufacturing, measured in national currencies and in US dollars, selected countries, 1973–1983 (average annual percent change)

Country	National currency basis			US dollar basis		
	1973–83	1973–80	1980–83	1973–83	1973–80	1980–83
United States	7.0	8.4	3.9	7.0	8.4	3.9
Canada	9.9	10.2	9.2	7.6	7.8	7.3
France	10.8	11.0	10.5	5.0	11.8	−9.3
Germany	4.4	5.2	2.5	4.8	11.0	−8.4
Japan	2.8	4.5	−1.1	4.1	7.2	−2.8
United Kingdom	14.5	18.5	5.9	9.2	17.6	−8.2

Source: BLS, *Trends in Manufacturing*, April 1985, Bulletin 2219.

Ray Marshall

Table 13.4 Hourly pay levels abroad in manufacturing industries as percentage of US average, 1981–1984

| | Percentage of US average | | | |
	1981	1982	1983	1984
West Germany	97	90	85	75
Sweden	108	87	73	72
Netherlands	91	85	78	67
Italy	68	63	62	58
France	75	68	63	56
Japan	57	49	50	50
United Kingdom	65	58	51	46
Ireland	51	49	46	42
Spain	51	46	38	37
Taiwan	14	13	13	15
Mexico	34	17	12	13
South Korea	10	10	10	10
Brazil	17	18	12	9

Source: US Bureau of Labor Statistics.

baby boom lagged ours. In fact, during the 1970s the US had twice as many immigrants and refugees as the rest of the industrialized world combined.

Comparing labor market developments in the US, Europe and Japan over the past 10 years (1973–82) reveals three main trends: (1) steady increases in European unemployment; (2) sharp fluctuations in US unemployment;/ and (3) virtual stability in Japanese unemployment. It is interesting to note that although US unemployment rates increased during the latter 1970s, the differences between US and European performance narrowed considerably (see figure 4.A). Furthermore, long-term un-

Table 13.5 Growth of productivity after recessions

| | Compared annual rates of change after 9 months (percent) | | |
Trough: quarter	Productivity	Employment	Unit labor cost
1949:4	−4.8	2.8	3.1
1954:2	2.6	2.5	1.6
1961:1	4.4	0.8	−0.2
1970:4	4.4	3.0	2.6
1975:1	3.5	3.1	4.2
1982:4	2.4	3.9	1.7

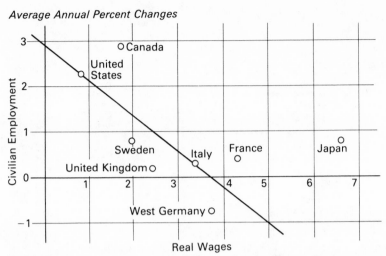

Figure 13.2. Changes in real wages and employment in eight countries,
1970–1978
Source: New York Stock Exchange Office of Economic Research, 'U.S. Economic
Performance in a Global Perspective', Feb. 1981, p. 44

employment has dramatically increased in Europe and, to a lesser extent, in the United States, suggesting structural realignments in employment opportunities in advanced industrial nations (see figure 13.4.B).

Relative to the US, however, the Europeans have done a better job maintaining real wages. The Japanese, by contrast, have done better than the US with real wage growth, but not as well with job growth; relative to the Europeans the Japanese have better performance in the growth of both jobs and real wages. The Japanese also have had relatively high rates of GNP growth and low levels of inflation (see figure 13.5).

However, despite declining real wages, the US has not had sufficient job growth to prevent unemployment from rising from an average of 4.8 percent from 1969 to 1970 and 6.3 percent from 1970 to 1980 and 7–10.8 percent so far in the 1980s.

Causes of Productivity Change

Despite numerous students using a variety of econometric and analytical techniques, there is little agreement on the weights to be attached to the

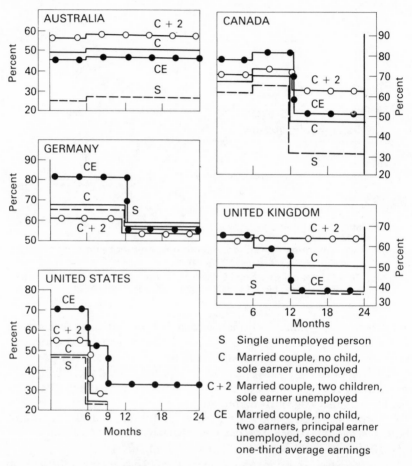

Figure 13.3. Income replacement ratios for households whose principal earner, previously on average earnings, is unemployed
Source: OECD, Employment Outlook, Sept. 1984, p. 95

A   Standardized unemployment rates

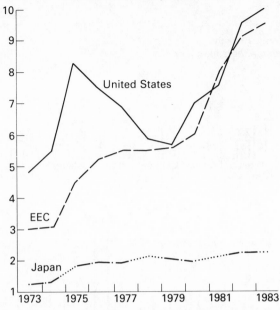

B   Long-term unemployment
(6-month and over)
as a percentage of total
unemployment

Figure 13.4. Unemployment rates 1973–1982
Source: OECD, *Economic Outlook*, Dec.

Real economic growth
Average annual percent change

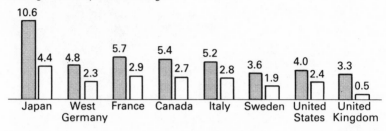

Consumer price index
Average annual percent changes

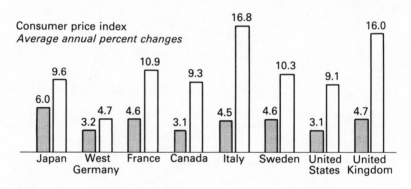

Unemployment rates
Average rate for period

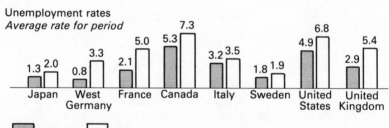

■ 1960–73   ☐ 1973–80

Figure 13.5. International comparisons of economic performance,
1960–1973 and 1973–1980

Source: US Department of Commerce, US Department of Labor, calculated by
the New York Stock Exchange in *US Economic Performance in Global Perspective*, 1951, p. 10

Table 13.6 US gross and net investment, 1956–1984 (percent of GNP)

	1956–60	1961–65	1966–70	1971–75	1976–80	1981	1982	1983	1984
Gross private domestic investment	15.4	15.3	15.5	15.7	16.5	16.0	13.7	14.27	17.41
Plant and equipment	9.9	9.5	10.6	10.4	11.2	11.8	11.4	10.68	11.62
Depreciation	7.3	6.6	6.6	7.3	8.3	9.0	9.4	6.75	7.52
Net investment	2.6	2.9	4.0	3.1	2.9	2.8	2.0	3.93	4.10
Residential construction	5.0	4.8	3.8	4.6	4.6	3.6	3.1	4.00	4.20
Inventory accumulation	0.6	1.0	1.1	0.7	0.7	0.7	-0.8	-0.41	1.58

Source: US Department of Commerce, Bureau of Economic Analysis.

various causes of the slowdown in productivity growth.[4] Unfortunately, neither our data nor our techniques are strong enough to account for these changes. My own assessment is as follows:

While there are monumental technical problems involved in making the assessment, the energy crisis undoubtedly played an important role in the slowdown. We should note, however, that the productivity slowdown started in the 1960s, long before the first energy price shock of 1973–74. However, something associated with the energy crisis appeared to have reduced measured productivity growth. For one thing, the energy crisis caused a substitution of labor and capital for energy, which would reduce productivity measured in terms of labor or capital. Moreover, the energy crisis caused some capital stock to become obsolete, reducing the net capital available. The energy crisis also contributed to economic instability, leading to economic policy confusion and recession; productivity growth always declines during recessions and increases during recovery. Moreover, recessions and economic uncertainty tend to reduce investments in human and physical capital.

There is, however, no agreement over the relative impact of investment on productivity. As can be seen from table 6, there appears to be no unambiguous relationship between changes in gross or net investment and changes in productivity growth – the period 1956–60, for example, was one of relatively low ratios of net investment to GNP and yet relatively high productivity growth. What is involved, of course, is a complex set of causal forces, no one of which has an unambiguous effect through time. Put another way, investment could have had a strong influence, but was counteracted by other forces or the lags between investments and productivity growth were such as to defy measurements taken at any given time.

Some economists argue that the relevant ratio is not aggregate investment, but capital-labor ratios. International comparisons suggest a rough relationship between relatively high rates of growth in capital per employee and productivity growth (see table 13.7). Moreover, as can be

Table 13.7 Annual average compound growth rates of capital per employee

	1960–1973	1973–1980
France	4.8	4.5
Germany	6.2	4.7
Japan	10.6	5.8
Netherlands	5.9	3.4
UK	4.2	3.4
US	2.1	1.0

Table 13.8 Gross fixed capital formation/GDP, selected countries

	Fixed capital formation as a percentage of GDP			
	1960	*1970*	*1975*	*1980*
United States	17	18	17	19
Canada	22	21	24	23
France	20	23	23	22
West Germany	24	26	21	24
United Kingdom	16	19	20	18
Japan	30	36	32	32
South Korea	11	24	26	32
Hong Kong	26	19	19	28
Singapore	n.a.	33	35	39
Malaysia	11	16	25	26
Brazil	17	21	25	21

Source: United Nations, *Yearbook of National Account Statistics*, 1972, vol. 3, table 2A (for 1960): ibid., 1981, vol. 2, table 3 (for 1970, 1975 and 1980).

seen from table 13.8, countries with relatively high rates of gross capital formation seem to have relatively high rates of productivity growth.

As noted, however, the relationship between capital formation and productivity is not clear. Table 13.1 shows the inconsistency of the relationship between capital–labor ratios and productivity. In 1973–83, capital per hour rose by 4 percent a year (from 2.2 percent between 1950 and 1973) while output per hour declined from 2.8 percent to 1.8 percent. Moreover, recent BLS studies have not established strong relationships between capital–labor ratios and productivity. To repeat, however, these data do not prove that there is no relationship between investment and productivity, only that it is difficult to measure. However, the relationship clearly depends on the *quality* of the technology involved in the capital investment, not just aggregate capital expenditure, and there are time lags between expenditures and results which are difficult to determine. Despite these measurement problems, there is no doubt in my mind that the proper introduction of technology can improve and has improved productivity growth. However, just *any* increase in capital spending will not necessarily improve productivity growth.

Other factors commonly assumed to have influenced the productivity slowdown are more questionable. These include the increased labor force participation of women and young people (who had less experience but were better educated than the average older male already in the work force) and environmental and occupational safety and health regulations (which diverted capital, but also had unmeasured benefits) and in some cases, like the cotton dust standard, actually forced productivity-enhancing technological improvements that short-run profit-maximizing companies were not otherwise inclined to make.

Behavioral Factors

Although econometric studies of the reasons for the slowdown of productivity growth have produced inconclusive and conflicting results, there is evidence that productivity can be improved by better management and industrial relations systems.[5] There is evidence, moreover, that *deteriorating* labor-management relations during the 1960s were associated with declining productivity growth.[6]

Studies of management systems in the US and Japan suggest a number of features that improve productivity: greater worker involvement in production decisions and in the development and introduction of technology; job security, which provides flexibility in internal labor utilization and strengthens employers' incentives to finance continuing human resource development programs as integral components of the production process; flexible bonus-based compensation systems that combine basic wages, more egalitarian compensation systems, and bonuses based on company performance; consensus-based decision mechanisms that provide better information to all participants in the production process, greatly improve the quality of decisions; enterprise-based industrial relations systems which, along with bonuses and job security, cause workers to identify more with their companies and to be more concerned with quality and productivity.

The Japanese management system also has achieved much higher employee identification and motivation, as measured by competitive outcomes and attitudinal studies of American and Japanese workers. For example, a 1983 study reported by Public Agenda found that only 9 percent of American workers thought they could benefit personally from improved productivity; 93 percent of similar Japanese workers thought they would derive personal benefit from improved productivity. Of particular importance to improving productivity are systems which give heavy weight to human resource development. There seems to be general agreement among economists that historically a very large part of all improvements in productivity come from improvements in the quality of human resources; physical capital generally has been found to account for no more than 20 percent of productivity growth.[7] This should not be surprising, because developed people are an almost unlimited asset, whereas undeveloped people can be tremendous liabilities. Educated, trained people are better able to deal with change and develop institutions and policies to make effective use of resources and solve problems. The quality of workers' education is, moreover, an important determinant of their ability to adapt to change and assimilate technology.

Table 13.9A Human resource quality

	United States	West Germany	Japan
Productivity			
Manufacturing output (per manufacturing worker in thousands of US dollars, 1981)	31.5	24.9	23.7
OECD rank	(2)	(9)	(11)
Productivity growth (average of annual percentage rates of change in real GDP per employee 1977–82)	−0.1	1.5	2.9
OECD rank	(20)	(10)	(4)
Education			
Education expenditures (Total as % of GDP, 1981)	8.3	4.7	5.7
OECD rank	(4)	(16)	(11)
Enrollment in secondary education (% of relevant age groups, 1980)	97	n/a	91
Enrollment in post-secondary education, 1979 (% of 20–24-year-olds)	55	26	30
OECD rank	(1)	(8)	(4)

Source: OECD, *Labor Force Statistics*, 1983; OECD, *Historical Statistics*, 1983.

Tables 13.9A and 13.9B provide some information on the quality of human resources in the US, Germany and Japan. The tables show that the US ranks high on the average level of productivity, but low on productivity growth. The US also ranks relatively high on school enrollments, though other evidence suggests that the US ranks lower on educational attainment in technical subjects. Enrollments in secondary schools are high in Japan but somewhat lower in the US. Japanese post-secondary enrollments are relatively low, but the Japanese have well-developed on-the-job training programs. Japanese blue-collar workers who are regular employees appear to be much better educated than their American counterparts, especially in technical subjects and mathematics.

The US rank is relatively low on industrial unrest, employee motivation and turnover. We rank slightly above Germany on the managerial talent index, but way behind Japan. Note, however, that Germany has fewer days

Table 13.9B Human resource quality

Labour/management relations	United States	West Germany	Japan
Industrial unrest (Days lost per 1,000 workers)	813	6	31
OECD rank	(15)	(3)	(4)
Absenteeism (non-vacation days lost per worker per year)	3.5	7.7	1.6
OECD rank	(4)	(14)	(1)
Employee motivation index[a]	61.0	65.3	85.3
OECD rank	(9)	(6)	(1)
Managerial talent index[a]	70.5	68.6	82.1
OECD rank	(3)	(5)	(1)
Employee turnover index[a]	59	71	90
OECD rank	(21)	(10	(1)

[a] 0 = low, 100 = high. These indexes are based on subjective assessments gathered from over 1,000 respondents to a survey conducted by the European Management Forum (EMF). Respondents included company chief executives, economic and financial experts, bankers, and the heads of foreign-owned subsidiaries of large multinational companies, as well as key personalities from the press, trade unions, and business associations.

Source: European Management Forum, from OECD, *Historical Statistics*, 1983; International Labor Organization; *Bulletin of Labor Statistics*, 1983; *Japan Labor Bulletin*, Nov. 1982.

lost due to strikes than Japan, though Japan is very low on this index among OECD countries.

Although there is no question that the Japanese have developed a very effective management system in its export manufacturing sector, I am persuaded that their main competitive advantage relative to the United States is public policy, not their management systems. In fact, few major industrial countries have been as handicapped by public policy as the United States. Some of the public policy contrasts with the United States that have caused the Japanese to gain competitiveness include:

(1) Well coordinated macroeconomic policies that have kept unemployment low and productivity and real wage growth high. The US has had uncoordinated macroeconomic policies and very high and unstable rates of unemployment. The instability of the US system has been a major factor making it possible for Japanese firms to target American markets by cutting prices during recessions and taking advantage of inadequate capacity by American firms to meet rising demand to gain market share

Table 13.10 Percentage average weighted cost of
capital to industry, 1971–1981

	1971	1976	1981
United States	10.0	11.3	16.6
France	7.5	9.4	14.3
West Germany	6.9	6.6	9.5
Japan	7.3	8.9	9.2

Source: US Department of Commerce, *Historical Comparison of the Cost of Capital*, April 1983.

during recoveries. Since American firms are more likely to respond to recessions by laying off workers, the Japanese have had the capacity to gain market share rapidly during recoveries, as they did in gaining over 92 percent of the 256K dynamic RAM market.

(2) The Japanese have followed policies of providing low interest rates and low capital costs through the banking system to their producers (see table 13.10). The US, by contrast, has followed policies that have led to huge federal budget deficits and high real interest rates, that not only raise the cost of capital, but also have caused an overvalued dollar and huge trade deficits. DRI, Inc. has estimated that the net after-tax cost of capital between 1973 and 1984 was 0.1 percent for Japanese companies and 5.1 percent for American companies.[8] Table 13.10 shows the average weighted cost of capital to American industry to have been consistently higher than for other major industrial countries between 1971 and 1981.

(3) Japan has followed policies to cause very high personal savings rates whereas the US has followed policies to encourage consumption and discourage savings. Many American policies with respect to credit, taxation and income maintenance are based on depression-oriented ideas that saving is bad for the country. Indeed, the main justification for US trade and other economic policies is that they encourage consumption. Japan's policies, by contrast, have encouraged the growth of productive potential, national economic power and real incomes. The 1981–82 recession shows demand still to be important, but in an internationalized information world we must give greater attention to the cost of capital – which means savings relative to investment demand.

(4) Japan has followed coordinated industrial as well as macroeconomic policies. These policies are designed to upgrade the productivity of Japan's economy by strengthening the competitiveness of Japanese industry by working with the private sector to encourage the development and use of technology and to bargain actively to get the best terms on foreign technology for Japanese firms. They are designed to develop consensus on economic policy, and protect the Japanese market for companies in

strategic sectors until they are strong enough to freeze foreigners out themselves. Freezing foreigners out of the Japanese market – the world's second largest – gives them an enormous strategic advantage in developing products, scale economies and financial resources to compete in international markets.

(5) Perhaps the most important contrast between US and Japanese policies besides the consensus-based character of the latter, is that the Japanese provide a much more stable economic environment where much risk is socialized.

The United States, by contrast, has passive trade policies which are no match for the active policies of Japan and other countries. Our "free trade" ideology encourages *ad hoc* protectionism, has no sense of strategy, and tends to respond timidly, belatedly and inadequately to strategic policies of other countries. Illustrations of the inadequacies of our policies are the unilateral opening of American telecommunications and financial markets to foreign companies, giving up one of our main bargaining chips in opening foreign markets to American companies. Japanese companies derive considerable strategic advantage from being able to operate unchallenged in the Japanese market – while being able to develop strategic positions in the American market.

A second illustration of our inadequate policies is the administration's recent announcement that it would file charges against Japanese companies for dumping in the sale of the 256K RAM chip after the Japanese had gained over 90 percent of the world market for that strategic component. Ironically, Japanese companies can overcome dumping charges by raising their prices.

We should, however, keep the trade problem in perspective. Although there is adequate room to challenge their compliance with international trade rules, Japanese policies are not mainly responsible for our problems – ours are. Moreover, they are following rational strategies, given irrational US policies. The Japanese recognize, as we do not, that international business is a *strategic* process – where governments and businesses must work closely together.

The whole world has much to gain from an open and expanding international economic systems operating within the framework of negotiated, transparent, enforceable rules. We should join with Japan and other countries to negotiate such a system, but we will not be able to do this if we continue an ideological commitment to unrealistic competitive market policies in a world of oligopolies, powerful multinational corporations and active strategic trade policies by other countries. Nor will we have much power to negotiate acceptable rules if we continue to take unilateral actions that give up our interests without a quid pro quo.

We should take particular pains to avoid worsening our relations with the Japanese, because, as Ambassador Mike Mansfield correctly observes, we have no more important relationship with any other country. This relationship can be improved by more rational US economic policies to improve our competitiveness while opening their markets.

Other Factors Responsible for Declining Real Wages

In addition to slow productivity growth and economic instability, there are other obstacles to the rapid increases in real wages in the United States.

1. The secular increase in unemployment depresses wages and causes large material (as well as human) losses that could be used to increase real wages and public and private physical and human capital formation.
2. Demographic factors – especially the large increase in the work force because of the baby boomers and the increased labor force participation of women, also have depressed wages.
3. The ability to maintain or increase American wages has been weakened by the internationalization of the American economy. Internationalization has opened up previously sheltered US markets to competition from low-wage workers in other countries who frequently have developed very competitive management systems and use the most advanced technology. Unless American companies have competitive advantages because of technology, skills differentiated products, or better management systems, international competition will erode American wages, assuming a relatively open international trading system.
4. The relative openness of the American economy to immigration (legal and illegal) increases labor supplies relative to job growth and therefore reduces wages and perpetuates marginal low-wage jobs. Of course, it is impossible to know the number of illegal immigrants but refugees and immigrants (legal and illegal) probably accounted for at least one-fourth of the growth in the American work force during the 1970s. There is some debate about the effects of immigration on employment, but there is little doubt in my mind that it depresses wages of US residents, especially in the absence of policies to maintain economic growth.[9]
5. The decline in union strength reduces workers' ability to improve their wages. Although the main obstacles to the rapid increase in real wages for American workers are the other matters discussed in this paper, declining union strength also is a factor. Some argue that unions have no independent power to increase wages because union wage gains are at the expense of non-union workers, but I think that argument is flawed. Unions can increase and have increased wages by strengthening productivity. Moreover, the "social-cost-of-union" argument

assumes competitive markets, which is rarely the case. Where techno-logical, product, or other factors give companies market advantages, unions can share these "rents" with companies, with no adverse impact on non-union wages. Moreover, unions play an important role in protecting and facilitiating worker participation in the work place and in public policy matters that are essential to free and democratic societies. Internationalization nevertheless requires unions to be more concerned about the competitiveness of firms than was true in a less competitive environment. Experience also suggests that competitiveness – productivity, quality, flexibility – requires managers to be more concerned about employee security and involvement in work processes. I do not believe workers can have effective involvement in companies without the independent sources of power that come from the effective right to organize and bargain collectively.

Conclusions

The most important obstacle to increases in real wages is the slowdown in productivity growth. Whatever the reasons for the slowdown, it is clear that productivity improvements will require investment in physical and human resources, improved management and industrial relations system and, most important, economic policies to promote more effective use of physical and human resources. Improved economic performance, will in turn, require much better international economic policies. We must, moreover, rebuild national consensus for economic growth to promote the full and efficient use of our human and physical resources. We must be concerned about the quality of jobs as well as the number. The most immediate macroeconomic policy objective should be to reduce real interest rates and the value of the dollar by reducing federal budget deficits. However, it would be unwise to reduce budget deficits at the expense of economic growth or public investments in human capital and physical infrastructures. The current account balance should be a specific policy objective in order to prevent growing external debt from undermin-ing the value of the dollar as a reserve currency for unduly burdening future real output and real incomes in order to service large external debt. The most direct way to reduce current account deficits is to return the value of the dollar to its 1979–80 levels by reducing real interest rates through less restrictive monetary policies while federal budget deficits are raised by increased taxes. This will increase exports and reduce imports. Lower real interest rates also would help reduce the budget deficit.

But macroeconomic policies alone will not be sufficient. We need to take measures to greatly strengthen the development of our human resources. Moreover, reducing the value of the dollar could generate long-run inflationary pressures. We therefore should develop selective anti-inflation policies *before* inflation becomes a problem.

We also should develop mechanisms to build consensus over economic policy and to encourage such processes at the industrial, regional and state and local levels. These mechanisms cannot substitute for legislation, management, collective bargaining or free markets, but they can improve all of these processes by narrowing the range of conflicts and providing much better information, especially about trade-offs and limits.

Other measures that would improve economic performance and real wages for workers include:

1. Strengthened investments in civilian research and development.
2. An *active trade policy* to develop an open and expanding trade and finance system within the framework of transparent, enforceable, negotiable rules.
3. A positive adjustment program to encourage the modernization of industry and the shift of human and physical resources out of noncompetitive industries in an orderly way.
4. Rationalization of federal loans and loan guarantee programs into a single entity with the power to make adjustment loans or loans for research and development not likely to be financed by existing financial institutions. This entity should be insulated as much as possible from the political process and allowed to raise resources from pooled pension funds, public bond sales, and other sources.
5. Encouragement of greater worker participation and ownership through labor–management cooperation, employee stock ownership plans and strengthening the ability of workers to organize and bargain collectively.

Notes

1. Jane Seabury, 'Typical family's income has fallen', *Washington Post*, Nov. 29, 1985.
2. US Department of Commerce, *Handbook of Cyclical Indicators*, 1984, p. 133.
3. US Department of Labor, Bureau of Labor Statistics, *Trends in Manufacturing*, April 1985, p. 53.
4. For a good summary, see Economic Policy Council, United Nations Association, *The Productivity Problem: U.S. Labor–Management Relations*, Oct. 1983.
5. See ibid., and Richard B. Freeman and James L. Medoff, *What Do Unions Do?*, (Basic Books, New York, 1984).
6. Thomas Weisskopf, Samuel Bowles and David Gordon, 'Hearts and Minds: A Social Model of U.S. Productivity Growth', *Brookings Papers on Economic Activity*, 2, 1983.

7. See Anthony P. Carnevale, *Human Capital: A High Corporate Investment* (American Society for Training and Development, Washington, DC, 1983).

8. DRI, *Impact of the Dollar on U.S. Competitiveness*, Joint Economic Committee Hearing, Subcommittee on Economic Goals and Intergovernmental Policy, March 12, 1985, p. 12.

9. See Ray Marshall, 'Immigration: An International Economic Perspective', *International Migration Review*, 19 (1984), Fall, pp. 593–612.

14

Managing Better

SHELDON WEINIG

It is quite obvious that if we are to retain any semblance of our international competitiveness, we must increase productivity in the United States. Our record to date is quite dismal and this, of course, was clearly evidenced by the 1.5 percent annualized decrease in productivity posted during the fourth calendar quarter of 1985.

We speak of productivity as the key to future prosperity. I am afraid that is too optimistic. Before prosperity, we had best consider sustaining some semblance of competitiveness in the international marketplace. Much has been discussed about the impact of the cost of capital (US cost of capital is threefold that of the Japanese), the level of corporate taxation (considerably higher for growth companies as compared to "smokestack industries"), and various tax incentives on productivity in the US (with productivity lagging, the Government desires to withdraw the investment incentives of the 1981 tax-cut law).

I don't mean to minimize the impact of financial factors on productivity. But of one thing I am certain, without committed employees in general and specifically comitted engineers, there cannot be any significant increase in productivity.

It is much too easy to forget the human dimension in the productivity equation as we become more and more computer and automation oriented in our thinking. Computerization and automation are the results of human effort, and in turn their ongoing successful operation in the flexible manufacturing environment required for the future is also highly people-dependent.

The human dimension is a somewhat different vantage point than the cosmic view of macro-economics. It is not as easy to formulate a quantitative analysis of the people effect on productivity. Capital cost, accelerated depreciation, investment tax credits and R&D tax credits lend themselves to a myriad of calculations and predictive equations of their single and collective effects on US industry; however, I am not so sure the relationship to productivity is clearly definable. All, of course, are important and definitely have some effect, but none is as critical as the human dimension.

It probably cannot be understood until you view the problem from the "enterprise level," or perhaps even lower at the "trench level," of doing business.

The task of developing committed employees, never easy, may be even more difficult in the future than it has been in the past. For example, managing human resources in the future will present entirely different challenges for corporations and the old methods will be, for the most part, anachronistic. The traditional workforce of yesterday, whose main focus was salary and salary-equivalent benefits, who found strength as part of a collective group that rarely *intellectually* challenged management, has been replaced by a non-docile, individualist, provocative and creative body of mixed gender, mixed language, and mixed work objectives. Even to think of applying the quick fox remedy of emulating Japanese management techniques is nonsense.

We are not a homogeneous people similar to the Japanese, and our culture is in many instances in direct opposition to many of their business practices. The heterogeneity of the US population is not a second-order effect, it is primary to our thinking and behavioral patterns. It must be an important aspect of our strategic planning of human resource management.

I recently asked a vice president of a major US semiconductor manufacturer with operating plants in both the US and Japan why the device (chip) yields in their Japanese facility was nearly 20 percent greater than in their US plants. He explained that the most critical factor in semiconductor yields is the quantity of particulate (dirt) that falls onto the surface of the silicon wafer. Each falling particulate can effectively destroy a chip. Particulate comes from the normal and continuous shedding of human skin, cosmetics worn by the operators, lung particulate from smoking and about every other source imaginable. Cleanliness and care are primary to running a semiconductor business.

In Japan, he explained, the company's workforce consists entirely of Japanese women and management has been able to train this homogeneous, dedicated employee group not to wear makeup, not to smoke for at least one hour before entering the clean room, to be fastidious about personal cleanliness and even to take fewer tea and toilet breaks because entry to and exit from the clean room exacerbates the particulate problem.

In contrast, he said, his US workforce consisted of a polyglot mixture of whites, blacks, hispanics, orientals, etc. "Can you imagine asking this heterogeneous group of American workers not to smoke for one hour before entering the clean room, not to wear makeup for women (no beards or mustaches for men), and to take fewer coffee or toilet breaks?" That the difference is only 20 percent is surprising. This doesn't mean that we have to give up manufacturing semiconductors in the US; it means our approach to human management must be vastly different.

Secondly, corporate America must rid itself of the illusion that technical superiority is an American birthright. In the 1950s and 1960s, US technology was so advanced that it was possible for US industry to ship almost anything without the necessity of troubling themselves with anything as mundane as product reliability or even operability. (I sometimes think that some process equipment shipped by my company to customers like Texas Instruments worked only on Thursday afternoons, during which time TI produced silicon wafers with semiconductor yields of 10 to 14 percent; and yet both TI and MRC, producer and supplier, grew rapidly and profitably during that era.)

The US as a country in that time frame truly had world dominance in technology. We perceived that technological leadership position as an absolute – we truly believed that our high-tech creativity could not be challenged, let alone equalled. Not only is this no longer valid, but Americans now understand that it *can* be invented there ("there" for the most part meaning Pan-Pacific countries like Japan and Korea). Perhaps the greatest danger to our society is that many Americans no longer believe that *it can be invented here*.

Is there a viable solution, or at least course of action, for this country if we aren't to witness the total disintegration of our technological and manufacturing capabilities. Are we really all going to end up as griddle men at local McDonalds? Are service industries going to be the only available source of employment for American youth? I would like to think not, and yet I must admit that this country's plans, actions and results to date have not been overly effective.

I believe that the key to any improvement in our technological and manufacturing position is strongly dependent upon the human dimension in industry and, more specifically, highly dependent upon the contributions of the engineering profession. If we don't improve the attitude, effectiveness and number of our engineers, then I do not believe that we can avoid industrial catastrophy in this country.

The United States requires a large number of high quality, committed engineers. Without them, there is no possibility of altering the downward spiral of our technological position or manufacturing base. Engineering skills are fundamental to a turnaround.

Shocking as it may seem, if I were beginning a new technological enterprise today, my play would be as follows:

Innovate in the United States
engineer in Japan
produce in Korea
sell like hell all over the world.

(Please note where I would do the engineering.)

Let us examine some aspects of the engineering problem in the United

States. First, let us deal with the numbers. Seven percent of college graduates in the US are engineering majors, whereas in Germany and Japan the total is approximately 40 percent. These numbers, although depressing, do not accurately reflect how really bad it is. For example, in Japan nearly 100 percent of graduating engineers go on to practice their profession. In the US, five years after graduation approximately 35 to 40 percent of the engineers are no longer practicing their profession. The five-year sticking ratio for the profession is about 0.6 (perhaps the worst sticking ratio for any profession).

The disillusionment of practicing engineering is manifested in many ways. For example, engineers are the single largest group of candidates pursuing MBA degrees. This course of study doesn't enhance the possibility of their continuing in real engineering positions. Thousands of engineers choose to go into sales because they perceive the monetary rewards as practicing engineers to be insufficient for their financial ambitions. Others go into medicine, law, anything, so they don't have to pursue an engineering career. Further, the relatively low salaries paid to engineers as compared to other professions make one question whether superior students are being attracted to the engineering schools.

And yet, despite the obvious shortage of qualified engineers in the US, thousands of engineers were *laid off* in 1985 when the electronics and computer industries experienced one of their periodic economic downturns. This country is the only free world nation that uses layoffs as a corrective method of countering the vagaries of the economic business cycle.

The real question then is how do we improve the plight of the engineers so that we can attract more and better students and then keep the motivated to remain engineers. It is obvious that employment security is an absolute necessity for American industry, especially technology firms and especially for the hard core of engineering and technical talent.

Dr Eric Block, president of the National Science Foundation and formerly vice president of IBM Corporation, noted that the productivity revolution which should result from the greater use of computer applications and robots should ultimately enrich all of our lives. Scientists, engineers, technicians and production workers will all benefit from the rapid changes occurring because of the computer revolution. Production workers, instead of operating machines, will control their operations and the factory will be process rather than product driven.

In productivity jargon, it means that the factory will be flexible and that rapid changeover to permit different products to be manufactured could be made in the shortest possible time. This, however, requires far better educated employees than we have ever had in the United States. It means that industry must make significant investments in employees to train and educate them so that they will be able to be productive in this new environment. Dr. Block's conclusion was that *"universal continuing employment could well be the result of this type of productivity revolution."*

This is a not surprising conclusion for a former employee of IBM, where employment security has been practiced for decades. My company, Materials Research Corporation, has also been practicing employment security for 25 years, and there are a scattering of other companies, such as Hewlett-Packard and Eli Lilly, who have pursued this enlightened policy. However, let us not believe that this practice is acclaimed by all. The investment community, for example, whom we depend upon for the capital required to sustain and grow the business is extremely critical of this policy of continuing employment. This was succinctly addressed in a January 9, 1986, *Fortune* Magazine article titled "Most Admired Companies". After significant business analysis of the most admired companies and their financial results, the author notes, "Once again, profits provided the shortest road to admiration."

Personally, I believe that employment security is a fundamental requisite to developing the commitment required by all employees, but particularly by engineers who are absolutely critical to the improvement of productivity in this country. However, employment security is only one part of the overall fabric of human asset management. For example, as Dr Block clearly noted, companies are required to make more significant investments in the education of their employees and, hence, when employment security is provided by a corporation, it is necessary to have an enlightened educational program as well.

MRC's eduational program is quite simple. "You pass, we pay." Our employees can take whatever courses they desire without any relationship to degree matriculation or job improvement. Again, I can assure you that this program has not met with acclaim by the investment community. They ask why stockholders should pay tuition for an engineer to study English literature. Well, frankly, there is no easy answer. But it is interesting that companies can provide gyms and support baseball and bowling teams without any need to justify their activities. Our educational program allows exercise for the brain which I believe is of value to the company equal to or greater than well-toned muscles and trim waists. It is not a case of either/or.

There is another aspect of management which I believe must be changed. Usually when economic conditions turn down due to cyclicality of an industry, everyone freezes wages. In other words, given the choice of management by stick or carrot, in tough times we throw away the carrot and use the stick. This is backwards. What we require is to continue wage increases which are performanced-based and where "fully satisfactory" is zero wage increase. But those who excel, be it in good times or bad times, let us continue to reward generously.

Finally, employees must participate in the fruits of their labor and the company's successes. Whether this is accomplished by means of profit sharing, stock options, stock purchase plans, any other or all of the above, it is an absolute and necessary part of involving employees in the company's activities. It is of critical importance in gaining their total commitment to the success of the enterprise.

Let us not ignore management's role in this new scenario. Warren Bennis,[1] a professor at UCLA, wrote a book called *Leaders* in which he notes that when we talk about business we refer to good or bad managers, whereas when we speak of government we refer to leaders. Conversely, I think American business needs leaders and government needs managers. (If all of the MBAs we produce in the United States were to go directly into government, American business would be markedly improved; I can't be certain what the impact would be on government.)

The only legitimate reason for a manager to exist, whatever the level, is to create, cause change for the better, or innovate new ideas, according to Rosabeth Moss Kanter.[2] We must throw away the concept that there is a limit to the number of people managers can have directly reporting to them. Superb leaders can lead vast numbers of people providing they don't try to make the decisions for all of their people. Push decision-making down. We need leaders in business who are prepared to dream, create, motivate, train, and have the courage to run their organizations in a counterculture manner when necessary. Quarterly results, short-term project planning, layoffs and other kneejerk reactions to business downturns are anachronistic and will accelerate the total destruction of our technology and industrial position.

Another problem of US industry that permeates the entire organization is the "we/they" syndrome. *They* refers to all the things wrong in a corporation. The servicemen visiting a customer: "*They* certainly shipped you a piece of garbage." The production person: "*They* screwed up this time in engineering." And so on ... Examples abound all around us in every phase of our lives.

We is taking responsibility for ourselves as well as our organization. The serviceman: "*We* have never had this type of problem, but don't worry, *we* will resolve it to your satisfaction."

How do we get this type of commitment from our employees and especially from our engineering staff? There is no single nostrum. It is the careful administration of all of the above. An environment must be created in which the employee feels important, in which employment security is a fact of life, in which participation in decision-making and profits is well understood and, most importantly, where there is a leader to convey the substance of dreams and point the way. It is an organization in which *We* matters and *They* refers only to the competition. *We* makes profits, *They* don't!

Some pundit defined commitment as "high productivity, low turnover, and a better chance of avoiding corporate death at the hands of the Japanese." I have no argument with that definition.

Notes

1. Warren G. Bennis and Burt Nanus, *Leaders: The Strategies of Taking Charge* (Harper & Row, New York, 1985).
2. Rosabeth Moss Kanter, *The Change Masters – Innovation & Entrepreneurship in the American Corporation* (Simon & Schuster, New York, 1983).

15

Toward a Bipartisan Competitiveness Strategy

KEVIN PHILLIPS

The subject of international competition has become a pressing one in the United States of late, and deservedly so. But much of the speculation is one-dimensional, basing remedies and solutions entirely on principles of economics and management theory.

This is inadequate. The argument can be made – and I will certainly make it here – that US policymakers also have to keep politics and political economy in mind. I'm not talking about US partisan politics, Republican or Democrat, but about the relevance of changing global political circumstances and currents to the future of US trade, trade policy and international economic strategy. For example, if we knew that the world was turning back towards mercantilism, we'd be wise to pursue different policies than if we knew that a new free trade era and mechanism was just over the horizon.

To be sure, those are extreme choices. We're not very likely to be able to "know" either option as a safe trend on which to operate. However, it is possible to look at world trade and the world economy over the last decade or so and see a definite pattern of (1) increasing direct and indirect participation in trade by government; and (2) increasing resort by nations to *neo*-protectionism – subsidies, tax breaks, administrative and regulatory devices *et al*. – in lieu of the tariffs of yesteryear; and (3) increasing speculation that the helpful or apathetic role of a nation's government may now be a factor, along with purely economic assets or circumstances, in what economists call a country's "comparative advantage."

These measurements and judgements are as much a matter of politics as economics – and in some cases, politicians may be better able to face these apparent trends than economists unwilling to abandon obsolescent theory. At any rate, a *political* analysis of the changing global competitiveness context suggests that the United States is now and has been for at least five to ten years caught up in a global realignment of who produces what and for how much. We're winning in some categories, but we seem to be losing in a *greater* number – and that includes some of the high-tech industries most important to America's future. Basic economic shifts are central, of course. But other factors are also involved. For example, one supporting reason for this ebb is the difficulty Americans have had in giving up our post-World War II nonchalance about trade matters and their importance. They didn't use to count; now they're vital. Another reason, which I'll come back to, is that we've been relying on world organizations set up in our heyday right after World War II – organizations from the United Nations and UNESCO to the World Court and GATT, the General Agreement on Trade and Tariffs. They don't work for us so well now because they reflect the new realities of global power relationships in the 1980s. We may not be able to change that. Finally, this new global competitiveness context raises the possibility that the United States cannot afford to remain the only major economic power *without* a trade department, *without* a border neutral tax system (able to tax imports and rebate for exports) and *without* serious governmental mechanisms for coordinating US international economic policy.

At a minimum, the changes taking shape would seem to require the US government to begin thinking strategically. That's particularily true of senior Executive Branch officials. Indeed, few needs will be so compelling over the next few years – and few omissions have been so detrimental over the last few years – as a serious, coherent national trade and industrial strategy. The damage is everywhere: in shuttered factories, an agricultural sector near bankruptcy, markets here and abroad lost to foreign competitors, and the emergence of the United States as a debtor nation. Fortunately, there are important signs of change in the Executive Branch – especially since September's official about-face in global currency intervention and trade commitment – and the more Congress can further this trend, the better.

Not that shaping this kind of strategic approach and commitment will be easy. Until September, for half a decade or so, the President and the Congress – at first in legitimate reaction against the federal regulatory over-involvements of the nineteen seventies – have sought to roll back government. Efforts were made to reduce not only tax rates and domestic economic regulation, but also the role of the US government in the international economy. Adherence to free markets and free trade has been the bye-word. Since September, a more sophisticated awareness seems to be taking hold. But skeptics will require action and implementation, not just an opportune season of rhetoric. And cynics will remember that previous proposals for a new Washington commitment to US international competitiveness – moderate, realistic ones largely shaped by the business community – were rejected by President Reagan and his advisers as late as February 1985. "Chilly" is a reasonable description of the reception given White House-commissioned blueprints like the late 1984 report of the

President's Task Force on International Private Enterprise and the early 1985 report of the President's Commission on International Competitiveness. The largely ignored Task Force report urged White House creation of an Economic Security Council to plot US global economic strategy in the manner of the existing National Security Council. And the Commission followed by calling for a new federal department to orchestrate international trade and another to deal with science and technology. Some such new instrumentality – be it a department or beefed-up council – may well be necessary for this Administration or any other Administration to coordinate trade, tax, budget and monetary policies and their collective domestic and international impacts.

Not surprisingly, during this same pre-September period, the notion of a "strategy" explicitly to coordinate the various strands of government policy was also rejected out of hand. Here, too, the consequences have been inauspicious. In mid-September, US International Trade Commission Chairman Paula Stern pleaded for change: "To win a war, you need a strategy. In international trade, however, we are operating with neither a battle plan nor a general staff. No wonder we are in full, disorderly retreat." Exactly. A few days later, the President and the Treasury Department finally took action both on shaping a tougher strategy and promoting a dollar devaluation. However, if the "full, disorderly retreat" Paula Stern referred to is over, orderly strategizing still seems too *ad hoc*.

The unfortunate truth is that today's international economic policy crisis has been emerging – largely unstrategized – for several years. By 1982–83, the interacting 1981 federal tax cuts and post-1981 defense build-up were splashing the national economy in red ink. But the implications of the mushrooming deficits were ignored or denied. The highest real interest rates in 50 years lured foreigners to finance the US deficit. Their demand sent the dollar rising on the currency markets. And, of course, the soaring dollar – until mid-1985 hailed by officialdom as a proud new stanza to the Star-Spangled Banner! – made imports into the US cheap while making US exports increasingly too expensive for previous overseas customers. So aided, the foreign rivals of US agriculture and industry began to make enormous inroads into previously US-dominated markets both here and abroad. Many of these will never be recovered; they are the price the United States paid for its early 1980s nonchalance.

Yet there is another, *systemic* reason for the United States to begin taking strategic political economics seriously. We are almost certainly in another one of history's periodic global economic watersheds. This is the world political-economics realignment to which I referred earlier. The geography of advanced production is shifting – painfully. What used to be made in Pittsburgh, Lancashire, Lorraine and the Ruhr is migrating from West to East, from Europe and North America to Asia and Latin America. So is the technological edge that underpinned that hegemony. In the process, the United States is losing the post-World War II manufacturing and commercial dominance that nurtured yesteryear's nonchalant trade policy approach. And without that American self-interest, the political basis of an international free-trade system (or pretense) may vanish, too. Cautions and caveats abound.

Open markets are a precarious phenomenon, for one thing. A serious perusal of modern history – defined in the *Cambridge Modern History* as beginning in 1493 – suggests that free trade may be a latterday aberration. British economic thinkers Adam Smith and David Ricardo first articulated the concept early in the Industrial Revolution. Britain thereupon become the first world economic power to fully embrace free trade after Parliament's repeal of the Corn Laws in 1846, a commitment maintained until the general tariff of 1932. The United States picked up the open markets banner soon thereafter. By contrast, the leading economic powers of the prior three centuries – first Spain and then France – had practiced the protective economic self-aggrandizement history describes as mercantilism.

So free trade is not necessarily a norm. US policymakers cannot afford to assume it is a probable or logical state of global affairs. Arguably, for a dominant power to uphold it over several decades or even generations requires rare circumstances: The world's foremost manufacturing nation must also be the world's leading naval, commercial and technological power. Until more or less the early twentieth century, Britain occupied that niche. Then the United States fulfilled those criteria for at least three decades after World War II. Now, however, the United States is being commercially threatened by East Asia much as this country and the Kaiser's Germany nipped at the heels of early twentieth century Britain. And US free trade commitment seems to be ebbing at more or less the same stages of manufacturing decline that eroded free trade backing in late Victorian and Edwardian Britain. Japan and the "little dragons" of East Asia are hardly likely to pick up the banner, given the similarity of their economic practices to those of sixteenth-century Spain or seventeenth-century France. Let me stipulate: the United States may well be able to set up a *regional* free-trade bloc with Canada. It's late twentieth-century reconstitution of an *international* free trade era that global political-economic circumstances suggest will be so tricky.

Interestingly, a considerable similarity between current-day US trade politics and the earlier British metamorphosis underscores our strategic conundrum. At its mid-nineteenth-century zenith, Great Britain boasted half the world's manufacturing production. By 1870, that share had declined to 32 percent, and by World War I, to about 15 percent. Demands for major modification of free trade were issuing from major segments of British heavy industry by the 1890s, and by the 1920s, most of the Conservative Party had gone over to protectionism. In 1932, tariffs and Empire Protection were finally enacted.

The parallel is all too obvious. Right after World War II, the United States, like Britain a century earlier, produced roughly half of world manufactures. That was when Washington really promulgated US commitment to free trade. As of 1980, with the US share of world manufacturing turning down to little more than 20 percent, support for protectionism was growing. Now, five years later, trade is arguably on its way to being a top issue in US politics, mirroring its prominence in British debate during the period (1890–1932) of that nation's late-stage, declining world economic preeminence. In short, the reasons for growing US concern with the competitiveness crisis are substantially systemic. Much more is involved than transient currency misalignment pressures.

Under pressure of global neo-mercantilist realities, even some US free trade economists have begun to wonder if their purely economic interpretation of the doctrine of "comparative advantage" – that goods are produced where economic advantage dictates – may not have to be modified to also allow for the benefits of a collaborative national government. And they should be wondering. Suppose for a moment that the cynical political-historical analysis of free trade *is* correct and the world *is* slipping into what could be called a "neo-mercantilist" era. Then countries like the United States with governments that have generally spurned pro-export policies, currency alignment attention, business-government collaboration and strategic economic thinking must suffer. Many of their industries and economic sectors will be comparatively *disadvantaged*. Unfortunately, large elements of this transition and related US sectoral slippage may *already* be a fact.

Under the circumstances, Washington's strategic abdication has become intolerable, and a three-pronged national industrial, trade and competitiveness agenda seems imperative to arrest and partially reverse these tides. Key components must include: (1) overt acceptance of both a necessary *pro-active* role of the federal government and high-level strategic coordination of US economic policies; (2) implementation of a specific US competitiveness agenda ranging from creation of a new trade agency to an overhaul and enforcement of the US trade laws, reform of obsolescent antitrust law limitations, expansion of export finance and stepped-up US attention to research and development and technological education; and (3) phased-in enactment of a new border-neutral US consumption tax to simultaneously reduce the deficit (and bring down the dollar in orderly fashion), shift the present burden of taxation away from savings toward consumption, and re-orient the US revenue system towards export–import sensitivity.

Fortunately, elements of the strategic transformation are already under way. No longer does the Executive Branch operate on its earlier presupposition that deficits and interest rates are unrelated, that tax reform and trade solutions need not contemplate one another, and that monetary policy can let the dollar strengthen without reference to the pain of farms and factories. The Treasury's new internationally coordinated effort to bring down the dollar is evidence of a profound transformation. This is all to the good. A globally oriented antitrust overhaul is also underway. At this writing, however, too many people in Washington still oppose what should be the next step: *a policy linkage by which tax overhaul also becomes a vehicle for dealing with the inter-related deficit and trade problems.*

Let me begin with the need for high-level policy coordination. As of January, 1986, it seems imperative to promote institutional coordination of the various economic policies and government economic involvements that the Administration earlier regarded as unrelated and separable. Watchers identify the new Economic Policy Council under Treasury Secretary James Baker III as a force for strategic thinking, albeit falling well short of the Economic Security Council role proposed by the President's Task Force on International Private Enterprise nearly a year ago. Let us hope so. If the world is indeed heading into something resembling a neo-mercantilist era, development of this new economic *realpolitik* machinery will be critical to the United States.

Even apart from this new *realpolitik* machinery, US policymakers should immediately undertake a study of the political-economic obsolescence of the whole range of international organizations the United States helped blueprint at the end of World War II – the UN, UNESCO, the World Court, GATT, etcetera. Because of changing global power equations – new countries, new alliances, new economic circumstances and relationships – these organizations no longer work as they once did. Certainly our interests are not being well-served. But the larger question is whether these organizations are still plausible policy vehicles. If not, are new ones in order – or politically achievable?

In addition to strategic thinking and global re-evaluation, new programmatic approaches are also necessary. For the United States to deal with the managed trade and neo-mercantilism increasingly apparent around the world, some new domestic organizational, developmental and legal weaponry is necessary. In my 1984 book, *Staying on Top: The Business Case for a National Industrial Strategy*, I suggested 15 measures. None was at all radical, and all were based on conversations with the heads of major national business organizations and on a synthesis of those organizations' policy agendas, as well as on my analyses of public opinion polls, of Congressional sentiment and other yardsticks of real-world political feasibility for a national competitiveness agenda. My thesis, directed at conservatives, was that policy activism does not have to conjure up economic planning councils and national industrial redevelopment banks.

There is substantial support – even the makings of a consensus – for a centrist blueprint. Here is the framework that I thought sensible or politically plausible two years ago, some of which has since been enacted into law as ordered by the Executive Branch. It is all feasible; it is all practicable.

Trade Law and Enforcement

1. Establishment of a federal Department of International Trade and Industry to foster US competitiveness. (The Administration has lost interest, but some centralized trade agency still seems necessary.)
2. Enactment of trade reciprocity legislation.
3. Fuller enforcement of existing US trade laws. (How much of a solution the tougher trade approach set forth by the Administration in September can represent remains to be seen.)
4. Stepped-up federal monitoring and analysis of foreign national industrial policies.
5. Revision of US trade laws to cope with subsidies and other aspects of foreign industrial policies.
6. Revision of US antitrust policy to redefine anti-competitive behavior using global market standards and to allow US corporations to collaborate on research and technology to meet foreign competition.
7. Expansion of the charter and lending activities of the US Export–Import Bank. (The larger "war-chest" now under consideration needs further expansion.)

Lobbying

8. Intensification of US business lobbying overseas, plus more effective regulation of foreign lobbying in the United States. (The new proposed Wolpe-Kaptur bill to prohibit top US officials from serving as foreign lobbyists for a period of ten years after their resignations from government has some merit.)

Tax Policy

9. Appointment of a national commision on trade and taxation to recommend US tax code revisions to spur international competitiveness. (With any luck, 1986 Senate Finance Committee hearings can serve much of the same purpose.)

Management–Labor Relations

10. Support for redirection of labor–management relationships with particular attention to productivity incentives.

11. Consideration of new non-statutory Federal approaches to ameliorating industrial plant closings. (The new US Labor Department Task Force look into the plant closing question has promise.)
12. Establishment of a displaced-worker retraining program modeled on veterans' benefits.

Research and Development and Education

13. Increased support of technological research, including creation of a "basic research trust fund."
14. Protection of US technology against theft and espionage and toughening of US intellectual property laws (copyright and patents).
15. Enactment of a Morrill Act (land-grant college) equivalent for scientific and technical education.

Public opinion polls show support for virtually all of these approaches. Indeed, the Reagan Administration is already moving on about half of these fronts. However, while individual measures are important, what's really needed is White House proclamation of a larger, cohesive competitiveness agenda. Piecemeal trade law revision is not enough. Neither is dollar-valuation gamesmanship. A program broad enough to rally public opinion is necessary – not just in its own right but to underscore the scope and depth of Washington's new commitment.

Ingredient number three in a US competitiveness strategy has become increasingly imperative: a tax increase – but not just *any* tax increase – to get the deficit under control. Enactment of a consumption tax, in particular, is the only way deficit reduction can be conjoined with the sort of major overhaul needed to point the Internal Revenue Code toward trade and international competitiveness goals. It doesn't point there very well now.

As of early 1986, the best option is what's being called a Business Transfer Tax (BTT). A variation on a value-added tax, most versions would impose a 5 percent or 10 percent tax on business transactions, excluding the retail level. Like other VATs used around the world, it would exempt exports and apply to imports. In addition, corporations with American payroll FICA obligations or some other US tax liabilities would be able to offset those liabilities substantially against their BTT payments. The net federal revenue proceeds, depending on the rates, exemptions and rebate mechanisms involved, would be somewhere in the $25–100 billion a year range. Calculations suggest that a large part of the burden could be made to fall on foreign firms sending goods into the United States.

A partial shift towards this type of taxation could benefit American competitiveness in three dimensions. First, it would raise revenue to begin reducing the deficit, thereby taking the pressure off real interest rates and the over-valuation of the dollar and its negative impact on trade. Secondly, movement towards a consumption tax could be used to reduce corporate income tax rates or retain various corporate tax incentives, thus assisting United States competitiveness by *decreasing* the burden on capital formation and savings while *increasing* the burden on consumption. Most of our trading partners raise a substantially higher percentage of their total revenues from consumption-type taxes. And thirdly, most value-added taxes, falling in imports and being rebatable against exports, encourage exports and tie national tax policy and national trade policy together. US companies, by contrast, have non-rebatable taxes built into their export costs. Product competitiveness suffers.

Can there be a useful national trade and industrial strategy built around only one or two of the three components? Obviously. Practical politics is, after all, an incremental game. This three-part blueprint calling for commitment to economic *realpolitik*, to a broad-based competitiveness agenda and to a new consumption tax aimed at the budget and trade deficits and the over-valued dollar is arguably an ideal unlikely to be reached. Partial progress is better than no action at all. But given the $150 billion dollar trade deficit that stares us in the face, with its resulting greater-than-necessary dislocation of America's farms and factories and the possibility of ill-considered Congressional remedies, the sooner and the more fully we move in these directions the better.

Bluntly put, the lack of a US competitiveness strategy has become intolerable – and dangerous.

PART V

Conclusion

16

The Task of Public Economics

SENATOR PAUL SARBANES

Policymakers in Washington, DC are forced by the circumstances of their jobs to respond to a rapid succession of pressing events. Sometimes these events are major, at other times relatively minor; sometimes they are close to home, at other times quite far away. In any case, the stream of demands for reactions and decisions is constant. In such an environment, the opportunity to sit back, observe and reflect on the long-term trends which are shaping our nation and world is both welcome and necessary. In the absence of a long-term perspective the events confronting us often appear to be without meaning or coherence, and only with such a perspective can we make day-to-day decisions with any confidence that we are on the right track. The Fortieth Anniversary Symposium of the Joint Economic Committee and the Employment Act of 1946 afforded members of the Committee and others in the Congress a rare opportunity for reflection and review. It is our hope that the publication of these papers will offer a similar one to readers throughout the nation and the world.

At the core of the US domestic political debate in this century has been the question of how to fulfill the long-term ideals of American individualism in a world that is ever more interdependent and connected. Chairman David Obey summed up this quest in his opening essay when he called for an "effective 'public economics'" to provide the "foundation necessary for private initiative," and thus long-term growth and opportunity. Just as the two halves of scissors are needed to cut a piece of paper, Chairman Obey suggested that individual initiative can only flourish when a degree of stability, opportunity and equity has been established by sound public policy.

The first half of the scissors comes almost naturally to most Americans. Our nation's commitment to individual rights and individual initiative is as old as the nation itself. It lies at the very heart of Thomas Jefferson's assertion, in the Declaration of Independence, that all human beings are entitled to their "unalienable rights to Life, Liberty and the Pursuit of Happiness."

In the early days of the Republic, this meant an opportunity to own land, participate in local government, and then in large part to be left alone. In a situation in which Americans faced a seemingly limitless frontier, the context for individual initiative was assumed. With some degree of justification, public policy was seen as a hindrance. Unfettered free markets were a logical and necessary extension of this principle. It was no accident that Jefferson's Declaration and Adam Smith's *Wealth of Nations* were written in the same year.

The twentieth century has presented us with the continuing challenge of how best to realize the abiding Jeffersonian promise in a world profoundly changed and changing. Whereas Jefferson himself had envisioned an American frontier enduring until the "thousandth generation," the frontier, in fact, did not survive five generations. It had all but disappeared by the turn of the century and America was by then in the throes of an industrial revolution that would change us forever. Our markets were becoming national rather than local, our lives urban rather than rural, and our products increasingly industrial rather than agricultural. Yet our values remained constant.

At the very first meeting of the American Economics Association in 1886, Richard T. Ely, a professor at the Johns Hopkins University, declared that "a political economy written before the introduction of railroads can hardly be sufficient in the year 1885. Adam Smith would have been the first to recognize this." This insight animated Americans from a variety of backgrounds and a variety of perspectives. A writer who had the ear of a great Republican President, Theodore Roosevelt, warned that industrial conditions required that "the goal of combining individual freedom and economic prosperity now had to be approached in new and innovative ways." Simply to repeat the past, he warned, would leave the Jeffersonian promise "stifled" rather than "fulfilled."

These same sentiments were echoed by Theodore Roosevelt's nephew, the great Democratic architect of the New Deal, Franklin Roosevelt, when he called on Americans to recognize "the new terms of the old social contract."

With the help of hindsight, we can see that this had indeed been the objective of much of the micro- and macroeconomic policy of the last 50 years. Consider the provocative papers in this volume by Walter Heller, James Tobin and Robert Eisner. The authors review the macroeconomic policies of the last two decades. Their concerns go far beyond the technical aspects of sterile GNP numbers, however, for they understand that GNP growth, or the lack of it, significantly increases – or diminishes – the possibilities that real men and women have to make meaningful lives for themselves and their families. Without belaboring the point, the authors make clear that the ability of individuals to realize their plans and dreams is very much dependent upon an environment which those individuals do not – by themselves – make.

Similarly, the papers in this volume by Bernard Anderson, Robert Kuttner, Ray Marshall, Michael Piore and others make the point that while in a dynamic, changing economy the individual worker is often the least flexible factor of production, this is not simply to be accepted as an immutable fact of nature like earthquakes or tides. Each of these authors demonstrates that judicious public policies can increase – and have increased – the opportunity for individual workers to learn new and improved skills and to participate more productively in the workplace. Thus, opportunity not only contributes to their own well-being but generates more growth – and hence opportunity – for society as a whole. Seen in this light, programs like the GI Bill of Rights, the National Defense Education Act, the Wagner Act, all of which appeared highly innovative at the time of their enactment, provided the framework for individual opportunity in a changing world. At the same time, these initiatives helped to solve economic problems that would otherwise have plagued the economy. In a similar fashion, innovative social insurance programs such as Social Security and Unemployment Insurance provided economic stabilizers for the economy, while also laying a foundation of security for individuals and their families.

As useful as our historical retrospective is, however, it is not enough; it is the first chapter, not the last. The clear message of this symposium has been that the economy continues to change, and we must therefore continue the tradition of "creative pragmatism" to which Representative Obey refers in the opening paper. Kevin Phillips, Lionel Olmer, Barry Bluestone, Chris Tilly and Bennett Harrison, Lester Thurow, Sheldon Weinig and others make the point in different and complementary ways that the United States is increasingly part of a world economy. Entire nations as well as individuals are now shaped by events beyond their borders and beyond unilateral control. Just as we confronted the challenge of a changing economy *within* our own borders in the earlier part of the century, we must do so now and into the next century, in global terms. We must think about new and flexible institutions to provide the stability, opportunity and equity we need in a rapidly changing environment. Concurrently we must not fall victim to the comfortable but dangerous illusion that it is the *absence* of institutions, rather than *appropriate* institutions which will help to solve our problems.

As a case in point, we have seen Members of Congress and the Administration engaged in recent months in discussions of how best to target international exchange rates, how best to coordinate programs to solve the international debt crisis, and how best to stimulate agricultural exports. Federal Reserve Board Chairman Paul Volcker recently called on "other strong countries, with little or no inflation, with excess capacity and historically high unemployment" to stimulate their economies for the sake of strong *international* economic growth. These developments indicate a movement in practice, if not yet in theory, toward the recognition that the world is changing and we must respond as creatively to it as we have responded to other changes in the past.

At some time our ideas must catch up with our behavior. If not, our actions will lack direction; over time they will serve no coherent purpose, and we will have failed to meet the challenge that our predecessors met so well in the past. If this collection of papers contributes to our understanding of the nature and magnitude of the challenge and contributes in ways that help us remain true to our values even as we develop new strategies and tactics, then it will have accomplished a great deal indeed.

Appendix
Charting Economic Change

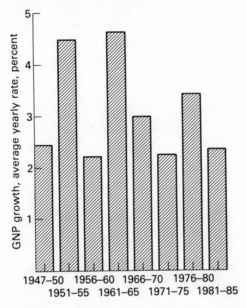

Figure A.1. Real GNP growth, 1947–1985

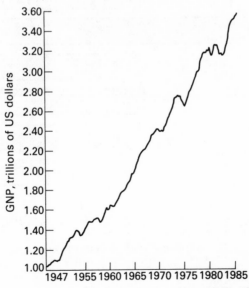

Figure A.2. Real Gross National Product, 1947–1985

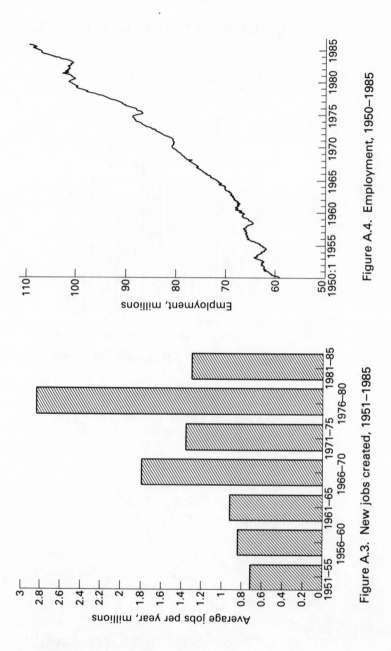

Figure A.3. New jobs created, 1951–1985

Figure A.4. Employment, 1950–1985

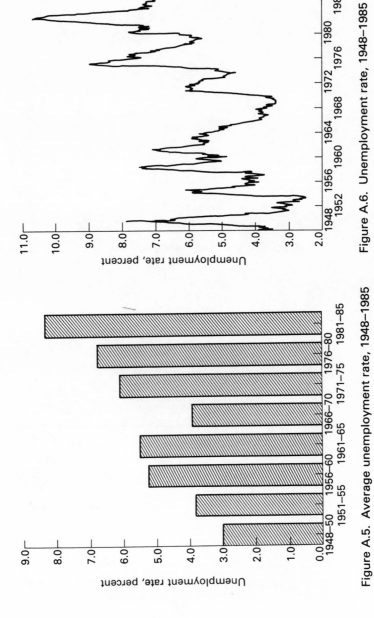

Figure A.5. Average unemployment rate, 1948–1985

Figure A.6. Unemployment rate, 1948–1985

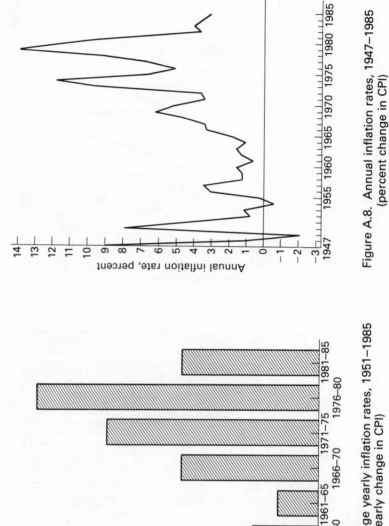

Figure A.7. Average yearly inflation rates, 1951–1985 (yearly change in CPI)

Figure A.8. Annual inflation rates, 1947–1985 (percent change in CPI)

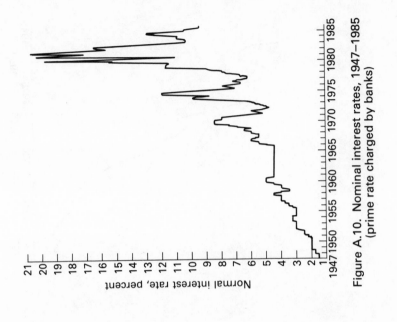

Figure A.10. Nominal interest rates, 1947–1985
(prime rate charged by banks)

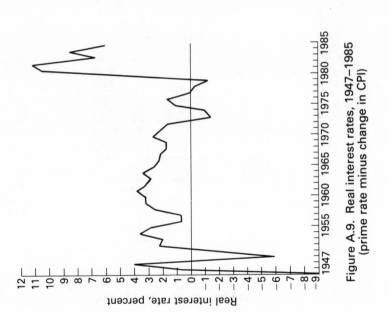

Figure A.9. Real interest rates, 1947–1985
(prime rate minus change in CPI)

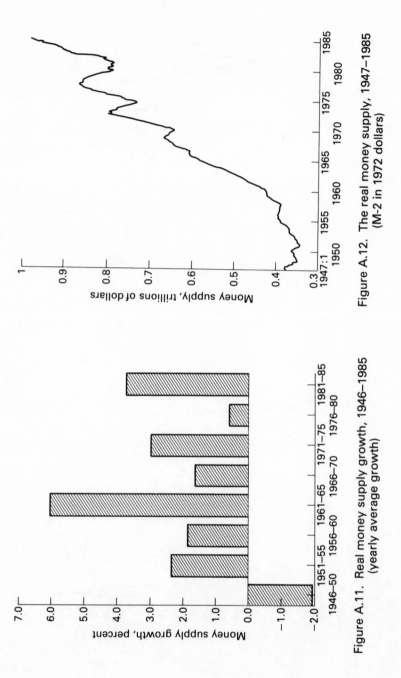

Figure A.11. Real money supply growth, 1946–1985
(yearly average growth)

Figure A.12. The real money supply, 1947–1985
(M-2 in 1972 dollars)

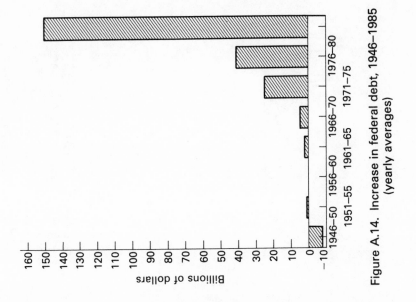

Figure A.14. Increase in federal debt, 1946–1985
(yearly averages)

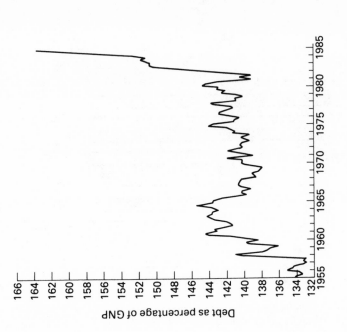

Figure A.13. Public and private debt outstanding,
1955–1985

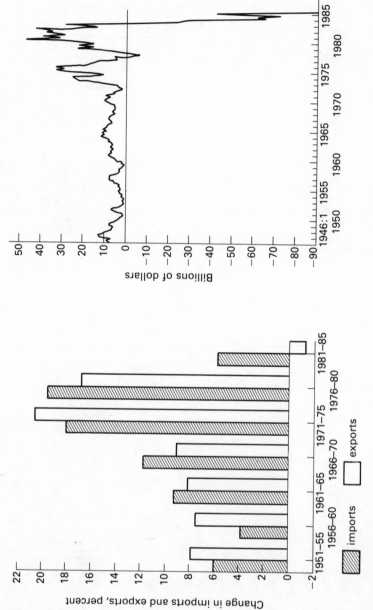

Figure A.15. Changes in imports and exports, 1951–1985
(average yearly rates)

Figure A.16. Trade balance, 1946–1985
(on current account basis)